$36⁰⁰

Crossing national borders

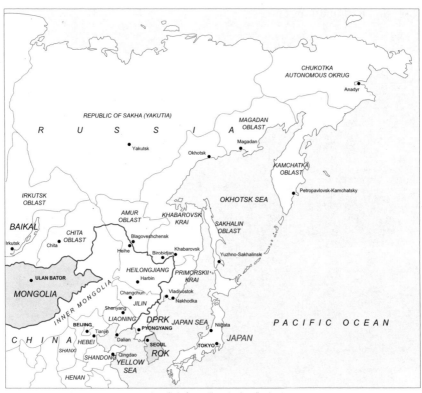

Source: Courtesy of the Economic Research Institute for Northeast Asia, Niigata, Japan.

Map of Northeast Asia

Crossing national borders: Human migration issues in Northeast Asia

Edited by Tsuneo Akaha and Anna Vassilieva

United Nations University Press

TOKYO · NEW YORK · PARIS

United Nations University Press
United Nations University, 53-70, Jingumae 5-chome,
Shibuya-ku, Tokyo, 150-8925, Japan
Tel: +81-3-3499-2811   Fax: +81-3-3406-7345
E-mail: sales@hq.unu.edu
General enquiries: press@hq.unu.edu
http://www.unu.edu

United Nations University Office at the United Nations, New York
2 United Nations Plaza, Room DC2-2062, New York, NY 10017, USA
Tel: +1-212-963-6387   Fax: +1-212-371-9454
E-mail: unuona@ony.unu.edu

United Nations University Press is the publishing division of the United Nations University.

Cover design by Mea Rhee

Printed in Hong Kong

UNUP-1117
ISBN 92-808-1117-7

Library of Congress Cataloging-in-Publication Data

Crossing national borders : human migration issues in Northeast Asia / edited by Tsuneo Akaha and Anna Vassilieva.
    p.   cm.
 Includes bibliographical references and index.
 ISBN 9280811177 (pbk.)
 1. East Asia—Emigration and immigration. 2. East Asia—Emigration and immigration—Statistics. I. Akaha, Tsuneo, 1949– . II. Vassilieva, Anna.
 JV8756.5.C76   2005
 304.8'095—dc22   2005022324

Contents

List of figures and tables vii

List of contributors x

Foreword xii
    Robert A. Scalapino

Acknowledgements xiv

List of abbreviations xvi

Introduction: Crossing national borders 1
    Tsuneo Akaha and Anna Vassilieva

**Part I: Population trends and migration patterns in
Northeast Asia** 9

  1 Population trends and migration patterns in Northeast Asia ... 11
    *Maurice D. Van Arsdol, Jr., Stephen Lam, Brian Ettkin and
    Glenn Guarin*

Part II: Chinese migration to the Russian Far East 45

  2 Chinese in the Russian Far East: Regional views 47
    Victor Larin

3 Migration and economic security: Chinese labour migrants in
  the Russian Far East 68
  Elizabeth Wishnick

Part III: Russian, Chinese and Korean communities in Japan 93

4 The Russian presence in contemporary Japan: Case studies in
  Hokkaido and Niigata 95
  Tsuneo Akaha and Anna Vassilieva

5 Chinese migrants in contemporary Japan: The case of Niigata   120
  Daojiong Zha

6 Koreans in Japan and Shimane 141
  Mika Merviö

Part IV: Migration issues in the Korean peninsula and Mongolia .. 163

7 North Koreans in China: Sorting fact from fiction 165
  Hazel Smith

8 The realities of South Korea's migration policies 191
  Shin-wha Lee

9 Foreign migration issues in Mongolia 215
  Tsedendamba Batbayar

10 Conclusion: Implications for regional international relations ... 236
   Tsuneo Akaha and Anna Vassilieva

Index 248

Figures and tables

Figures

Map of Northeast Asia... ii

1.1   Population size, East Asian and Northeast Asian states:
estimates and projections, 1950–2050 15

1.2   Vital rates and epidemiologic transition, Northeast Asian
states: estimates and projections, 1950–2050 18

1.3   Population pyramids, Northeast Asian states: estimates and
projections, 1950–2050 19

2.1   Chinese tourism in Amur Oblast and Primorskii Krai (000
people), 1997–2003 52

2.2   Chinese visits to Amur Oblast (000 people), 1997–2002 53

2.3   Chinese registered in Primorskii Krai by purpose of visit,
2000 53

2.4   Attitudes towards the idea of "Chinese expansion" in the
Russian Far East, summer 2003 61

2.5   RFE residents' attitudes towards different categories of
Chinese people in Russia, 2003............................... 62

2.6   Future developments in Russia's relations with Asia-Pacific
countries: Views of the southern RFE, summer 2003 62

7.1   Map of DPRK provincial boundaries 168

7.2   Population of North Korea by province and percentage,
2000 175

Tables

1.1 Recent population data for Northeast Asia states and East Asia states 12
1.2 Migration indicators, Northeast Asian states, 1990–2000 22
3.1 Population of the Chinese Northeast, 2002 72
3.2 Full-time employment in north-eastern Chinese provincial capitals compared to other Chinese cities, 2002 73
3.3 Reasons for Chinese workers to go to Russian Far East for work 73
3.4 Monthly salary of Chinese workers in Russian Far East, 2004 75
3.5 Occupation of Chinese workers in Russian Far East, 2004 .. 75
3.6 Influence of Chinese workers' experience in RFE on their life in China 81
4.1 The number of Russian nationals entering Japan, 1995–2002 99
4.2 The number of new Russian visitors to Japan by purpose of entry, 2002 100
4.3 The number of new temporary Russian visitors in Japan, 2002 100
4.4 The number of registered Russians in Japan by prefecture, end-2003 101
4.5 The number of Russians registered in Hokkaido, 1991–2003 (at year-end) 102
4.6 The number of Russians registered in Niigata, 1991–2003 .. 103
4.7 The number of Japanese and Russian interviewees and survey subjects in Hokkaido and Niigata City, 2001 and 2003 106
5.1 Registered Chinese in Niigata, 2001 123
5.2 Occupations/professions of Japanese survey respondents ... 126
5.3 Age of Japanese survey respondents 126
5.4 Highest level of education obtained by Japanese survey respondents 126
6.1 The largest concentrations of Koreans in Shimane, 2001 152
6.2 Korean residents in Shimane, 1913–1990 152
6.3 Shimane Korean respondents to 1996 survey 153
6.4 Marital status of Koreans in Shimane (%) 154
6.5 Educational background of Koreans in Shimane, 1996 155
6.6 Respondents' facility in Korean language (%) 156
6.7 Respondents' practice of Korean customs at home (%) 157
6.8 Awareness of respondents' Korean ethnic background among co-workers and neighbours (%), 1996 157
6.9 Ethnic Koreans' use of Japanese aliases (%) 158

6.10 Shimane Koreans' plans (%)   159
8.1   Overseas Koreans, 2003   194
8.2   The increase in overseas Koreans, 1971–2003   195
8.3   Countries with more than 2,000 overseas Koreans, 2003   196
8.4   Koreans "temporarily" going abroad, by purpose, 1985–
      2001   196
8.5   Overseas Korean associations, 1997 and 2000   197
8.6   Educational institutions abroad for overseas Koreans   201
8.7   Foreign residents in South Korea, 31 December 2002   205
8.8   Acceptance of refugees by South Korea, 1994–2003   209
9.1   Number of arrivals and departures in Mongolia by country,
      2000–2002   222
9.2   Outbound Mongolian passengers by point and purpose,
      2002   228
9.3   Mongolian attitudes towards Russians and Chinese (%)   229
9.4   Mongolian attitudes towards Japanese and Koreans (%) ...   229
9.5   Perceived changes in the number of foreigners in Mongolia
      (%)   230
9.6   Desirability of Mongolian partnerships with countries and
      international organizations (%)   231
9.7   Mongolian preferences in dealing with foreigners (%)   231
9.8   Mongolian attitudes towards Russians and Chinese by age
      and gender (%)   232

Contributors

Tsuneo Akaha is a Professor of International Policy Studies and Director of the Center for East Asian Studies, Monterey Institute of International Studies, California, USA.

Tsedendamba Batbayar is a Counsellor, Mongolian Embassy, Beijing, China.

Brian Ettkin is a graduate student, Graduate School of International Policy Studies, Monterey Institute of International Studies, California, USA.

Glenn Guarin is a graduate student, MA Politics, Security and Integration, School of Slavonic and Eastern European Studies, London.

Stephen Lam is a PhD candidate, Department of Geography, King's College, London.

Victor Larin is Director, Institute of History, Archaeology and Ethnology of the Far Eastern Peoples, Russian Academy of Sciences, Vladivostok, Russia.

Shin-wha Lee is an Associate Professor of Political Science, Korea University, Seoul, Korea.

Mika Merviö is a Professor of Political Science, the University of Shimane, Hamada, Japan.

Robert Scalapino is a Robson Research Professor of Government Emeritus, Institute of East Asian Studies, University of California, Berkeley, California, USA.

Hazel Smith is a Reader in International Relations, University of Warwick, UK.

Maurice D. Van Arsdol, Jr. is an Adjunct Professor, Graduate School of International Policy Studies, Monterey Institute of International Studies, California, USA, and a Professor of Sociology Emeritus, University of Southern California, USA.

Anna Vassilieva is an Associate Professor and Russian Studies Program Head, Monterey Institute of International Studies, California, USA.

Elizabeth Wishnick is an Assistant Professor of Political Science, Montclair State University, New Jersey, and Research Associate, Weatherhead East Asian Institute, Columbia University, New York.

Daojiong Zha is an Associate Professor and Director, Center for International Energy Security, Renmin University of China, Beijing, China.

Foreword

Robert A. Scalapino

For centuries, the societies of Northeast Asia have alternated between closer interaction, including the flow of people across ethnic and political borders, and aloofness, sometimes involving maximum isolation. Migration, in search of a better livelihood or for other reasons, was a vital part of the region's history as empires rose and fell. Yet for long periods of time, Korea's efforts to preserve its identity caused it to be known as the Hermit Kingdom, and Japan under the Tokugawa sought to exclude outsiders for nearly three centuries. Imperial China also attempted to protect itself, against the "Western barbarians", but in vain.

Today, isolation is no longer possible, as even North Korea's leadership is coming to realize. Thus the task of interacting in a more intensive fashion, economically, culturally and in all facets of security, confronts every society. Ours is a time when three semi-conflictual forces are rising: internationalism, nationalism and communalism. As is well known, internationalism takes many forms: institutional and less formal, official and non-official, regional and global. At the same time, nationalism is re-asserting itself in Asia as elsewhere. Sometimes it assumes anti-foreign characteristics, thereby making conditions for immigrants more difficult. Moreover, in a revolutionary era when individuals are often seeking to find and preserve a meaningful identity, a stronger commitment to ethnicity, religion or localism is prevalent.

Under these circumstances, the human flows taking place in a region such as Northeast Asia present both opportunities and challenges. The chapters in this volume deal with a wide range of issues, and they present four comprehensive themes worthy of note.

The first theme pertains to how well or how poorly the people of a country have absorbed migrant populations and to what are the current trends in this matter. For example, to what extent have Japanese citizens accepted Koreans, Chinese and the much smaller number of Russian immigrants, or visitors, and what is the larger political impact? As will be noted in several chapters of this book, Koreans, even second- and third-generation residents, face problems of integration in Japan; and for many Japanese, Russians remain distinctly "foreign" despite somewhat greater acceptance.

A second consideration is the threat factor. Current attention is focused here primarily on China in view of the massive size of its population and its continuous problem of unemployment, especially in rural areas. In the Russian Far East and Mongolia, whose populations are small and, in the case of the former, have declined in recent years, will Chinese migration, legal or illegal, be a threat in a variety of ways? Several chapters deal with this issue insightfully. It should be noted that this matter involves not only the number of immigrants but also their type. In some settings, Chinese entrepreneurs rapidly assume a critical role in an economy.

Yet another factor of basic importance has to do with certain domestic conditions, among them the ageing of societies, as in Japan. The need for immigrant labour in Japan will clearly loom ever greater in the years ahead. Meanwhile, although China too has a growing senior population, its current priority must be on reducing unemployment and the still expanding rural–urban gap. Migration in China will be greatest within its borders, with millions of rural people continuing to move into the cities. But China will also continue to have an ample number of available workers for other countries in the region, causing apprehension despite their needs.

A final consideration that takes the attention of various contributors to this book concerns human security of the most basic types. The trafficking in women and the exploitation of migrant workers, especially those without legal status, are growing problems. As several chapters make clear, human flows have both benefits and liabilities, and there is a need for much greater international cooperation in order to mitigate their negative features. Increased human flows throughout Northeast Asia in the years ahead are virtually certain. Thus the research that informs the findings and conclusions presented here is a pioneering undertaking that warrants careful attention and much study.

Acknowledgements

This book is a product of international collaborative research efforts that began in 2001. Our review of the existing literature on international migration and on Northeast Asian affairs revealed that there were many fine studies of global migration patterns and regional migration developments in Europe, the Western hemisphere and Southeast Asia but that studies which focused on Northeast Asia were very rare. Those that did exist were mostly either single-country studies written in the local language and inaccessible to outsiders or studies of narrowly delineated streams of migration from China and Southeast Asia to Russia, Japan and South Korea.

We invited several foreign and US-based researchers to join forces with us and undertake a serious comparative study of people crossing borders in Northeast Asia and their impact on host communities and societies. The chapter authors of this book agreed to join the project at different phases of its development since 2001.

We were fortunate in obtaining the United Nations University's (UNU) co-sponsorship of the project, including funding for some of the field research and for organizing meetings among project participants, twice in Tokyo and once in Monterey, California. We are very grateful for their support.

We particularly wish to thank four individuals in UNU's Peace and Governance Programme: Dr Ramesh Thakur (Senior Vice-Rector), Dr Hazel Smith (Senior Academic Programme Officer at the time of her support of and participation in the project) and Dr Ted Newman (Academic

Programme Officer) for their intellectual contribution to the project and Ms Yoshie Sawada (Administrative Assistant) for her timely logistical assistance. We are also grateful to the United States Institute of Peace for giving us a grant to support some parts of the field research and to hold meetings in Washington, DC in May 2004 and in Seoul in April 2005 in order to disseminate the project's findings and policy recommendations.

Finally, we thank five graduate assistants at the Center for East Asian Studies, Monterey Institute of International Studies, Monterey, California, for their tireless help in carrying out this project – in data collection, in editing research reports and in conducting meetings in Monterey and elsewhere. We acknowledge their contribution by listing their names here: Lora Saalman, Brian Ettkin, Chris Hulick, Richard Sedgwick and Oksana Chikina.

Tsuneo Akaha and Anna Vassilieva

Abbreviations

CIS   Commonwealth of Independent States
DPRK   Democratic People's Republic of Korea
ILO   International Labor Organization
IUJ   International University of Japan
MOFAT   (South Korean) Ministry of Foreign Affairs and Trade
MSF   Médecins sans Frontières
OKF   Overseas Koreans Foundation
RENK   Rescue the North Korean People: Urgent Action Network
RFE   Russian Far East
ROC   Republic of China
ROK   Republic of Korea
SAR   Special Administrative Region
SARS   Severe acute respiratory syndrome
SOEs   State-owned enterprises
TBCs   Trans-border cities
TBSs   Trans-border systems
UNHCR   United Nations High Commissioner for Refugees
WFP   World Food Program
WTO   World Trade Organization

Introduction: Crossing national borders

Tsuneo Akaha and Anna Vassilieva

The landscape of international relations in Northeast Asia is changing, and migration and other types of human flow within and between the countries of the region are becoming an important part of it. The state-centric approach to and view of international relations that prevailed in this part of the world during the Cold War can no longer describe or explain the logic and shape of emerging realities. The Cold War, as the ideological order of the state-centric world, has become a thing of the past, although its remnants can still be seen on the divided Korean peninsula. Old and new manifestations of nationalism are interacting with expressions of nascent regionalism.[1] Non-state actors such as multinational corporations and environmental NGOs that have transformed global politics have become important agents of change in this region as well. They are giving rise to new issues, new perspectives and new identities among the peoples of Northeast Asia, although resistance to the forces of change is also visible. Topics such as human security, labour migration, human trafficking and refugees are emerging as a focus of political debate and policy discussion in the region.

It is time for scholars in Northeast Asia to understand the above changes according to a new analytical paradigm, to explain their dynamic and to discuss their consequences for the future of the region. This book is a first step in meeting the challenge. The shared goal of its contributors is to lay bare the challenges that cross-border human flows pose. The book will illuminate the cases of Chinese migrants in the Russian Far East; Russians, Chinese and Koreans in rural Japan; North Koreans in

1

China; and migration issues in South Korea and Mongolia. These cases give us a glimpse of the dynamic changes under way in the relationships between peoples who have long been separated by national borders.

More specifically, the authors are concerned with several basic questions. What issues does cross-border migration raise in each of the Northeast Asian countries, and how are their governments and societies responding to them? Is cross-border migration contributing to the development of a regional identity among the peoples of Northeast Asia – a sense that they share a common future? How likely is it that the Northeast Asian countries will move beyond their current unilateral (internal) responses and bilateral adjustments and engage in serious multilateral cooperation? What is the impact of international migration on the security concerns of the governments and peoples of Northeast Asia?

At the end of the twentieth century, there were an estimated 175 million international migrants, nearly 3 per cent of the world's population and twice the number of 1975. Some 60 per cent of them, about 104 million, were in developed countries, and the remaining 71 million were in developing countries.[2] In 2000, about 1,627 million people, approximately 28 per cent of the world's population, were living in the Northeast Asian countries of China, Japan, North Korea, South Korea, Mongolia and Russia. There were 19,029,000 migrants living in these countries, which was only 11.7 per cent of the global migrant stock.[3] This relatively small number of migrants reflects the tight control that the Northeast Asian governments have traditionally maintained over the movement of people across their national borders, and it suggests the potential for substantial future growth in cross-border migration in the region. Indeed, Northeast Asia has lagged behind other regions of the world in the voluntary movement of individual citizens across state borders.

However, there are signs throughout the region that a major change is afoot. Increasing numbers of ordinary citizens in all Northeast Asian countries are finding it necessary, desirable and indeed possible to travel to neighbouring countries. Some of them decide to settle permanently in the host society, others find temporary employment as migrant workers and still others travel simply as tourists.

In Northeast Asia's modern history, the interests of central governments have long dictated the substance and pattern of international relations.[4] As the most powerful political institutions in the nation-states of the region, the central governments controlled political relations, commercial ties and human contacts across national boundaries. Accidental or unintended border crossings by individual citizens were exceptions, such as in times of war or crisis when state control of borders was weak. In the post–Cold War period, however, the voluntary movement of individual citizens across national borders has become a visible aspect of the region's international relations, and it is growing. This development is challenging national authorities' power to control their frontier areas, exposing their inability to limit the impact of migrant communities on their societies and even threatening the host countries' ethnic and national identities.

The growing cross-border human flows in Northeast Asia have far-reaching implications at various levels. First, they have the potential to change the nature of the region's international relations. On the one hand, the cross-border movements of people may promote the development of a regional identity among the countries' leaders: they may create opportunities for international cooperation to address migration-related challenges such as migrant labour, transnational human resources development, human rights violations against migrants, infrastructure development for international education and tourism, international crime, trafficking in people, drugs and weapons, and the spread of HIV/AIDS and other infectious diseases. On the other hand, regional governments' inability to forge effective international cooperation in addressing these problems may highlight disagreements, contradictions and conflicts between their perspectives and interests. In addition, the movement of people across national borders has the potential to exacerbate the enmity and suspicion that have long characterized state-to-state relations in the region.[5] The absence of a global framework for the management of movements of people across national borders is well recognized.[6] What is the likelihood that the opportunities and challenges associated with cross-border human flows will give rise to multilateral cooperation? The authors in this volume directly or indirectly address this question not at the global level but within the regional context of Northeast Asia.

Second, cross-border human flows in Northeast Asia present both opportunities and challenges to individual citizens, be they the people crossing borders or members of the host communities. As the final report of the Commission on Human Security states, "For many people ... migration is vital to protect and attain human security, although their human security may also be at risk while they are migrating."[7] Migrants and other people crossing borders are known to expand opportunities for economic exchange between businesses and individuals, to enlarge social networks between different nationalities and to promote the development of transnational communities made up of people of the same ethnic and cultural heritage living in separate countries. The cross-border movement of people may also contribute to the development of transnational identities that are based not on nationality or ethnicity but on shared professional interests and practices.[8]

On the other hand, international human flows can also threaten the material well-being of members of host communities, by, for example, putting stress on their natural and social environment or displacing local workers. The influx of foreigners can heighten social tension at the community level by threatening or being perceived as threatening the communal identity and social order of the host societies; and, in addition, emigration reduces the pool of human resources and disrupts social networks in the sending communities.[9] The welfare of migrants and other individuals crossing borders may be endangered too by outright violation of their human rights or by more subtle forms of injustice and discrimination.

This volume is the product of an international research project – "Cross-border human flows in Northeast Asia: A human security perspective".[10] The case studies from it presented here show the diversity of issues that the cross-border movement of people presents to migrants and other individuals and to affected communities and also national policy-makers in Northeast Asia.

The authors' emphases vary depending on the nature of the case they analyse and the methodology of their analysis. Chapter 1 gives a brief overview of the population trends and migration patterns in each of the Northeast Asian countries and in the region as a whole. The studies of Chinese migration to the Russian Far East in chapters 2 and 3 highlight perceptions of the costs and benefits among the Chinese migrants and members of the host community and also the policy implications for the Chinese, Russian and other regional governments. Chapters 4 and 5 examine the interaction between Russian and Chinese residents respectively and provincial communities in Japan and the cultural and social challenges it presents, as well as the implications for Japan's relations with Russia and China. Chapter 6 deals with the well-established Korean communities in Japan and Shimane Prefecture and discusses the issues of cultural identity, social assimilation and generational change. The analysis of North Koreans in China in chapter 7 is concerned principally with the acute human security problems facing them, and calls for solutions that require a national and international policy response. Chapter 8 examines immigration and emigration issues in South Korea and highlights the difficulty of balancing the interests of South Korea's national identity with the demands of the international community regarding the rights of migrants. Chapter 9 is a study of immigration policy issues in Mongolia; it describes the evolution of Mongolian policy and key concerns regarding in-migration and out-migration.

The gravity of problems and the criticality of concern regarding migration issues also vary from case to case. Concern for national security is most pronounced in the case of Chinese migration to the economically fragile Russian Far East, although the analyses by Larin and Wishnick expose some of the exaggerated fears there about the consequences of the influx of Chinese migrants. In contrast, the case of Russians in Japan examined by Akaha and Vassilieva, the situation of Koreans in Japan studied by Merviö and the circumstances of Chinese in Japan analysed by Zha present not security questions but cultural and social issues regarding negative stereotypes about and discrimination against foreign residents in provincial areas of Japan. The same can be said about the ill treatment of foreign migrants in South Korea examined by Lee and about Mongolian women, who are vulnerable to human trafficking, as noted by Batbayar. The most serious human security problems are found in the case of North Koreans in China, analysed by Smith.

Before presenting the cases, we should describe the boundaries of this collective endeavour. First, "migration" refers in this volume only to voluntary migration; it does not include forced migration. The exclusion of forced migration makes sense because migration within Northeast Asia is mostly of a voluntary nature – largely a result of the gradual opening of national borders to foreign travel and the growing number of ordinary citizens searching for economic opportunities in neighbouring countries. There is one important exception. It could be argued that the North Korean migration to China and elsewhere in the past several years has not been entirely "voluntary". As Smith notes, there may indeed be some cases of defection for fear of political persecution. However, it is clearly not the case that all North Korean migrants in China are subject to political persecution. Indeed, as also noted by Smith, the overwhelming majority of North Koreans moving into north-eastern China have left their country voluntarily, and there is also an undetermined number of North Koreans who move back and forth between North Korea and China. Another case that has attracted much international attention of late is that of North Korean abduction of South Koreans and Japanese citizens during the Korean War and in the 1970s and 1980s respectively. These cases of the forced movement of people are not included in this volume.

Second, with the exception of some references to South Koreans outside Northeast Asia in chapter 8, the studies in this book are focused on the cross-border movement of people within the region. The geographical boundaries are justified by our central concern with the impact of international human flows on the countries and communities of Northeast Asia.

Also, most case studies in this book discuss both conventionally defined "migrants", i.e. individuals who have established or plan to establish a long-term or permanent residence in a foreign country, and those who establish temporary residence there but plan to return to their home country after a certain period of time or who are short-term visitors as tourists or for business, educational or other purposes. The inclusion of short-term visitors is justified by the fact that in many cases, they have as much, if not more, impact than long-term migrants on host countries or communities and on host nationals' perceptions of and attitudes towards foreigners in their areas. Local residents also often fail to differentiate between long-term residents and short-term visitors from neighbouring countries.

In his 2002 report *Strengthening of the United Nations: An Agenda for Further Change*, Kofi Annan, the Secretary-General of the United Nations, called for a comprehensive examination of the different dimensions of migration, as well as of the causes of population movements and their impact on development.[11] We hope that the analyses in this book will encourage discussion and further investigation of the growing cross-border human flows in Northeast Asia and their implications for the region's governments and peoples, for the relations between its countries and also for the interests of individuals crossing borders and members of host communities.

Notes

1. Tsuneo Akaha, ed., *Politics and Economics in Northeast Asia: Nationalism and Regionalism in Contention*, New York: St Martin's Press, 1999.
2. Commission on Human Security, *Human Security Now*, New York: Commission on Human Security, 2003, p. 41, available at http://www.humansecurity-chs.org/finalreport/ (retrieved 12 August 2004).
3. See Maurice D. Van Arsdol, Jr., Stephen Lam, Brian Ettkin and Glenn Guarin, chap. 1, in this volume.
4. See Akaha, ed., *Politics and Economics in Northeast Asia* and Samuel Kim, ed., *The International Relations of Northeast Asia*, Oxford: Rowman & Littlefield, 2004.
5. For a comprehensive examination of factors stunting the development of regional cooperation, see Gilbert Rozman, *Northeast Asia's Stunted Regionalism: Bilateral Distrust in the Shadow of Globalization*, Cambridge: Cambridge University Press, 2004.
6. World Commission on the Social Dimension of Globalization, *A Fair Globalization: Creating Opportunities for All*, Geneva: World Commission on the Social Dimension of Globalization, 2004, p. 95.
7. Commission on Human Security, p. 41, available at http://www.humansecurity-chs.org/finalreport/ (retrieved 12 August 2004).
8. Peggy Levitt, "Transnational Migrants: When 'Home' Means More Than One Country", Migration Information Source, Washington, DC, 1 October 2004, available at http://www.migrationinformation.org/feature/display.cfm?ID=261 (retrieved 20 January 2005).
9. The World Commission on the Social Dimension of Globalization cautions that the promotion of international labour migration should be tempered by a recognition of the costs associated with it, for both sending and receiving countries. World Commission on the Social Dimension of Globalization, *A Fair Globalization*, p. 97.

10. The project was jointly sponsored by the Center for East Asian Studies, Monterey Institute of International Studies, and the Peace and Governance Program, United Nations University (UNU), and supported by grants from UNU, the Freeman Foundation and the US Institute of Peace. Akaha and Vassilieva were co-directors of the project.
11. United Nations, General Assembly, Fifty-seventh Session, *Strengthening of the United Nations: An Agenda for Further Change, Report of the Secretary-General*, New York, 20 September 2002 (A/57/387), p. 10.

Part I

Population trends and migration patterns in Northeast Asia

1

Population trends and migration patterns in Northeast Asia

Maurice D. Van Arsdol, Jr., Stephen Lam, Brian Ettkin and Glenn Guarin

Introduction

Human population flows within and across national borders in Northeast Asia affect the balance of the region's populations, economies, cultures and resources. They are important for state security and human welfare alike. As these flows involve the citizens of states, Northeast Asian governments are concerned with the stability and cohesion of the social fabric and the security of their borders. Population changes, however, occur as a result of individual and collective actions. Accordingly, the security of the state is affected by the welfare of its citizens. State security and human welfare are intertwined and sometimes complementary, but one does not guarantee the other.

The ultimate (root) causes of disharmony between state security and human welfare result from failures of the social contracts that bind countries and populations together in cooperative activity. The proximate causes of this discord apply to specific situations, and can include both changes in population stocks (size, composition and distribution) and population flows (births, deaths and international and intrastate migration). "Human flows" include international and intrastate migrants who have more or less permanently settled in new locations. They also include short-term migrants: migrant workers, traders, tourists, business persons, educators, students, "entertainers" (including sex workers), refugees and internally displaced persons. The links between population dynamics, state security and population welfare are indirect and reciprocal. Popula-

11

Table 1.1 Recent population data for Northeast Asia states and East Asia states[a,b]

	Population mid-2004 (millions)	Natural increase (annual, %)	Projected population 2025	Infant mortality rate	Total fertility rate	% population <15	% population 65+	Life expectancy at birth (years)	% urban	GNI PPI per capita, 2002 (US$)
Northeast Asia states	1,675.1	–	–	–	–	–	–	–	–	–
East Asia states	1,531.0	0.6	1,709.0	30	1.6	21	9	72	46	6,790
(Northeast Asia area: NE China provinces, Japan, DPRK, Mongolia, Russian Federation)	312.5	–	–	–	–	–	–	–	–	–
China	1,300.1	0.6	1,476.0	32	1.7	22	7	71	41	4,520
NE provinces[c]	104.9	–	–	–	–	–	–	–	–	–
Liaoning	41.8	–	–	–	–	–	–	–	–	–
Jilin	26.8	–	–	–	–	–	–	–	–	–
Heilongjiang	36.2	–	–	–	–	–	–	–	–	–
China, Hong Kong SAR	6.8	0.1	8.4	2.4	0.9	15	12	81	100	27,490
China, Macao SAR	0.4	0.4	0.5	3.0	0.8	20	8	77	99	21,910
Taiwan	22.8	0.4	24.4	6.0	1.2	20	9	76	78	–
Japan	127.6	0.1	121.1	3.0	1.3	14	19	82	78	27,380
DPRK	22.8	0.7	24.7	45	2.0	27	6	63	60	–
ROK	48.2	0.5	50.6	8	1.2	20	8	77	80	16,960
Mongolia	2.5	1.2	3.4	30	2.7	36	5	65	57	1,710
Russian Federation	144.1	–0.6	136.9	13	1.4	16	13	65	73	8,080
Russian Far East[d]	7.0	–	–	–	–	–	–	–	–	–

[a] *Major source*: Population Reference Bureau, 2004 World Population Data Sheet, Population Reference Bureau, Washington, DC, 2004.

Definitions: mid-2004 population: estimates are based on a recent census, official national data or UN and US Census Bureau projections.

Rate of natural increase: birth rate minus the death rate, implying the annual rate of population growth without regard for migration. Expressed as a percentage.

Projected population 2025: based on official country projections, series issued by the UN, US Census Bureau or Population Reference Bureau projections.

Infant mortality rate: the annual number of deaths of infants under age 1 year per 1,000 live births.

Total fertility rate: the average number of children a woman would have assuming that current age-specific birth rates will remain constant throughout her childbearing years (usually considered to be ages 15–49).

% Population: <15 and 65+ in age, often considered to be the "dependent ages".

Life expectancy at birth: the average number of years a newborn infant can expect to live under *current* mortality rates.

Urban population: percentage of the total population living in areas termed urban by that country.

GNI PPP per capita, 2002: gross national income in purchasing power parity (PPP) by mid-year population, based on value of goods and services in US which can be purchased in referenced country with US dollars.

[b] Do not reproduce without permission from Population Reference Bureau, Inc.

[c] 1 November 2000 Census enumerated population, *Tabulation of the 2000 Population Census of the Peoples Republic of China*: compiled by the Population Census Office of the State Council Department of Population, Social, Science and Technology Statistics, National Review of Statistics of China, 2002, Beijing.

[d] Mid-2002, "Russian Statistics Yearbook 1999–2002", Russian Federation National Statistics; Economic Research, Institute for Northeast Asia (ERINA), Niigata, Japan, available at http://www.erina.or.jp/En/Asia/Bask2002/Bask2002.htm.

–: data unavailable or inapplicable.

13

tion policies and dynamics tend to affect proximate rather than ultimate determinants of security and welfare.[1]

The size of Northeast Asian countries' populations and economies magnifies the global consequences of the region's population dynamics. The Northeast Asian states – China, the Hong Kong Special Administrative Region (SAR), the Macao SAR, Japan, the Democratic People's Republic of Korea (the DPRK, or North Korea), the Republic of Korea (the ROK, or South Korea), Mongolia and the Russian Federation (Russia) – were the homelands of approximately 1,627,000,000 people in the year 2000. China, Japan and Russia held the earth's first, ninth and seventh largest populations respectively in that year. They then ranked seventh, second and fourteenth in terms of gross national product.[2]

The Northeast Asian states and all Asian countries contained approximately 27 per cent and 61 per cent respectively of the earth's population in 2000. According to United Nations medium variant population projections, the Northeast Asian countries and the East Asian countries (the Northeast Asian countries less the Russian Federation) will each have larger populations than any non-Asian continent until approximately 2040, when they will be overtaken by Africa.[3]

The population characteristics of the Northeast Asian states circa 2003 are summarized in table 1.1. Approximately 312 million people, or one-twentieth of the earth's population, lived in Northeast Asia, defined here to include the Heilongjiang, Liaoning and Jilin provinces of China, the Russian Far East's main administrative areas – Primorsky Krai, Khabarovsky Krai, Amurskaya Oblast, Jewish Autonomous Oblast, Sakhalinskaya Oblast, Republic of Sakha (Yakutia), Chukhotsky Autonomous Okrug, Magadanskaya Oblast (including Koryaksky Autonomous Okrug – and the entirety of the other Northeast Asian countries).

Figure 1.1 indicates the great disparity in population size among Northeast Asian states. China's estimated population of 1,275,000,000 in 2000 far exceeded that of the other Northeast Asian and East Asian states; it was more than 500 times the size of the Mongolian population. China has approximately 78 per cent of the population of all the Northeast Asian countries. The three north-eastern Chinese provinces have about one-third of the population of Northeast Asia. When the higher population density in China's border regions is contrasted with the less densely populated border regions in adjacent Mongolia and Russia, it becomes even more apparent that China dominates Northeast Asia in terms of population.

The late twentieth-century transition from high to low fertility and mortality rates is complete in most Northeast Asian countries. National populations have also aged, urbanized and diversified. As a result, fertility is no longer the major population concern in the region. Ageing, ur-

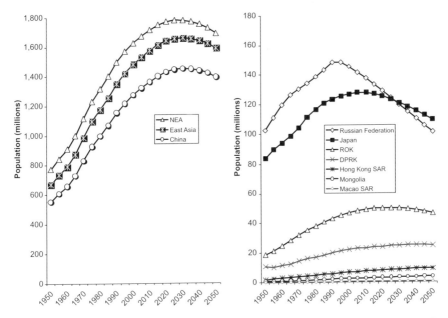

Figure 1.1 Population size, East Asian and Northeast Asian states: estimates and projections, 1950–2050 (*Source*: From *World Population Prospects, The 2002 Revision, Vol. 1*, by Population Division, © 2003 United Nations. Reprinted with the permission of the publisher.)

banization, population diversification, and internal and international migration, including refugee movements and other cross-border flows, are fuelling new debates about the future of populations in Northeast Asia.

This chapter considers the following questions about how changes in population stocks and flows affect state security and human welfare in Northeast Asia. First, what is the background and nature of current population changes in Northeast Asia? Second, what are the migration trends in and policies of the Northeast Asian states? Third, how do cross-border flows respond to or affect other population changes in those states? Fourth, what new migration policy frameworks might enhance both state security and population welfare in the region?

Population change in Northeast Asia

Background

Current population transitions in Northeast Asia reflect past conflicts in the region, and cross-border flows are no exception.[4] "Civilizational" conflicts between Russia and China reflect migratory activity in border regions beginning with indigenous tribes and continuing with Mongols, Russians, Koreans, Han Chinese, Europeans, Americans, Japanese and Manchus. Russians began settling the Russo-Chinese border regions under the aegis of the Treaty of Nerchinsk of 1689. The majority of the Mongol population was subsequently incorporated into the Chinese and Russian empires. The Russian empire expanded after the Sino-Russian treaties of 1858 and 1860, which extended Russian territory to the northern bank of the Amur River and to the Sea of Japan. Russia thereby obtained territory equal in size to one-third of the United States. The Qing dynasty was weakened in the nineteenth century by British victories in the opium wars of 1832–1842 and 1856–1860 and by other European and American invasions and occupations. Civilizational conflicts between Russia and Japan included the Russo-Japanese war of 1904–1905, after which Russia surrendered claims to Korea, Port Arthur and South Sakhalin, and the Soviet annexation of the then Japanese-controlled Sakhalin and Kurile islands at the end of World War II.[5]

The displacement of populations by demographic engineering and by past conflicts can be proximate causes of conflict, especially if displaced populations define and exert a "right of return". Stalinist demographic "engineering" (forced relocation policies) expelled Chinese from the Russian Far East and displaced Korean migrants to Central Asia. World War II, nationalist conflicts between China and Japan and between Korea and Japan, the state conflict between the DPRK and the ROK, and changing borders have left Chinese, Japanese, Mongolian and Korean populations and their descendents stranded outside their traditional homelands. The 1950–1953 conflict between the DPRK and the ROK, which expanded to include China, the United States and other countries, shifted Koreans between the DPRK and the ROK. Northeast Asian policy-makers' views regarding relations with their neighbours and the treatment of migrants are affected by this history of conflict and demographic engineering.

Recent population transitions

How can recent population changes in Northeast Asia be accounted for? The changes in population stocks and flows in Northeast Asia, East Asia and elsewhere are linked to modernization – from agricultural to industrial to post-industrial economic activity. These changes have been associated with a series of linked population transitions. In the absence of migration, the vital rates and epidemiologic transition represents death and birth rate decreases and the occurrence of population growth through natural increase (an excess of births over deaths). A labour force and ageing transition results from an increase in the proportion of the population of labour force age and subsequent ageing. An urbanization and diversification transition occurs as more people move from rural areas to cities, resulting in the mixing of dissimilar populations.[6] The effects of these transitions will continue throughout the twenty-first century.

Vital rates and epidemiology

The change of the pattern of vital rates and epidemiology is essentially complete in all Northeast Asian states except the DPRK and Mongolia. However, some Northeast Asian populations will grow for several decades as a result of population momentum, which occurs when a population with low fertility experiences growth because past high fertility has concentrated the population in the childbearing ages. Figure 1.1 indicates that the Northeast Asian and East Asian regions face population declines after 2035, as has Europe since around 1990. Figure 1.2 suggests that all Northeast Asian states except Mongolia will experience net natural decreases (an excess of deaths over births) by 2050.

Ageing of the population and the labour force

The age–sex population pyramids in Figure 1.3 reflect the "demographic bonus" in some Northeast Asian countries that resulted from birth- and death-rate declines in the early stages of the change of vital rates and epidemiology. This bonus was a temporary increase in the ratio of the age of the labour force population to the total population. It accompanied improved public health, family planning, education, openness to trade, and investment and savings. It helped to fuel the Asian "economic miracle" in Japan, the ROK, the Hong Kong SAR, the Macao SAR and the ROC prior to and into the 1990s.[7]

Population ageing in Northeast Asia has also resulted in the ageing of national labour forces, labour shortages and a shift from youth dependency to old age dependency. Population ageing has recently provided a rationale for Northeast Asian countries to import migrant labour. Figure 1.3 indicates that Northeast Asian states are moving from isosceles triangle-shaped population pyramids – with wide bases denoting relatively many children and narrow apexes denoting relatively few older people – towards mushroom-shaped pyramids, whose caps reflect a high proportion of older people.

Population ageing is a "predicament, and not a problem with a solution".[8] Japan and South Korea, for example, will not be able to import enough workers by 2050 to maintain current (2000) support ratios of the working-age population (15–64) to the old-age population (65 and older).[9] These support ratios could possibly be increased by raising retirement ages.[10] The ageing predicament is more acute in Russia, where no relief from population decline is in sight, and in rural China, where the potential economic benefits of the demographic bonus are still unrealized.

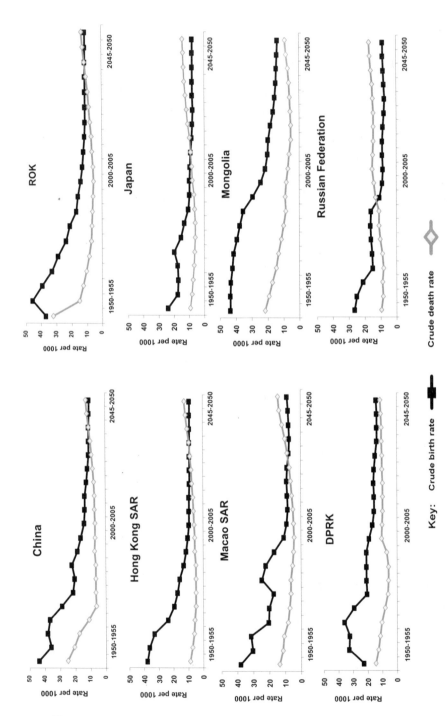

Figure 1.2 Vital rates and epidemiologic transition, Northeast Asian states: estimates and projections, 1950–2050 (*Source:* From *World Population Prospects, The 2002 Revision, Vol. 1,* by Population Division, © 2003 United Nations. Reprinted with the permission of the publisher.)

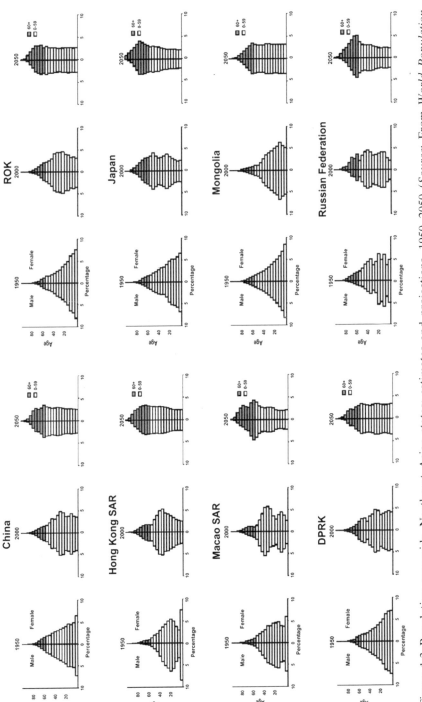

Figure 1.3 Population pyramids, Northeast Asian states: estimates and projections, 1950–2050 (*Source:* From *World Population Ageing, 1950–2050*, by Population Division, © 2002, United Nations. Reprinted with the permission of the publisher.)

Urbanization and diversity

The percentages of Northeast Asian national populations termed "urban" by their governments circa 2003 ranged from 39 per cent in China to 100 per cent in the Hong Kong SAR (see table 1.1). A "world cities" network in Northeast Asian countries organizes and services economic activity. The network includes the "world class" or "alpha" cities Tokyo and Hong Kong, followed by the "beta" cities Moscow and Seoul and then by the "gamma" cities Osaka, Beijing, Taipei and Shanghai.[11]

Migration between adjacent states can enhance the development of trans-border cities (TBCs): they sprawl across nation-state boundaries and are based on increasingly borderless economies. Adjacent TBCs sometimes coalesce into trans-border systems (TBSs), comprised of two or more TBCs. TBCs and TBSs have diverse, and sometimes transnational, populations. They organize transactions between countries and stimulate migration.[12]

Northeast Asian TBSs include the Hong Kong SAR, the Macao SAR, Guangzhou (China) TBS and the Tokyo–Seoul–Pyongyang–Beijing TBS urban corridor. Small TBCs may develop in the Blagoveshchensk (Amur Oblast, Russia)–Heihe (Heilongjiang, China) and the Pogranichnyi (Primorskii Krai, Russia)–Suifenhe (Heilongjiang, China) special trade zones. A TBS linking the ROK and the DPRK could follow the development of the Kaesang Industrial Complex north of the demilitarized zone. Although TBCs and TBSs pose difficult questions regarding national sovereignty, they enhance regional stability by integrating human and economic resources.

Migration

The change in the pattern of migration does not explain migration, and migration does not follow or lead the vital rates and epidemiological transition in any specific manner.[13] Migration refers to a change of the *de jure* or usual place of residence that crosses city, county, provincial, state or international boundary lines (internal and international migration). Migration is linked to other flows, of capital, communications, and goods and services, and can be a cause or consequence of changes in population stock. International migration flows include "conventional" flows of more permanent settlers and reunited families, as well as short-term "non-conventional" migrants. Refugee migration and internal (intrastate) population displacement are forms of forced migration. Most persons crossing international borders are not migrants; they are travellers (e.g. traders, other business persons and tourists) who will return home.[14]

Migration trends and policies

Migration trends

Migration systems are defined by population flows between groupings of countries. Northeast Asian migrations reflect the historical penetration by European capitalist markets and the flows of Europeans from the "older (European) core" to the "world periphery (including Northeast Asia)" for economic activity. These flows were followed by migrations of Northeast Asian nationals to "older" and "newer" core areas, including newer core areas in Northeast Asia and East Asia.[15]

The migration and development tiers relevant to Northeast Asia have been defined by Skeldon as follows: (1) the "new core" for economic activity and migrants (Japan, the ROK and Taiwan [Republic of China]); (2) "core extensions and potential cores" (coastal China, the Hong Kong SAR, the Macao SAR and the more settled coastal areas of the Russian Far East); (3) the "labour frontier" migrant source (e.g. the populous near interior of eastern China and the DPRK); and (4) the "resource niche" (e.g. Mongolia, the remainder of China, including western China and Tibet and the rest of the Russian Far East). The Northeast Asian labour frontier contains a reservoir of potential migrants, some of whom migrate to extract resources from the resource niche and to engage in manufacturing and service activities in Northeast Asian core extensions and potential cores.[16] The Northeast Asian new core and the core extensions and potential cores are now experiencing increasing migration pressures from lower-income Asian countries.[17]

Migration indicators for Northeast Asian countries for 1990 and 2000 are summarized in table 1.2. Total migrant stock increased in each Northeast Asian state between 1990 and 2000. Northeast Asian states had approximately 28 per cent of the world's population in 2000, but its migrant stock amounted to an estimated 19,029,000 people, or only 11.7 per cent of the world's total migrant stock of approximately 175,000,000. If the Russian Federation's stock is subtracted from the Northeast Asian countries, the region's migrant stock was only about 3.4 per cent of the world total. Russia had the largest estimated migrant stock among Northeast Asian countries: 13,259,000, about 68 per cent of that of the regional total and 9 per cent of Russia's population, largely owing to the recent return of former residents of other republics of the former USSR. Russia's migrant stock was followed in size by the Hong Kong SAR (2,701,000); Japan (1,620,000); the ROK (597,000); China (513,000); the DPRK (37,000); the Macao SAR (16,000); and Mongolia (8,000).[18]

Table 1.2 indicates that there are relatively few refugees in Northeast Asia. In 2000, China had the largest number of refugees (294,000), fol-

Table 1.2 Migration indicators, Northeast Asian states, 1990–2000*

Indicator	China 1990	China 2000	Hong Kong SAR 1990	Hong Kong SAR 2000	Macao SAR 1990	Macao SAR 2000	Japan 1990	Japan 2000
Population								
No. (000s)	1,155,305	1,275,133	5,705	6,860	372	444	123,537	127,096
Natural increase/1,000 population	11.1	9.3	5.8	4.8	12.3	6.5	2.8	2.1
Rate of growth/1,000 population	10.8	9.0	17.0	19.9	22.5	13.0	3.1	2.6
Migrant stock								
No. (000s)	380	513	2,218	2,701	204	294	877	1,620
% of population	–	–	38.9	39.4	54.9	66.1	0.7	1.3
Refugees								
No. (000s)	287.3	294.1	8.2	1.0	0.2	–	6.8	3.8
% of migrant stock	75.6	57.4	0.4	–	0.1	–	0.8	0.2
Net migration								
No. (000s)	–381	–381	66	99	4	3	3.7	56
Rate/1,000 population	–0.3	–0.3	11.1	15.1	10.1	6.5	0.3	0.4
No./100 births	–2	–2	98	147	60	60	3	5
Workers' remittances								
Total (US$m)	124	556	"	"	"	"	"	505
% of gross domestic product	–	0.1	"	"	"	"	"	–
Per capita (US$)	–	–	"	"	"	"	"	4
Projected population in 2050 (000s)	1,462,058	–	9,648	–	527	–	109,220	–
Projected population in 2050 (000s)*	1,480,836	–	6,104	–	401	–	105,418	–

	DPRK		ROK		Mongolia		Russian Federation	
Population								
No. (000s)	19,956	22,268	42,869	46,740	2,216	2,533	148,292	145,491
Natural increase/1,000 population	13.7	8.2	10.0	8.2	20.5	16.2	−2.7	−5.6
Rate of growth/1,000 population	13.7	8.2	9.5	7.8	17.0	9.7	−0.2	−3.6
Migrant stock								
No. (000s)	34	37	572	597	7	8	11,689	13,259
% of population	0.2	0.2	1.3	1.3	0.3	0.3	7.9	9.1
Refugees								
No. (000s)	"	"	0.2	—	"	"	—	26.3
% of migrant stock	"	"	—	—	"	"	—	0.2
Net migration								
No. (000s)	—	—	−23	−18	−8	−16	372	287
Rate/1,000 population	—	—	−0.5	−0.4	−3.5	−6.5	2.5	2
No./100 births	—	—	−3	−3	−12	−27	24	22
Workers' remittances								
Total (US$m)	"	"	488	63	"	78	"	"
% of gross domestic product	"	"	0.2	—	"	0.8	"	"
Per capita (US$)	"	"	11	1	"	3	"	"
Projected population in 2050 (000s)	28,038	—	51,560	—	4,146	—	104,258	—
Projected population in 2050 (000s)*	28,038	—	51,961	—	4,210	—	101,680	—

Source: From *United Nations International Migration Report 2002*, by Population Division. © 2003 United Nations. Reprinted with the permission of the publisher.
*Assuming zero migration after 2000.

23

lowed by the Russian Federation (26,000) and Japan (4,000). The highest rates of net migration were experienced by the Hong Kong SAR (15 per 1,000 of the population), followed by the Macao SAR (6 per 1000) and Russia (2 per 1000). Net migration was negative in China, the ROK and Mongolia.[19]

Human flows in Northeast Asia, including "conventional" (permanent) migrants and "non-conventional" (short-term) migrants, now present a number of state security and human welfare issues. Human flows from China to the Russian Far East have led to nationalist fears and security concerns in Russia.[20] The new presence of Russians in northern Japan has resulted in unfavourable reactions by Japanese citizens, which could hamper closer relations between Japan and Russia and further postpone the resolution of the Japan–Russia sovereignty dispute over the Northern Territories/southern Kurile Islands.[21] The importing of Chinese labour into Japan raises issues regarding the lack of assimilation of Chinese in Japan that may negatively affect bilateral relations between Japan and China.[22] The lack of assimilation of Koreans in Japan and their failure to gain full legal protection may impede Japan's successful globalization.[23] The passive migration policies of the ROK government have been detrimental to the welfare of overseas Koreans and foreign migrants to Korea, and may lead to tensions with Russia, China and Japan.[24] Incidents involving DPRK migrants and asylum seekers in north-eastern China, some of whom seek to migrate to the ROK, China and elsewhere, pose serious legal, economic and humanitarian issues for Northeast Asian countries.[25] In Mongolia, the recent increase in migration, combined with a lingering Russian presence and an upsurge in Chinese influence, is a matter of concern.[26] More generally, the increasing feminization of migration, including migration for domestic service, mail-order marriages, sex work, and also the sex trafficking of women and children, complicates a number of human welfare issues.[27]

Migration policies

The public and private sectors share the management of migration in Northeast Asia.[28] Some state-managed migration in Northeast Asia has given way to demand-driven migration serviced by labour contractors who also provide cross-border services in lieu of labour.[29] Policy-makers in Northeast Asia and East Asia, driven by the demand for labour, tend to favour the circulation of unskilled workers and highly skilled personnel, to restrict permanent settlement[30] and to reject government recruiting of migrants owing to perceived threats to cultural homogeneity.

The increasingly restrictive migration policies of industrialized states outside Northeast Asia are lessening demands abroad for unskilled labour from the Northeast Asian labour frontier. Nevertheless, growing migration pressures in Northeast Asia are increasing the legal and ir-regular cross-border flows to and within the region, heightening state security concerns and threatening the welfare of migrants. In 2003, all Northeast Asian governments except that of the Russian Federation re-ported that their levels of immigration were satisfactory and that they also planned to maintain their immigration policies or not to intervene to change migration levels. Russia reported its level of immigration as too high and had a policy for lowering it. China and Russia indicated that they encouraged the return of their nationals; Japan and the ROK did not encourage their return. All Northeast Asian countries stated that their levels of emigration were satisfactory, and intended either to main-tain the current level or not to intervene.[31]

The migration policies of Northeast Asian countries appear to give low priority to the rights and well-being of migrants. China, Japan and the ROK do not favour the integration of non-nationals, and, excluding refu-gee agreements, there are no significant international governance re-gimes in place in Northeast Asia to regulate the cross-border movement of people. Moreover, as of 2003 no Northeast Asian countries had rati-fied the 1990 Convention on the Protection of Rights of Migrant Workers and Family Members, the 2000 Protocol to Prevent, Suppress, and Punish Trafficking of Persons or the 2000 Protocol against the Smuggling of Migrants. China, Japan, the ROK and the Russian Federation have rati-fied the 1951 Convention relating to the Status of Refugees and the 1967 Protocol relating to the Status of Refugees.[32]

National cases

China

China's sheer numbers have a great influence on Northeast Asian popu-lation stocks and flows (see figure 1.1). China successfully engineered rapid mortality and fertility declines in the second half of the twentieth century. It is now experiencing massive rural–urban migration, rapid population ageing and increasing social and economic diversity. It is ex-porting large numbers of its population and assimilating the Hong Kong and Macao SARs. The New Economic Reform has resulted in impressive economic growth, but it has also led to new social problems. There is a growing disparity in standards of living. Universal access to healthcare has ended, threatening the health of poor urban and rural populations. The deterioration of the public health infrastructure has increased the vulnerability of China's populations to HIV/AIDS, severe acute respiratory syndrome (SARS), influenza and tuberculosis.[33]

China's ageing population is now inspiring a national dialogue on its economic future.[34] A rise in the support ratio of the old-age population to the working-age population will adversely affect social services, pensions and healthcare. China's policy-makers have called on the government to examine and learn from Japan's experience with ageing.[35]

A combination of redundant farm labour, rural poverty, environmental stress, developmental differences between regions and higher wages in economically booming urban areas in China has recently generated the aforementioned massive rural–urban migration.[36] Rural–urban migrants have challenged the household registration (*hukou*) system, which had tied internal migrants to their birthplace. The geographic movement of rural residents, including relocation to cities, was formally restricted. Barred from moving to the cities, internal migrants were ineligible for work there. Internal migrants were also denied educational opportunities, and they had restricted access to healthcare.[37] Excluding Beijing and Shanghai, the Chinese government relaxed *hukou* registration on 1 October 2001. This left undisturbed many of the "floating population" of 130 million migrants then estimated to be living outside their place of registration and created new opportunities for China's population.[38]

The Chinese government is now turning internal migration into a means of modernization and easing the plight of migrant workers.[39] Many urban migrants now circulate between cities and villages, helping to decrease urban–rural economic and cultural differences.[40] Nevertheless, the economic divide between rural and urban areas continues to contribute to growing socio-economic inequalities throughout the country.[41]

Minority ethnic affiliation and trans-border contacts among ethnic minorities are increasing in China.[42] The Chinese government has encouraged internal migration in order to modernize the economy and build up underdeveloped provinces. Economic development notwithstanding, internal migration has also facilitated efforts by the government to increase the Han population in peripheral areas, particularly in Xingjian Province in the north-west, the Inner Mongolia Autonomous Region, Heilongjiang Province in the north-east and the Tibetan Autonomous Region.[43] Ethnic, religious and political tensions have escalated in the Tibetan Autonomous Region and Xingjian Province because incoming Han Chinese have appropriated local resources.[44] In north-eastern trans-border regions such as the Amurskaya Oblast in the Russian Far East and the Tumen River basin near the DPRK, the presence and migration of Han Chinese threaten to harm China's relations with its neighbours.[45]

China is a leading global source of international migration, with as many as 33 million ethnic Chinese living abroad. Rural–urban migration has caused some of this migration. China's economic growth has resulted in attempts by Beijing to attract skilled foreign workers and Chinese students who have been educated abroad. There is also more undocumented migration (largely from Viet Nam and the DPRK) and more international travel by Chinese.[46] The Chinese government is developing policies to further manage immigration and emigration, and is engaging more in international dialogue regarding migration.[47] These changes will improve the welfare of Chinese migrants.

Hong Kong SAR

The transformation of the global economy since the 1970s resulted in the rapid economic development of the then British-controlled Hong Kong, which has now completed the vital rates and epidemiological transition.[48] The economic integration of Hong Kong with the rest of China, as well as border and immigration controls similar to other trans-border systems, is facilitating development of the Greater China economic bloc (China–Hong Kong SAR and Macao SAR–Taiwan) and increasing China's global interdependence.[49] Illegal migration to Hong Kong has been relieved by the creation of special economic zones near the city, which attract residents from mainland China. Many Hong Kong citizens have established residences on the mainland. Immigration issues concern the rights of some mainland Chinese, especially those born to Hong Kong residents, to live in Hong Kong, and also migration pressures on Shenzhen, a site of extensive economic activity across the border from Hong Kong.[50]

Macao SAR

The Macao SAR, which reverted from Portuguese to Chinese administration in 1999, is experiencing rapid population ageing. Macao's economy is based largely on tourism, gambling and the export of clothing.[51] China is undertaking infrastructure development in order to integrate Macao into its economy. Foreign labour is used in lieu of mainland Chinese labour because laws now restrict the flow of mainland Chinese to the area. (Macao Chinese are free to enter and exit the mainland.) In order to decrease reliance on outside labour, the Macao government is giving hiring preference to locals and reducing the number of outside workers.[52] Nevertheless, Macao's low fertility rate suggests that hiring only local residents will not solve the labour shortage.

Taiwan (ROC)

The population of Taiwan (ROC) is ageing, and the government is now promoting higher fertility. Urbanization is increasing in already densely populated places while new urban areas have sprouted up beyond the official limits of major cities.[53] The economy is moving from labour-intensive to capital- and technology-intensive industries. Taiwan is a large investor in other Asian economies, including mainland China and the Hong Kong SAR. Labour shortages have led to the import of illegal as well as legal foreign workers, but in 1998 the government halted labour imports because of rising unemployment.[54] There is an increasing interchange between Taiwan and mainland Chinese populations. According to one source, "800,000 of Taiwan's 22 million people lived full-time or part-time on the Mainland in 2002".[55]

Japan

Since World War II, Japan has transformed its economy and population. Economic recovery and development focused largely on the Pacific area rather than Northeast Asia. Its population has changed rapidly in profile, from high to low rates of fertility and mortality. Japan is beginning to experience population decline as a result of low fertility and population ageing. Young Japanese are delaying marriage and having fewer children, which has led to below-replacement fertility. Also, the dependency burden on the labour force is increasing as more resources are focused on support of the increasing older population.[56] Japan has recently experienced reduced trade surpluses, rising unemployment and falling standards of living. Recognizing that an increasing ratio of aged population to working population will severely limit public contributions to pension plans as well as hamper funding for possible expansion of the military, the Japanese government is attempting to shift responsibilities for the care of older people back to families.[57]

The dependence burdens on its labour force suggest a need for Japan to import foreign labour in numbers that would be culturally and politically unacceptable owing to the high value placed on ethnic homogeneity.[58] During the 1980s and 1990s, Japan became a labour-importing country, with the focus on less-skilled workers. It also attracted illegal migrants, particularly for the "3-K" (kitanai, kiken and kitsui) or dirty, dangerous and demeaning jobs and for jobs for female "entertainers".[59] In addition, it experienced large increases in circulating travellers, including Russians in Niigata and Hokkaido, some of whom came to stay.[60] These experiences, as well as past and current migrations of Koreans and Chinese to Japan, are raising new questions about the well-being and assimilation of migrants.[61] However, Japan discourages the assimilation of foreign nationals and has yet to resolve questions of national identity. Migration issues can jeopardize Japan's relations and economic ties with other Northeast Asian countries.

What can Japan do to ameliorate the problems arising from its declining population? One policy option is to encourage higher fertility. Another option is to increase participation in the labour force on the part of women and older people. Japan may also continue to invest in increasing its labour productivity and developing more of its productive capacity abroad. The final option is to continue to recruit foreign workers (sometimes illegally) through private contractors.[62] Domestic NGOs in Japan are now assisting foreign workers, and act as advocates for their rights and welfare, regardless of whether they are highly skilled European professionals or Asian labourers.[63] Japanese immigration policies may now be moving towards greater accommodation to the needs of foreign nationals, but not at the expense of tighter oversight in order to address national security concerns.[64]

The DPRK

North Korean migration to China, motivated largely by the failures of the North Korean economy, poses serious political, humanitarian and economic problems for Northeast Asian countries. Famine resulted in 500,000 to 1,000,000 deaths in the DPRK in the 1990s.[65] Although it has strict migration controls, a worsening political or economic situation and civil strife could result in state implosion and/or massive refugee migration to the ROK and China.[66] The DPRK is linked diplomatically to China and retains trade ties with the Russian Federation. In 2003, an estimated 10,000 North Koreans were reported to be working in the Russian Far East, living in segregated facilities under harsh working conditions and the surveillance of North Korean security agents.[67]

An increasing emphasis on trade and economic integration, including well-managed non-coercive labour flows between the DPRK and the ROK and between the DPRK and the Russian Federation, could enhance the DPRK's development and also regional stability. A rural market economy has taken root on the DPRK–Chinese border.[68] Some recent DPRK migrants to north-eastern China have been treated as economic migrants, but others have become asylum seekers and have sought refuge in foreign embassies and consulates in China.[69] Authorities in north-eastern China have refused these migrants access to UNHCR representatives since 1999.[70] Bilateral treaties between China and North Korea enable Chinese authorities to seek out and repatriate North Koreans to the DPRK, where they may be subject to persecution by the authorities.[71] The welfare of North Koreans in China affects the international relations of all Northeast Asian states.

The ROK

The ROK is now a major labour importer and a declining labour exporter. "Irregular migration" has been the norm in South Korea, as imported labour was formerly unacceptable to its trade unions.[72] The ROK government has recently decided to admit migrant workers from China, Kazakhstan, Indonesia, Viet Nam, Sri Lanka, Thailand, Mongolia and the Philippines in order to replace undocumented workers and make up for labour shortfalls.[73] Undocumented workers are acknowledged to have helped to prevent a crisis in the country's labour market but will nonetheless be extradited if they do not leave voluntarily.[74] Trade unions supported the protests in spring 2004 by Korean-Chinese workers, who were seeking more equitable access to the ROK labour market. Although mandatory health insurance for foreign workers came into effect in August 2004,[75] other rights are absent, in particular education and other benefits for the workers and their dependants.

Ethnic Korean migration to the ROK, from China and the DPRK, also raises international questions.[76] The Emigration and Immigration and Legal Status of Overseas Koreans Bill of January 2000 allows ethnic Koreans to stay in South Korea for two years, with the possibility of extending their visas and integrating into ROK society. In contrast to the more accepting legal environment they find in the ROK, ethnic Koreans in either China or Japan, whose ancestors left Korea before and during the Japanese occupation (1910–1945), may find it almost impossible to preserve their Korean identity. The ROK no longer directly accepts North Koreans who have migrated to China. Instead, it negotiates with foreign embassies in Beijing to accept these asylum seekers, who are later redirected to Seoul.[77]

On the Korean peninsula, more than in other Northeast Asian areas, economic development is strongly linked to the prevention of massive refugee movements. Economic ventures between the two Koreas include the construction of a trans-peninsula railway, which will eventually connect with the Trans-Siberian railway.[78] The planned Kaesong Industrial Complex north of the demilitarized zone may, if realized, further boost cross-border economic trade and population flows.[79] However, the persistent nuclear threat that looms over the peninsula deters the ROK from investing more heavily in the DPRK, especially in the north-east (whose collapsed industrial base is the main source of refugees). Continuous tension over the nuclear question may further aggravate economic conditions in the DPRK, thereby generating refugee flows.

Mongolia

Approximately 85 per cent of Mongolia's 2.5 million residents in 2004 (see table 1.1) were Mongol Khalkha. Other ethnic categories included Turkic groups, primarily Kazakhs (7 per cent), the Tungusic (5 per cent) and others, primarily Chinese and Russians (3 per cent).[80] Approximately 4.8 million Mongol citizens of China were concentrated in Inner Mongolia and in Liaoning, Jilin, Hebei, Heilongjiang and Xinjiang provinces.[81] Approximately half a million Mongols were also found in the Lake Baikal area and the lower Volga area of the Russian Federation.[82] The Mongolian government has relaxed foreign travel for Mongolians to the extent that large numbers of citizens of Kazakh ethnic origin have returned to Kazakhstan.[83]

During the twentieth century, Mongolia changed from a feudal pastoral society to a Soviet-influenced agricultural-industrial society and then, in the 1990s, to a democratic-capitalist system with an emphasis on social welfare.[84] Urbanization was rapid and well controlled from the 1950s to the 1980s. Current major problems in Mongolia include poverty and hunger.[85] Recent internal migration has been driven by harsh winters, by poor harvests and droughts and by a lack of rural employment opportunities. Internal migration has been from the western and central regions to Ulaanbaatar, Darkhan and Erdenet.[86] Migrants often settle with their livestock in crowded urban and suburban areas, burdening the environmental and socio-economic infrastructures (health services, education, housing and jobs) and inhibiting economic growth.[87]

Modernization is increasing pressures for both immigration and emigration, with their attendant hazards and benefits. Mongols in Mongolia have long-standing concerns about the assimilation of ethnic Chinese, but Russian immigrants have been more readily accepted. If migration into Mongolia increases significantly, it will be largely from China and particularly from Inner Mongolia.[88]

The Russian Federation

The Russian Federation's population in 2004 was the second largest among Northeast Asian states, but regionally the Russian Far East's (RFE) population is the smallest of the various geographic areas comprising Northeast Asia. Russia faces disconcerting demographic trends. Since the dissolution of the Soviet Union, it has experienced unusually high mortality from preventable causes (e.g. alcoholism, violence and accidents), decreasing life expectancy, increased morbidity, high induced abortion rates and low fertility rates. Revolution, wars, famine, urbanization and political changes in the twentieth century are reported to "have already cost Russia about a half of its possible population in 2000'', and continued low levels of reproduction could lead to a further halving of the population.[89] Russia's population issues are amplified in the sparsely populated Russian Far East, where, even at its population peak of 8.1 million people in 1991, only 5 per cent of the national population lived in a region that comprises 35 per cent of the total national area.

The government of the Soviet Union pursued an intensive programme of demographic engineering in the Russian Far East – to deploy and quarter Soviet army contingents, to construct a regional military-industrial complex, to extract natural resources for European Russia and to provide a place for criminals and the politically undesirable.[90] The population of the Russian Far East, which increased from 1.6 million to 8.1 million between 1926 and 1991, consists primarily of ethnic Russians.[91] In 1937, the Chinese and Korean residents of the region were subjected to security deportations; 172,000 Koreans of the RFE were relocated to Kazakhstan and Uzbekistan.[92]

After the Russian Far East's population peaked in 1991, immigration effectively stopped. Economic depression, as well as the ending of subsidies, served as a stimulus for many to begin leaving the region. Between 1992 and 2002, the population of the RFE declined from 8.1 million to less than 6.7 million (see figure 1.1).[93] Population decline was more severe in the northern part of the RFE than in the south.[94]

It is in the context of these broader demographic trends that concerns about Chinese immigration to Russia, in particular the Russian Far East, have emerged over the past decade. Reactions among Russians to the ostensibly increasing Chinese presence vary from fear of invasion to considering possibilities for economic development.[95] Inconsistencies and weaknesses in Russia's immigration policy, legislation and enforcement over the past decade are associated with these concerns. Normalization of relations between the Soviet Union and China in the late 1980s, followed by the adoption of visa-free exchange between the two countries in 1992, led to unanticipated mass movements across the Russia–China border in the Russian Far East.[96] The RFE economy grew dependent upon illegal as well as legal Chinese shuttle traders, and the number of illegal aliens increased.[97] The competing political and juridical objectives of the national government in Moscow and the Russian Far East regional governments resulted in negative economic consequences for the RFE. In a region of less than 7 million citizens, the liberal estimate of 200,000 migrants (only 3 per cent) there created a perception of uncontrolled cross-border crime and illegal migration. Growing tension among the populace prompted the governments of Russia and China to create in May 2003 joint working groups whose purpose was to put into effect curbs on the uncontrolled movement of people across their common border.[98]

Russian authorities have attempted to improve both the reporting and the control mechanisms of migration. In 2002, the Duma passed a new citizenship law that introduces additional reporting and control requirements, but it does not provide for any clear mechanism for their implementation.[99] The law effectively prevents about 4 million potential Russian repatriates living in the Commonwealth of Independent States after the fall of the USSR from receiving Russian citizenship.[100]

Conclusions and policy implications

Can Northeast Asian countries work together to develop and implement policies regarding changes in population stocks and flows that will preserve state security and increase the welfare of their populations? Northeast Asian policy-makers, aware of the advantages of population stabilization, have successfully used national policy frameworks to help facilitate a regional equilibrium of low birth and death rates. But questions remain. Will Northeast Asia avoid pandemics of infectious and parasitic diseases? How will the region deal with population ageing? How will it adjust to the shrinking population in the Russian Far East? Ultimately, how will Northeast Asian policy-makers guide changes in population stocks and flows in ways that will effectively balance state security concerns with the well-being of the populations of the region?

The following approaches to migration would appear to enhance population welfare and state security in Northeast Asia: (1) facilitate trade, investment and human rights for both native and migrant populations; (2) facilitate migrants' integration into labour forces and social life at destination; (3) help to maintain stability at home by way of facilitating migrants' remittances; (4) provide ways for migrants to return home and to contribute to their countries of origin; and (5) enhance relations between areas of origin and destination.[101]

Most governments give scant attention to how the welfare of migrants is linked to economic development and state security. The Global Commission on International Migration argues that "Fair rules for trade and capital need to be complemented by fair rules for the movement of people."[102] The General Agreement on Trade in Service is a global governance framework for the cross-border movement of goods and services. But, with the exception of refugees, there is no comparable international governance framework for the protection of the welfare of migrants.[103]

Multilateral migration policies

An effective multilateral governance framework for the cross-border movement of people is prerequisite for enhancing the welfare of migrants in Northeast Asia. In order for such a framework to work, Northeast Asian countries must provide stability and public goods for both their citizens and migrants. Creating a cross-border framework will require extensive activity by international organizations, including the United Nations High Commission for Refugees, the International Labor Organization and the International Organization for Migration as well as non-governmental organizations. Pivotal to this task will be the development of migration management systems that also take into account and involve the different concerns of commercial enterprises, non-governmental organizations and the governments of origin, transit and destination countries. An example is the Berne Initiative, which is an attempt to develop a balanced approach so as to facilitate regular migration and prevent irregular migration and to obtain benefits from migration between countries.[104]

Northeast Asian governments, international organizations and non-governmental organizations are faced with a number of cross-cutting issues regarding human flows in Northeast Asia. These issues include the rights of foreign nationals and host community citizens; migration impacts on bilateral relations between origin and destination countries; and migration impacts on Northeast Asian economies and the regional security environment. An understanding of the sources of these issues is increasing, and some migration-responsive policies are now in place. The next step in averting the problems these issues are giving rise to is the development of coordinated, region-wide migration-determining policies and also migration-responsive policies.

The rights of foreign nationals

For China, the dilemma relates to how to take advantage of its huge pool of internal migrants and improve its economy without sacrificing its control over their movement. Another problem is Chinese migration into the Russian Far East, an issue over which it will have to enter into full political dialogue with Russia if migration is to benefit both sides. The welfare of migrants from China (and Russia) in Mongolia may also be an issue.

For Japan, migration is also tied to economic performance. The primary barrier for it is how to reconcile the growing presence of foreigners (absolute numbers are still small) and their welfare in a country that prides itself on its unique national character.

The ROK shares with Japan the problems of reconciling the presence of migrants with cultural uniqueness. In addition, the ROK has to continue to engage its northern neighbour in political dialogue regarding migration and other issues. But despite the sometimes heated rhetoric of the DPRK and the ROK, rapprochement can continue.

The majority of Chinese (and Vietnamese and North Koreans) in the Russian Far East provide inexpensive labour and transport, and the Chinese also sell inexpensive consumer goods to the region. The overarching welfare issue facing the Chinese in the Russian Far East involves abuses of labour standards.

The rights of affected host-community members

For China, Japan and the ROK, migration and foreign workers pose short-term problems; most of the stresses have to do with how the governments handle perceived threats to established political and collective control. So far, foreign workers have caused only minor problems. For Mongolia, the activities of Chinese traders are posing problems for the local economy.

For Russia, Chinese migration to the Russian Far East poses a number of problems for the host community, the least of which is potential Chinese territorial expansion. The Chinese presence adds tension to the social fabric, but the real future impact of the Chinese presence on the region will be economic. Employing illegal Chinese labour at deflated wages will prevent long-term improvements in the competitiveness of local Russian business.

Impacts on relations between origin and destination countries

The issue of Chinese migration to the Russian Far East is one of the most significant sticking points in bilateral relations between China and Russia. It is unlikely that Chinese migration to the Russian Far East threatens state security in Northeast Asia, but failure to resolve this issue is impeding the integration of the RFE into Northeast Asia. Nevertheless, political dialogue between Russia and China is increasing.

Although foreign workers in Japan come from many countries, the large number of Chinese suggests that policy-makers in Tokyo and Beijing need to talk more about migration policies. Problems related to the Korean presence in Japan are tied to Japan's concept of its racial purity. Japan's political relations with its Asian neighbours will not improve fundamentally unless it acknowledges its role in World War II more publicly.

Impacts on the regional security environment

A Northeast Asian economic zone, like ASEAN for Southeast Asia, would bolster regional state security if provisions were made for the welfare of migrants. Such a zone (perhaps leading to closer political cooperation) could increase labour and capital flows by encouraging the freer movement of workers and the factors of production.

Sources of the problem(s)

The proximate sources of the problems outlined above include a population decline in the Russian Far East and unemployment in more densely populated areas in north-eastern China. The root source of the problems of migration/foreign workers is not migration/foreign workers as such. It is how slowly the Northeast Asian governments are addressing the issue. They are still dealing with the aftermath of civilizational, nationalist and state-to-state conflicts.

Policies in place

The governments of China, Japan and the ROK are creating and implementing policies to deal with migration/foreign workers. The slow pace of the policies is due to a political hesitancy to lose control over population movement/immigration and in effect increase the strain on the social fabric. However, economic necessity is forcing the three governments to rethink past policies. The government in Moscow has focused on the enforcement of migration rather than first devising long-term plans for the role of migration in Russia's development. There is a need for China and the Russian Federation to include Mongolia fully in the migration policy process.

Possible policies

New migration policies are clearly needed. The government of China can grant internal migrants the freedom to move to and settle in regions where they can find jobs. In the end, some version of the *hukou* system will remain, but it will be greatly adjusted to exigent economic necessity. The governments of Japan and South Korea can further loosen their foreign worker laws, but how fast they can do this will probably depend on the global economy. The ROK has the additional task of trying to live peacefully with the DPRK. China is attempting to promote peace on the Korean peninsula, which may augur more active policies on its part in the future. China and the Russian Federation, as well as the ROK and the DPRK, can develop potential trans-border cities, and all Northeast Asian countries can take further advantage of the Tokyo–Beijing urban corridor.

Overcoming obstacles

The real obstacles to state security and individual welfare posed by migration and the assimilation of migrants are the fixed political positions of the governments of Northeast Asia. Nevertheless, political controls are gradually loosening. An example is China, where internal migrants are granted more and more rights. The question is, can these changes occur rapidly enough to keep up with migration/foreign worker issues, which are increasing daily? The proximate obstacles to state security and population welfare include the low level of economic development in Mongolia and the Russian Far East, population ageing, the influence of HIV/AIDS and SARS and the tendency of "short-term" migrants to remain where they have come to work. Successful guidance of the cross-border movement of peoples now requires coordination of the increasing number of migration-relevant public and private sector institutions so as to ensure a multilateral governance framework for regulating human flows.

Acknowledgements

Sections of this chapter are based on Maurice D. Van Arsdol, Jr., "Demographic Changes in Northeast Asia and Their Implications for Regional Stability", in Tsuneo Akaha, ed., *Politics and Economics in Northeast Asia, Nationalism and Regionalism in Contention*, New York: St Martin's Press, 1999, pp. 277–324. Thanks go to Professor Tsuneo Akaha, to Kae Dae Choi, a student at the Monterey Institute of International Studies, and to the following students in Professor Van Arsdol's spring semester 2004 class "Population and Migration in Northeast Asia": Donelle Di-Lorenzo, Marjorie Gelin, Christopher Hulick, Byungwook Jun, Sung-jin Kim, Doune Porter, Richard Sedgwick, Hiroko Shimota, Keeli Sorensen and Marcelyn Thompson. The assistance of Marian C. Van Arsdol, Pebble Beach, California, and Fern and Jon Price, Price Business Services, Monterey, California, is gratefully acknowledged.

Notes

1. Nazli Choucri, *Population and Conflict: New Dimensions of Population Dynamics*, United Nations Fund for Population Activities, Population Development Series No. 8, New York, 1983, p. 25.
2. The World Bank, *The 2002 World Bank Atlas*, Washington, DC: The World Bank, 2002.

3. United Nations, *World Population Prospects The 2002 Revision Volume I: Comprehensive Tables*, New York: United Nations, 2003. For statistical purposes, data for China do not include the Hong Kong SAR and the Macao SAR. Population projections should be interpreted with caution; they rely on unknowable assumptions, increase in error with successive time periods and are not particularly reliable for long time periods. Michael S. Teitelbaum, "The Media Marketplace for Garbled Demography", *Population and Development Review* 30 (2), 2004, pp. 317–327.
4. Leszek Buszynski, "Historical Perspectives of Relations within Northeast Asia", in Tsuneo Akaha, ed., *Politics and Economics in Northeast Asia: Nationalism and Regionalism in Contention*, New York: St Martin's Press, 1999, pp. 3–30.
5. John J. Stephan, *The Russian Far East: A History*, Stanford: Stanford University Press, 1994, pp. 31–32, 47–49.
6. The sequence of these population transitions has varied among Northeast Asian countries. See Ronald Skeldon, "On Mobility and Fertility Transitions in East and Southeast Asia", *Asia and Pacific Migration Journal* 1 (2), 1992, pp. 220–249.
7. Andrew Mason, "Will Population Change Sustain the Asian Economic Miracle?", in Elisa W. Johnston, ed., *AsiaPacific Issues: Analysis from the East–West Center*, Honolulu, Hawaii, 34, 1997, p. 3.
8. F. Landis MacKellar, "The Predicament of Population Aging: A Review Essay", *Population and Development Review* 26 (2), 2000, pp. 365–397.
9. "The UN Population Division on Replacement Migration", *Population and Development Review* 26 (2), 2000, pp. 413–417.
10. United Nations Population Division, *Replacement Migration: Is It a Solution to Declining and Aging Population? Country Results Section*, New York: United Nations Population Division, Department of Economic and Social Affairs, ESA/P/WP.160, 2000, available at ⟨http://www.un.org/esa/population/unpop.htm⟩ (retrieved 20 April 2004).
11. Peter J. Taylor, D.R.F. Walker and J.V. Beaverstock, "Firms and Their Global Service Networks", in Saskia Sassen, ed., *Global Networks, Linked Cities*, New York, London: Routledge, 2002, pp. 93–115.
12. Jane R. Rubin-Kurtzman, Roberto Ham-Chande, Maurice D. Van Arsdol, Jr. and Qian-wei Wang, "Demographic and Economic Interactions in Trans-border Cities: The Southern California–Baja California Mega-City", *Proceedings, XXIInd International Population Conference, International Union for the Scientific Study of Population, Montreal, Canada, 24 August–1 September, 1993*, Vol. 3, Liege, Belgium, 1993, pp. 131–142.
13. Wilbur Zilensky, "The Hypothesis of the Mobility Transition", *Geographical Review* 61, 1971, pp. 219–249.
14. David M. Heer, "International Migration", in Edgar F. Borgatta, editor in chief, Rhonda J.V. Montgomery, managing editor, *Encyclopedia of Sociology, Second Edition*, Vol. 2, New York: Macmillan Reference, 2000, pp. 1431–1438 and Philip Martin and James Widgren, "International Migration: A Global Challenge", *Population Bulletin* 55, Population Reference Bureau, Washington, DC, 1996, p. 19.
15. Saskia Sassen, *The Mobility of Labour and Capital*, Cambridge: Cambridge University Press, 1988 and Douglas S. Massey, "International Migration at the Dawn of the Twenty-first Century: The Role of the State", *Population and Development Review* 25 (3), 1999, pp. 303–322.
16. Ronald Skeldon, *Migration and Development: A Global Perspective*, Harlow, Essex, England: Addison Wesley Longman, 1997, pp. 41–193.
17. Graeme Hugo, "The Demographic Underpinnings of Current and Future International Migration in Asia", *Asia and Pacific Migration Journal* 7 (1), 1998, pp. 1–25.

18. United Nations, *International Migration Report 2002*, New York: United Nations, 2002, pp. 64, 138–140, 151, 203, 230, 262 and 266.
19. Idem.
20. Please see in this book Victor Larin, chap. 2, "Chinese in the Russian Far East: Regional views" and Elizabeth Wishnick, chap. 3, "Migration and economic security: Chinese labour migrants in the Russian Far East".
21. See in this volume Tsuneo Akaha and Anna Vassilieva, chap. 4, "The Russian presence in contemporary Japan: Case studies in Hokkaido and Niigata".
22. Please consult in this book Daojiong Zha, chap. 5, "Chinese migrants in contemporary Japan: The case of Niigata".
23. See in this volume Mika Merviö, chap. 6, "Koreans in Japan and Shimane".
24. Please see in this book Shin-wha Lee, chap. 8, "The realities of South Korea's migration policies".
25. See in this volume Hazel Smith, chap. 7, "North Koreans in China: Sorting fact from fiction".
26. Please consult in this book Tsedendamba Batbayar, chap. 9, "Foreign migration issues in Mongolia".
27. Sally Cameron, "Trafficking of Filipino Women to Japan: A Case of Human Rights Security Violation in Japan", Center for East Asian Studies, Monterey Institute of International Studies, 2003, available at ⟨http://gsti.miis.edu/CEAS-PUB/2003_Cameron.pdf⟩, retrieved 6 February 2005.
28. Stephen Castles and Mark J. Miller, *The Age of Migration: International Movements in the Modern World*, 3rd edn, New York: The Guilford Press, 2003, p. 154.
29. Ashwani Saith, "Migration Perspectives and Policies: South Asian Perspectives", *Asia and Pacific Migration Journal* 8, 1999, pp. 285–311 and Philip Martin, "Labor Contractors: A Conceptual Overview", *Asian and Pacific Migration Journal* 5, 1996, pp. 201–218.
30. Castles and Miller, *The Age of Migration*, pp. 162–163.
31. United Nations, Department of Economic and Social Affairs, Population Division, *World Population Policies, 2003*, New York: United Nations, 2004.
32. Idem.
33. Nancy Riley, "China's Population: New Trends and Challenges", *Population Bulletin* 59 (2), Population Reference Bureau, Washington, DC, 2004, pp. 7–8.
34. Yuan Zhi Gang, *Renkou Nianling Jiegou, Yang Laonian Baoxian Zhidu yu Zuiyou Chuxulu* [Population age structure in supporting pension insurance and favorable savings rate], *Jingji Yanjiu* [Economic research] 11, 2000, pp. 24–32.
35. Zuo Xue Jin, "21 Shiji Zhongguo Renkou Zhangwang" ["Forecast of China's demographic issues in the 21st century"], "*Xin Shiji Zhongguo Renkou Wenti Zhanwang, Taolun 3*" ["Outlook on China's population problem in the new century, discussion, part 3"], *Xinhua Wenzhai* [New China excerpts], pp. 16–18.
36. Delia Davin, *Internal Migration in Contemporary China*, London: Macmillan, 1999, pp. 51–52, 75 and Cheng Li, "Surplus Rural Labor and Internal Migration in China: Current Status and Future Prospects", *Asian Survey* 36, pp. 1122–1145.
37. Xiaogang Wu and Donald J. Treiman, "The Household Registration System and Social Stratification in China: 1955–1996", *Demography* 41 (2), 2004, pp. 363–384.
38. "China, Hong Kong", *Migration News* 9 (1), January 2002, available at ⟨http://migration.ucdavis.edu/mn/archive_mn/jan_2002–13mn.html⟩ (retrieved 19 October 2002) and "China, Hong Kong Migrants", *Migration News* 8 (4), April 2001, available at ⟨http://migration.ucdavis.edu/mn/archive_mn/apr_2001–13mn.html⟩ (retrieved 19 October 2002).

39. See Wang Gui Xin, "Renkou Qianyi: Jiang Chengwei Tuidong Zhongguo Xianzai Wenhua Fazhan de Zhongyao Yinqing" ["Human movement: The most important engine to power China's economic development"], in *Xin Shiji Zhongguo Renkou Wenti Zhanwang, Taolun 3* [Outlook on China's population problem in the new century, discussion, part 3], *Xinhua Wenzhai* (New China excerpts), June 2000, pp. 18–19. See also Baogang Guo, "Transforming China's Urban Healthcare System", *Asia Survey* 43 (2) 2003, pp. 385–403, "A Shot in the Arm", *Far Eastern Economic Review*, 12 June 2003, pp. 24–25 and "*Hukou* System and Discrimination against Rural Population in China", available at ⟨www.harvardchina.org/SpecialEvents/11–20–2001.htm⟩ (retrieved 1 September 2003).

40. Susan W. Lawrence, "Untying the Knot", *Far Eastern Economic Review*, 11 September 2003, pp. 30–31 and Nancy Riley, "China's Population".

41. Riley, "China's Population", pp. 29–31.

42. Ibid., pp. 26–27.

43. See Ching Huai Niu and Chao Kun, "Xibu Da Kai Fa: Ying Zhuyi Shi ge Guanxi" ["Western development: Ten important issues"], *Zhongguo Gaige* [China reform], June 2000, pp. 30–31 and Ming Shan Zhou and Ran Yu, "Xibu Kaifa: Que Qian Haishi Que Ren?" ["Western development: Lacking money or lacking people?"] *Zhongguo Gaige* [China reform], June 2000, p. 32.

44. Justin Jon Rudelson, *Oasis: Uyghur Nationalism Along China's Silk Road*, New York: Columbia University Press, 1997, p. 132.

45. Peggy Falkenheim, "The Russian Far East's Economic Integration with Northeast Asia: Problems and Prospects", *Pacific Affairs* 72, 1999, pp. 209–226 and Alexander Lukin, "Russia's Image of China and Russian–Chinese Relations", *East Asia: An International Quarterly* 17, 1999, pp. 5–41.

46. "China, Hong Kong," *Migration News* 9 (7), July 2002, available at ⟨http://migration.ucdavis.edu/mn/Achive_MN/july_2002–14mn.html⟩ (retrieved 19 October 2002); "China, Taiwan, Hong Kong", *Migration News* 8 (10), October 2001, available at ⟨http://migration.ucdavis.edu/mn/archive_mn/oct_2001–15mn.html⟩ (retrieved 19 October 2002); and "China, Hong Kong, Taiwan", *Migration News* 8 (12), December 2001, available at ⟨http://migration.ucdavis.edu/mn/archive_mn/dec_2001–14mn.html⟩ (retrieved 19 October 2002).

47. Ronald Skeldon, "China, from Exceptional Case to Global Participant", Migration Policy Institute, Washington, DC, April 2004, available at ⟨http://www.migrationinformation.org/profiles/display.cfm?ID219⟩ (retrieved 5 May 2004).

48. Ronald Skeldon, "International Migration and the Escafe Region: A Policy-Oriented Approach," *Asia–Pacific Population Journal* 7, 1992, pp. 3–22; Ronald Skeldon, "Hong Kong's Response to the Indochinese Influx, 1975–93", *The Annals of the American Academy of Political and Social Science, Strategies for Immigration Control: An International Comparison* 534, 1994, p. 92.

49. Cheng-yi Lin, "The Taiwan Factor in Asia, Pacific Regional Security", in Takashi Inoguchi and Grant B. Stillman, eds, North-East Asia Regional Security, Tokyo: United Nations University Press, 1997, p. 95.

50. "More Prostitutes in Shenzhen", *Far Eastern Economic Review*, 21 August 2003, p. 9.

51. CIA, *The World Factbook, 2002*, Pittsburgh, PA: Superintendent of Documents, p. 311.

52. "Hong Kong, Macau, China", *Migration News* 7 (9), September 2000, available at ⟨http://migration.ucdavis.edu/mn/archive/mn/sep/2000–16mn.html⟩ (retrieved 20 October 2001).

53. Taiwan (ROC), Ministry of Interior, available at ⟨http://www.gio.gov.tw/info/book2000/cho2_1.html⟩ (retrieved 20 October 2001).

54. "Taiwan Sets Up New Migration Bureau", *Migration News* 5 (11), November 1998, available at ⟨http://migration.ucdavis.edu./mn/archive_mn/nov_1998–mn.html⟩ (retrieved 19 October 2001).

55. "China, Taiwan, Hong Kong", *Migration News* 8 (9), September 2001, available at ⟨http://migration.ucdavis.edu/mn/archive_mn/sep_2001–14mn.html⟩ (retrieved 19 October 2002).

56. Milton Ezrati, "Japan's Ageing Economics", *Foreign Affairs* 76, 1997, pp. 96–105.

57. Naohiro Ogawa and Robert D. Retherford, "Shifting Costs of Caring for the Elderly Back to Families in Japan: Will it Work?", *Population and Development Review* 23 (1), 1997, pp. 59–93.

58. "UN Population Division on Replacement Migration", *Population and Development Review* 26 (3), 2000, pp. 413–417.

59. See Wayne A. Cornelius, "Japan: The Illusion of Immigration Control", in Wayne A. Cornelius, Philip L. Martin, and James F. Hollifield, eds, *Controlling Migration: A Global Perspective*, Stanford, CA: Stanford University Press, 1994, pp. 376–410 and Philip Martin, "Migrants on the Move in Asia", *Asia Pacific Issues, Analysis from the East–West Center*, No. 29, Honolulu, East–West Center, 1996, p. 7.

60. Please see in this volume Tsuneo Akaha and Anna Vassilieva, chap. 4, "The Russian presence in contemporary Japan: Case studies in Hokkaido and Niigata".

61. See in this book Mika Mervio, chap. 6, "Koreans in Japan and Shimane" and Daojiong Zha, chap. 5, "Chinese migrants in contemporary Japan: The case of Niigata".

62. Yoshiro Okunishi, "Labor Contracting in International Migration: The Japanese Case and Implications for Asia", *Asian and Pacific Migration Journal* 5, 1996, pp. 219–240.

63. Apichai W. Shipper, "Foreign Workers, NGOs and Local Government", available at ⟨www.aasianst.org/absts/2000abst/Japan/J–149.htm⟩ (retrieved 2 September 2003) and Koichi Ogawa, "The Organization of Foreign Workers in Japan: A Case Study of the Kanagawa City Union", available at ⟨www2u.bigobe.ne.jp/~ctls/bulb/article6–20.html⟩ (retrieved 1 September 2003).

64. "Japan: Migrants and Refugees", *Migration News* 4, April 2001, available at ⟨http://migration.ucdavis.edu/mn/archive_mn/apr_2001–14mn.html⟩ (retrieved 19 October 2002) and "Japan, Korea", *Migration News* 9 (5), May 2002, available at ⟨http://migration.ucdavis.edu/mn/archive_mn/may_2002–17mn.html⟩ (retrieved 19 October 2002).

65. Daniel Goodkind and Loraine West, "The North Korean Famine and Its Demographic Impact", *Population and Development Review* 27 (1), 2001, pp. 219–238.

66. Byung-joon Ahn, "The NPT Regime and Denuclearization of the Korean Peninsula", in Takashi Inoguchi and Grant B. Stillman, eds, *North-East Asian Regional Sovereignty: The Role of International Institutions*, Tokyo: United Nations University Press, 1997, p. 127.

67. Leonid Petrov, "North Korea Touts Cheap Labor in Russian Far East", CIS and North Korea (June 2003–October 2003), North Korean Studies, The Academy of Korean Studies, Australian National University, Canberra, available at ⟨http://north-korea.narod.ru/cis_nk_11.htm⟩ (retrieved 21 April 2004).

68. Holger Wolf, "Korean Unification: Lessons from Germany", in Marcus Noland, ed., *Economic Integration of the Korean Peninsula*, Special Report 10, Institute for International Economics, Washington, DC, January 1998, pp. 165–189.

69. "China: Migrants", *Migration News* 9 (10), October 2002, available at ⟨http://migration.ucdavis.edu/mn/Archive_MN/oct_2002–14mn.html⟩ (retrieved 19 October 2001) and Hazel Smith, chap. 7 in this volume, "North Koreans in China: Sorting fact from fiction".

70. Christian F. Mahr, "North Korea: Scenarios From The Perspective of Refugee Displacement", Working Paper No. 11, February 2002, The Inter-University Committee on International Migration, Massachusetts Institute of Technology, Cambridge, MA, available at ⟨http://web.mit.edu/cis/www/migration/pubs/rrwp/11_north.doc⟩ (retrieved 21 April 2004).

71. Idem and "North Korea Write-up: Summary and Recommendations", Human Rights Watch Publications, Human Rights Watch, Washington, DC, 2002, available at ⟨http://www.hrw.org/reports/2002/northkorea/norkor1102.htm⟩ (retrieved 21 April 2004).

72. Shin-wha Lee, "The realities of South Korea's migration policies", chap. 8 in this volume, and R. Isberto, "Illegal Migration in Asia", in Robin Cohen, ed., *The Cambridge Survey of World Migration*, Cambridge: Cambridge University Press, 1995, p. 399.

73. "South Korea to Accept Migrant Workers", 26 March 2004, available at ⟨http://www.countrywatch.com/@school/as_wire.asp?vCOUNTRY=118&UID=1050647⟩ (retrieved 19 April 2004) and "Japan, Korea Migration News", Migration Dialogue: *Migration News*, available at ⟨http://migration.ucdavis.edu/mn/more.php?id=2982_0_3_0⟩ (retrieved 19 April 2004).

74. Byun Duk-kun, "Korea to Allow 79,000 Migrant Workers", *Korea Times*, available at ⟨http://www.mongolembassy.com/eng_news/list.asp?tb=eng_news&num=807&page=1&colname=&text=⟩ (retrieved 19 April 2004).

75. "Japan, Korea Migration News", Migration Dialogue: *Migration News*, available at ⟨http://migration.ucdavis.edu/mn/more.php?id=2982_0_3_0⟩ (retrieved 19 April 2004).

76. Jeanyoung Lee, "Ethnic Korean Migration in South Korea: Issues and Its Political Implication", in Tsuneo Akaha, ed., *Human Flows across National Borders in Northeast Asia, Seminar Proceedings, Center for East Asian Studies, Monterey Institute of International Studies, Monterey, California, 2–3 November 2001*, Center for East Asian Studies, Monterey Institute of International Studies, Monterey, California, 20 January 2002, p. 118, available at ⟨http://gsti.miis.edu/CEAS–PUB/200108Lee.pdf⟩ (retrieved 10 February 2005).

77. Hong Young Lee, "South Korea in 2002", *Asia Survey* 43 (1), 2003, pp. 64–77 and "China Briefing", *Far Eastern Economic Review*, 26 June 2003, p. 25.

78. "A Railway Line in Limbo", *Far Eastern Economic Review*, 12 June 2003, pp. 22–24.

79. Aidan Foster-Carter, "A Bumpy Road Ahead?" *Comparative Connections* 5 (1), April 2003, available at ⟨http://www.csis.org/pacfor/cc/0301Qnk_sk.html⟩ (retrieved 1 August 2003).

80. Central Intelligence Agency, *The World Factbook – Mongolia*, available at ⟨http://www.cia.gov/cia/publications/factbook/geos/mg.html⟩ (retrieved 24 November 2001).

81. National Bureau of Statistics, comp., *China Statistical Yearbook, 2001*, Beijing: China Statistics Press, 2001, p. 42.

82. Ralph Gilberg and Jan Olof Svantesson, "The Mongols, Their Land and History", in Ole Bruun and Ole Odegaard, *Mongolia in Transition*, Nordic Institute of Asian Studies in Asian Topics, No. 22, Copenhagen, Denmark, pp. 5–22.

83. Ricardo F. Neupert, "Population Projections for Mongolia: 1989–2019", *United Nations Population Programme Asia–Pacific Population Journal* 7, 1992, p. 6.

84. Ricardo F. Neupert and Sidney Goldstein, "Urbanization and Population Redistribution in Mongolia", *East–West Center Occasional Papers*, Population Series, No. 122, December 1994, Honolulu, p. 4.

85. National Statistical Office of Mongolia, "Goal 1. Reduce Extreme Poverty and Hunger", 2003, available at ⟨http://www.nso.mn/mdg/eng_goals1.htm⟩ (retrieved 20 April 2004).

86. "Migration Network", *Fact Sheet No. 6, "Causes of Migration and Problems faced by Migrants", Fact Sheet No. 7, "Information about the 2000 Population and Housing*

Census and About the Micro Study on Internal Migration in Mongolia – 2000", Ministry of Social Welfare and Labor, The National Statistical Office, and UNFPA, Ulaanbaatar, Mongolia, no date.

87. Jörg Janzen, "Summary: Mongolia: Sedentarization of Pastoralists in Settlements of Ulaanbaatar. Background and Consequences for the Country's Development", IUAES 15th Congress, Florence, 7–8 July 2002, available at ⟨http://users.ox.ac.uk/~cnpc/jansen.html⟩ (retrieved 20 April 2004).

88. Tsedendamba Batbayar, "Foreign Presence in Mongolia: Current Status and Problems", in Tsuneo Akaha, ed., *Human Flows across National Borders in Northeast Asia*, 2002, p. 141, available at ⟨http://gsti.miis.edu/CEAS–PUB/200109Batbayar.pdf⟩ (retrieved 10 February 2005).

89. Dalkhat Ediev, "Application of Demographic Potential Concept to Understanding the Russian Population History and Prospects, 1897–2100", *Demographic Research* 4, 1999–2001, Herstellung: Books on Demand, pp. 289–336.

90. "Russia: Cross-Border Migration in the Russian Far East (October 1997)", p. 7, available at ⟨http://www.unhcr.ch/refworld/country/writenet/wrirus03.htm⟩ (retrieved 2 October 2003) and Fiona Hill and Clifford Gaddy, *The Siberian Curse: How Communist Planners Left Russia out in the Cold*, Washington, DC: Brookings Institution, 2003.

91. "Russia: Cross-Border Migration in the Russian Far East" (October 1997), p. 4.

92. Terry Martin, "Stalinist Forced Relocation Policies: Patterns, Causes, Consequences", in Myron Weiner and Sharon Stanton Russell, eds, *Demography and National Security*, New York: Berghahn Books, 2001, pp. 321–322.

93. Federal Statistics Service, "Permanent Population of the Russian Federation by Region", *2002 Census Initial Results*, available at ⟨http://www.gks.ru/PEREPIS/tabl_1.htm⟩, accessed 25 January 2005.

94. Authors' calculations based on Goskomstat data, available at ⟨http://www.gks.ru⟩.

95. See Larin, chap. 2, and Wishnick, chap. 3, in this volume.

96. Viktor Larin, "Chinese Emissaries in the Far East: A Response to the Alarmists", *Diasporas*, nos. 2–3, 2001, p. 80 (in Russian).

97. Ibid., pp. 81–83.

98. Bertil Linter, "Spreading Tentacles", *Far Eastern Economic Review*, 2 October 2003, pp. 54–56.

99. Zhanna Zayonchkovskaya, "Chinese Immigration to Russia in the Context of the Demographic Situation", Center for East Asian Studies, Monterey Institute of International Studies, 2003, available at ⟨http://gsti.miis.edu/ceas–pub/zayonchkovskaya20030914.pdf⟩ (retrieved 6 October 2003); Zhanna Zayonchkovskaya, "Institut grazhdanstva i migrasionnaya politika Rossii" ["The Institution of Citizenship and Russia's Migration Policy"], March 2003, available at ⟨http://antropotok.archipelag.ru/text/a219.htm⟩ (retrieved 6 October 2003); and Zhanna Zayonchkovskaya, "Igra v migratsionnie karty" ["The Migration Card Game"], *Ekspert* [Expert], 2 June 2003.

100. President Vladimir Putin has acknowledged the problems with this law, and called for its correction in his "Address to the Federal Parliament of the Russian Federation", 16 May 2003. Zayonchkovskaya, "Chinese Immigration to Russia in the Context of the Demographic Situation".

101. J. Edward Taylor, Joaquín Arango, Graeme Hugo, Ali Kovaouci, Douglas S. Massey and Adela Pellegrino, "International Migration and Community Development", *Population Index* 62, 1996, pp. 181–214 and 397–418 and E. Barth and D. Noel, "Conceptual Frameworks for the Analysis of Race Relations: An Evaluation", *Social Forces* 50, 1972, pp. 333–348.

102. Global Commission on International Migration, "A Fair Globalization: Creating Opportunities for All", summarized as "The World Commission on the Social Dimension of Migration: On the Cross-Border Movements of People", *Population and Development Review* 20 (2), 2004, pp. 375–380.
103. The GATS' "Mode 4" provision covers some service providers, and some international conventions attempt to protect migrant workers and stem human trafficking.
104. Michele Klein Soloman and Kerstin Bartsch, "The Berne Initiative: Toward the Development of an International Policy Framework", 1 April 2003, Migration Policy and Research Programme, International Organization for Migration, Geneva, Switzerland and Migration Policy Institute, Washington, DC.

Part II

Chinese migration to the Russian Far East

2

Chinese in the Russian Far East: Regional views

Victor Larin

The Chinese in the Russian Far East (RFE), who are already a part of the region's economy and local life, have yet to become accepted as constituents of its local society. They remain an integral part of the "Heavenly Kingdom" or "Greater China", which encompasses the Chinese population not only in its motherland but also throughout the rest of the world. Therefore, the growing importance of migration issues in modern life is not the only reason to pay close attention to the Chinese presence in Russia.[1] Of much greater significance, however, are questions about who will be the future proprietor of Siberia's vast resources and possibly even Russia's destiny. The Chinese presence in the RFE keeps these questions alive today.

In the 1990s, speculation emerged in Russia and abroad about its imminent disintegration and the dividing up of Siberia and the Russian Far East between the United States, China and Japan. At the same time, the idea of a "Chinese threat" emerged again in Russian society, gradually influencing its perception of the economic growth and political rise of China. It is no wonder that some assumed that Chinese migration to Russia was the first step in a far-sighted and pragmatic plan by leaders in Beijing to restore China's control of the territories north of the Amur River ceded to the Russian empire in the nineteenth century. This idea found many adherents among officials, journalists and ordinary people in Russia. Alexander Gol'bakh, commander of the Far East Border Guard, asserted that the Chinese authorities used the export of labour to Russia in order to promote a policy aimed at the "subsequent expansion into the Far East region to win strong economic, trade, and demographic positions there".[2]

The contemporary presence of Chinese in Russia has not affected the RFE's demography and economics as much as was the case at the end of the nineteenth century and the beginning of the twentieth.[3] However, its impact on local public attitudes is comparable to that of a century ago. Historically, Russians along Chinese borders have perceived and interpreted the Chinese presence in Russia, particularly in the RFE, as a political and strategic phenomenon rather than a social, economic or cultural one. Deep cultural differences between the two civilizations became apparent as growing individual contacts in the border regions strengthened Russians' suspicions of the Chinese. As a result, distorted pictures of a "potentially expansionist China" and "millions of insidious Chinese in Russia" prevail in public sentiment and strongly influence Russian policies towards China and Russian–Chinese relations.

Chinese migration to the Russian Far East was, and still is, different from the migration patterns we observe in the United States, Europe and many other places in the world. Although a basic motivation to go abroad informs Chinese people's migration to the RFE as elsewhere, a number of other factors contribute to the unique nature of their migration to Russia. These factors include the controversy over how they enter Russia (mainly as tourists) and what they do once they are in the country (often as illegal workers); Chinese perceptions of the host country as a place of temporary stay; and the paradox of the geographical proximity of the two countries but cultural gap between the two peoples.

The history of Russian–Chinese relations and competing trends in Russia's and China's economic, political and demographic development today make Russians suspicious about Beijing's long-term interests, especially in the territories north and south of the Amur River. These suspicions fuel the widespread perception of "unpredictable, ambitious China" and cause Russians in the Far East not to trust the Chinese who come to their country.

This chapter focuses on the sources of those fears, compares the perceptions and realities regarding the Chinese in Russia and concludes with possible scenarios for the transformation of the social and political landscape of the Russian Far East. Because much has already been written about Chinese in Russia since the 1990s, I shall focus mostly on developments in the new century.

China's approach to the Russian Far East

Two basic factors explain the Chinese public's and government's perceptions of the Russian Far East. The first one is political tradition. According to an ancient Chinese view of the outside world, the territories that are now part of the RFE belonged to the Middle Kingdom's vassal periphery. These outlying districts, inhabited by barbarians, were unfit for settlement by *hanren* (original Chinese), although they could serve as a means of improving their welfare. The second factor is a modern one: China's rapidly growing demand for natural resources and need for new markets for its goods and labour. These factors are reflected in the two main principles the Chinese central government follows in conducting its relations with Russia: to make the lengthy northern border peaceful and secure and to gain access to the natural resources of Siberia and the Russian Far East in order to support China's internal economic development. Moreover, contemporary Chinese policy-makers consider this vast area to be "economically complementary to China's northeast region".[4] Hu Yaobang was the first Chinese leader to visit Harbin, in August 1982, and approved the resumption of border trade with Russia. Hu Jintao, the current leader, initiated a programme to review the old industrial base of north-eastern China, and he encouraged and supported the activities of the north-eastern provinces in developing direct economic and political relations with the neighbouring territories of Russia.

China's two north-eastern provinces, Heilongjiang and Jilin, became active in expanding their relations with Russia. Jilin has not been very successful in this effort, having paid more attention to relations with the Koreas and Japan, but Heilongjiang Province has put the Russian Far East at the centre of its economic development plans. Procurement of Siberian natural resources, as well as involvement in the Russian commodity, labour and tourist markets, has become an important source of Heilongjiang's economic development; it has provided an opportunity to create a great number of new jobs on both sides of the border. Thus, internal economic and social development needs have been the objective reasons for the provincial governments to organize and support the activities of individual Chinese in the RFE.

Between 1988 and 2000, more than 113,000 contract workers sent to Russia by Heilongjiang Province carried out contracts valued at US$2 billion. Eighty per cent of them were concentrated in the border territories.[5] In 2001–2003, another 20,000 people from Heilongjiang were recruited to work abroad, and most of them were employed in construction and agricultural projects in Siberia and the RFE.[6] In 2003, Heilongjiang Province's trade with Russia grew to US$2.96 billion, representing 55.5 per cent of its foreign trade and 18.7 per cent of Russian–Chinese trade.

Provincial authorities have not only served as a conduit for the export of labour to Russia but also encouraged and supported individual initiatives to conduct business there. Between 1997 and 2002, more than 1.1 million Chinese visited border territories of the Russian Far East (Primorskii and Khabarovsk krais and Amur Oblast [*krais* and *oblasts* are main administrative units]) as tourists. Most of them (as well as Russian tourists travelling to China) used this channel for private business and temporary (mostly illegal) employment in Russia. The annual volume of "shuttle trade" (the Chinese call it "people's trade") between the Russian Far East and Heilongjiang Province reached US$500–US$600 million, three times the level of officially declared exports to the Russian Far East from China. Nobody knows how many people were involved in this unofficial trade, but this business has become an important part of the local economies and has supported the livelihood of tens of thousands of people on both sides of the border. Therefore, the north-eastern provinces of China have been vitally interested in promoting human exchange with the border territories of Russia in various forms, such as group and individual tourists, business, contract workers, students etc.

Chinese workers, peasants and intellectuals living in immediate proximity to the Russian border have their own interest in these territories. Since the beginning of the 1990s, two motives have stimulated ordinary Chinese citizens to travel north of their own accord. On the one hand, there are demographic pressures and unemployment in north-eastern China.[7] On the other hand, news of the opportunity to make fast money through business in Russia has long since spread through the cities and villages of the region. The second of these factors has always been, and continues to be, the more important motivation for migration,[8] although conventional Russian views on the matter suggest the opposite.

Channels of migration

There are three official channels the Chinese use to come to Russia: visa-free tourism, contract work and business. Tourism remains the most important and popular channel. The first "visa-free group tourism" agreement, providing for affordable tour prices and relatively easy procedures for gathering documents,[9] was concluded in December 1992 in Beijing. It opened the way for a massive and completely uncontrolled movement of Chinese tourists, mostly shuttle traders, to Russia. This channel was the major source of illegal migration to Russia, and brought significant problems to the local authorities and population. Eventually, it became a symbol of "Chinese expansion" into Russia. The fears and the realities of the mid-1990s pushed the local authorities to undertake measures to bring the situation under control. The measures, both juridical[10] and practical,[11] were mainly restrictive and prohibitive, and helped to reduce tension in the region.

On 29 February 2000, the Russian and Chinese governments signed a new agreement on visa-free group tourism to regulate tourist companies' activities and to stop illegal migration and illicit work on the part of tourists. According to the agreement, a tourist group must include at least five people, and companies offering visa-free travel are required to get a licence for international tourism and to have at least three years of experience in the business. Visa-free tourists cannot stay in the destination country for more than 30 days.

The new agreement did not affect the scale of border tourism as much as substantial changes in the rouble–yuan exchange rate did. After the rouble depreciated by a factor of four during the autumn of 1998 and most Russians instantly became too poor to buy even cheap Chinese goods, the number of Chinese "business tourists" dropped in 1999. At the same time, it became much more affordable for real Chinese tourists to come to Russia. The year 2000 marked a peak in Chinese tourism in the Russian Far East. About 240,000 tourists from China entered Russia, most of them using the border crossings in Amur Oblast and Primorskii Krai. About 20,000–30,000 tourists visit Khabarovsk Krai annually,[12] but a substantial number of them cross the border in Amur Oblast and Primorye.[13]

At the beginning of the new century, the number of tourists crossing the Russian–Chinese border in Primorye increased slowly, reaching 162,000 in 2002. Around ten per cent of them went to other territories of the Russian Far East; and 145,000–147,000 visited cities and villages in Primorye. In the same period, the number of tourists visiting Amur Oblast decreased slowly because of the lack of interesting sites as well as the low quality of service. Thus, in 2001 and 2002 the number of Chinese tourists in Amur Oblast was smaller than in 1996–2000 (see figure 2.1). The 2003 SARS (severe acute respiratory sydrome) scare hurt tourism along the border but could not stop it, as 65–70 per cent of Chinese "tourists" visited Russia not for sightseeing but for trade and illegal work.

In 2000, only 82 Chinese evaded the control of the Department of Internal Affairs of Primorskii Krai and did not return home. They represented 0.03 per cent of the total number of Chinese visiting the region that year. The number went down to 15 people in 2001 (0.01 per cent).[14] In 2002, according to the Passport and Visa Services of Primorskii Krai, the percentage of Chinese tourists who returned home by the time of their tour deadline reached 99.87 per cent.[15] Still, 210 Chinese tourists (the remaining 0.13 per cent) stayed too long in Russia, and most of them worked there illegally.

Contract work is the second channel through which Chinese come to Russia. In August 1992, Russia and China signed an agreement on the main principles for recruiting Chinese citizens to work in Russia. The accord limited the maximum period of work to three years, guaranteed

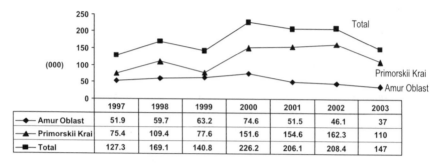

	1997	1998	1999	2000	2001	2002	2003
◆ Amur Oblast	51.9	59.7	63.2	74.6	51.5	46.1	37
▲ Primorskii Krai	75.4	109.4	77.6	151.6	154.6	162.3	110
■ Total	127.3	169.1	140.8	226.2	206.1	208.4	147

Figure 2.1 Chinese tourism in Amur Oblast and Primorskii Krai (000 people), 1997–2003 (*Sources: Itogi i tendentsii sotsial'no-ekonomicheskogo razvitiya Primorskogo kraya v 2002 godu* [The Results and Trends of Primorskii Krai Social and Economic Development in 2002], Vladivostok: TCSR, 2003, p. 131; *Amurskii statisticheskii ezhegodnik* [Amur Oblast Administration Reference], Blagoveshchensk: Amur Oblast Administration, 2003, p. 8; and *Amurskaya Pravda*, March 2004).

Chinese workers "all rights and liberties according to Russian law", required them to observe Russian laws and rules for foreigners and made the companies and enterprises that employed them responsible for their number, quantity and the conditions of their work and stay.[16] In the 1990s, the number of contract workers from China employed in the Russian Far East ranged from 7,500 to 10,000 per year. Most of them (6,000–8,000 annually) worked in Primorye; other territories usually had fewer than 1,000 Chinese labourers each. The percentage of Chinese citizens of the total number of foreign workers in Primorye was between 60 per cent and 63 per cent (23–30 per cent in Amur Oblast).

In November 2000, Russia and China signed a new agreement on their citizens' "temporary work" in the other country. The agreement sets the main conditions of employment, payment, permanent residence in the other country, social security etc. for Chinese workers in Russia and Russian workers in China. It is hard to say that this agreement stimulated the use of Chinese labour in the RFE at the beginning of the new century. Most likely, it was the improvement in Russia's economic situation that increased the demand for foreign labour and caused Chinese employment in the region to grow slowly. In Primorskii Krai, the number of Chinese workers increased from 6,374 in 1999 to 9,639 in 2001 and 10,227 in 2003 (amounting to 70.2 per cent of all foreign workers). In Amur Oblast, the number rose from 468 in 2000 to 2,397 in 2002.

As the two aforementioned channels for entry by Chinese were more or less under the strict control of the local authorities by the end of the 1990s, the third channel, commercial and business trips, became a more important source for increasing numbers of illegal Chinese workers to

gain access to the Russian labour market. Overstaying commercial visas
became the main kind of violation committed by Chinese in the RFE.[17]

The different sources of Chinese entry into Russia were not of the
same significance for the different territories of the RFE. Primorskii
Krai attracted many Chinese tourists, predominantly for sightseeing and
for the shuttle trade, but the proportion of Chinese tourists in Blagoveshchensk did not exceed that of the other categories of Chinese citizen
there (see figures 2.2 and 2.3).

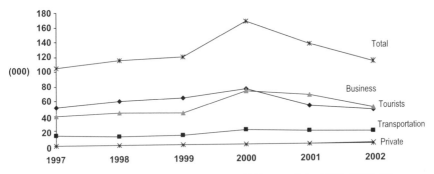

Figure 2.2 Chinese visits to Amur Oblast (000 people), 1997–2002 (*Sources*:
Osnovniye pokazateli vneshneekonomicheskikh svyazei Amurskoi oblasti i KNR
[Main Indexes of Amur Oblast and PRC Foreign Economic Relations], Blagoveshchensk: Amur Oblast Administration, 1999, pp. 2–3 and *Amurskii statisticheskii ezhegodnik* [Amur Oblast Administration Reference, 2003], Blagoveshchensk: Amur Oblast Administration, 2003, pp. 8–9).

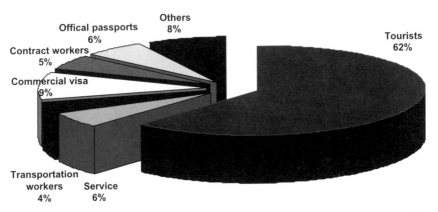

Figure 2.3 Chinese registered in Primorskii Krai by purpose of visit, 2000
(*Sources*: *Analiticheskii otchet Territorial'nogo organa Minfederatsii Rossii v Primorskom kraye za 2000 god* [Analytical Report of the Territorial Unit of
the Ministry of the Russian Federation in the Primorskii Krai in 2000], p. 27,
unpublished).

Chinese communities in the Russian Far East

Relatively stable communities of Chinese emerged in the Russian Far East by the end of the 1990s. Although they are not well organized or territorially settled yet, they have economic or social ties with Russia. Some of the Chinese who cross the Russian–Chinese border are a part of these communities. Among others, contract workers, students, businessmen and legal and illegal traders become part of these communities for various lengths of time. As a result, the scale and activities of these communities have become a hotly debated question.

At present, specialists estimate the total number of Chinese living in Russia to be between 300,000 and 400,000 people. Of these, 50,000–70,000 have settled in Moscow.[18] According to semi-official statistics, which one can extrapolate from occasional publications and interviews with officials, in the second half of the 1990s the number of Chinese who settled in Primorskii Krai was estimated to be 30,000–36,000,[19] including 5,000–6,000 staying there illegally.[20] An official police database reported that about 2,700 Chinese were living more or less permanently in Amur Oblast.[21]

The official statistics about Chinese migrants provided by immigration and police authorities disprove the typical conclusions widely put about by some officials that millions of Chinese have already settled in Russia. The real number of Chinese workers and students in the Russian Far East, as well as the number of Chinese tourists who stayed there illegally, had decreased by the end of the 1990s. Thus, for accuracy, all official figures should be reduced substantially. I would estimate that the RFE has 25,000–30,000 Chinese, including 10,000–12,000 contract workers, 10,000–15,000 traders, several hundred students and several hundred medium-scale businessmen.

Various sources provide crude assessments of the scale of the illegal presence of Chinese in the labour market of the Russian Far East. Chinese migration to the region is predominantly commercial. A majority of Chinese migrants are engaged in wholesale and retail trade; the next largest percentage is engaged in study or training, followed by those working on a contract basis. However, some Chinese who come for study or training do not study or, shortly after arrival, give up their studies to start trading or to engage in other business. They usually circumvent the law to do so. The overwhelming majority of Chinese who have legally or illegally settled on Russian territory do varying amounts of trading in Chinese goods. According to official statistics concerning Chinese in Amur Oblast, 40 per cent of them are employed in trade. However, unofficial estimates put the share of Chinese tourists involved in trading at market places of that region at 95 per cent,[22] excluding Chinese workers and students who are employed part-time to sell Chinese goods. Ponkratova states that the number of Chinese citizens who were actually employed in Amur Oblast towards the end of the 1990s might have been five to six times higher than the official number of those legally employed. According to her, approximately 700 Chinese worked every day just in the market places in Blagoveshchensk, the capital city of Amur Oblast.[23]

One of the biggest Chinese markets in the RFE is in the city of Ussuriisk in Primorskii Krai. The officials of the market say that there are about 800 to 1,200 Chinese who have official permission to work there. However, rumours have it that about 10,000 Chinese gather at the market. Many Russian and Chinese employers are interested in hiring illegal workers in order to save on wages. They often violate Russian legislation when they engage Chinese coming as tourists or with short-time commercial visas to work in construction and agriculture or as cooks, dishwashers and so on. In 1999, the Regional Migration Service identified 1,486 foreign citizens (mainly Chinese) who were illegally involved in trade, consumer services and construction in the border regions and cities of Primorye. In 2000, this number amounted to 1,318. In 2002, the regional police uncovered 92 organizations that illegally employed foreign labour and 596 foreign citizens working unlawfully in Primorye.[24] These statistics show that although the number of illegally employed foreign citizens in Primorye is steadily decreasing, there are still many Russian employers who are prone to violate the law if it means higher profits. As Wishnick mentions, "although regional officials blame the Chinese government for encouraging illegal immigration to the Russian Far East, corruption in Russia makes it possible for the Chinese economic migrants to remain there".[25]

In the areas of the Russian Far East far from China, the issue of the illegal Chinese presence is not as urgent as in the border territories. According to statistics of the Migration Services of Sakhalin Oblast, in 2001 only a few dozen Chinese were illegally employed on the island.[26] Insignificant numbers of Chinese traders compete with Russians in the markets of Yuzhno-Sakhalinsk, Magadan and Petropavlovsk–Kamchatsky. Nevertheless, in 2002 dozens of Chinese traders in Petropavlovsk upset their Russian colleagues, who believed that the Chinese were driving down prices, and provoked their protests against the Chinese presence.

In the 1990s, the scale and possible consequences of attracting Chinese labour into the RFE were the topic of numerous discussions in academic, political and other circles. But the total annual percentage of Chinese workers employed in the region has never exceeded 0.2 per cent of the total labour force there, and thus cannot have any serious impact on the general social situation. Even if we take into consideration the Chinese

tourists who are illegally involved in trade and other forms of entrepreneurship, this figure will not be higher than 0.5 per cent of regional
employment.[27]

Their illegal presence and work in Russia are not the only disturbing
issues related to the Chinese in the Russian Far East. By the beginning
of the new century, regional Russian communities were more anxious
about the criminal activities of certain Chinese than about their number.
"Criminal Chinese", "dishonest Chinese", "Chinese who destroy the
ecology of the region" – these became the characterization of the Chinese by the local mass media. Primorye newspapers described them as
thieves and "untidy citizens of China", who reaped profits mostly by
smuggling liquor and drugs.[28] *Parlamentskaya Gazeta* asserted that
"China's peaceful expansion to Russia" is criminal in nature.[29] Khabarovsk's governor Victor Ishaev is quoted as having alleged that "drugs,
narcotics, and crime poured into the region following the Chinese traders
who came there".[30]

In 2002, police statistics in Primorskii Krai recorded 177 crimes committed by foreign citizens, more than 130 of them by Chinese, including
21 cases classified as serious or extremely serious.[31] Most of the crimes
were committed against other Chinese. However, the statistical information from the Department of Internal Affairs differed significantly from
reality. Only a few crimes committed by Chinese against other Chinese
were reported to the police because Chinese victims of crimes went to
Russian authorities only as a last resort.

Since the end of the 1990s, government officials and the local press
have discussed the issue of Chinese criminal groups operating among
the Chinese in the Russian Far East. They used to refer to them as traditional Chinese secret societies, but their claims were not substantiated by
reliable information. The newspaper *Vladivostok* claimed that Ussuriisk
had turned into the capital of the "Chinese mafia" in the region and was
collecting money generated by Chinese organized crime.[32] It is hard to
imagine that Chinese gangsters provided the journalist (or his informant
in official agencies) with any information about their activities so that
such a conclusion could be reached. However, the perception of "criminal Chinese society in Russia" was given a new life.

Given the public perception of the criminality of some Chinese activities in the region, occasional reports of criminal offences *against* Chinese
businessmen in the Russian Far East[33] add to the negative views of local
Russian citizens. Nor do they encourage the police to become advocates
of Chinese people's presence and business in Russia, although some
police officers receive illegal payments from Chinese markets and businesses. On the other hand, the Chinese cannot feel secure because they
fall prey to both Russian and Chinese criminal groups, which are be-

lieved to coordinate their activities much more effectively than their governments, and to private security agencies. Also, the Chinese cannot feel secure because often the Russian police cannot determine the true perpetrator of a crime.

In addition to expressing concern about the negative impact of Chinese migration on local labour markets and the social environment, many in the RFE blame the Chinese for ruining their natural environment. They assert that the Chinese "unproductively pillage valuable forest and aquatic resources of the Far East". These perceptions are held by many ordinary people, who deliberately or subconsciously reject the possibility of Chinese settlement in Russia. They are also shared by politicians and intellectuals, who are responsible for developing policies concerning security and relations between the two countries. As a result, various proposals have been made for political and juridical measures to limit and control Chinese migration.

Ethnic characterization of "typical Chinese", found in public opinion in the Russian Far East, is another source of Russians' fears, prejudices and gloomy expectations. This image is mixed. According to a 2003 opinion poll conducted in the southern part of the Russian Far East, the characteristic attributed most often to the Chinese (by over 65 per cent of respondents) was "hard-working". Their enterprising nature was also highly valued by 48 per cent. Also mentioned were politeness and reliability (9 per cent and 7 per cent respectively). On the negative side, "cunning" (41 per cent) was among the highest-ranked characteristics of Chinese. Aggressiveness was rated fourth, at 21 per cent. Only 2 per cent of respondents considered Chinese to be honest and generous.

Many Russians believe that the Chinese are not cultured in their everyday behaviour, but they hold this notion along with a general recognition of and respect for the cultural heritage of Chinese civilization. Most of the Chinese contract workers in the agricultural, construction and consumer service sectors since the beginning of the 1990s have come from the less educated and poorer strata of China's north-eastern provinces. The same can be said about the Chinese tourists who have come to sell consumer goods in Russian markets. Many Russians have formed their images of Chinese people based on their impressions of these contract workers and market traders. A high-ranking Primorye official wrote at the end of the 1990s that "the cultural level of the majority of Chinese visiting Primorskii Krai was very low ... Chinese citizens do not exert any positive cultural influence on the life of the region."[34]

The mixed images above, along with other factors such as China's growing economic and military potential as well as sharp contradictions in the two states' relations in the recent past, produce both growing respect for China as a state and worsening attitudes towards its citizens.

Thirty-four per cent of the respondents in the 2003 poll said that their attitudes towards China had improved over the previous 10 years, and only 9 per cent admitted that their attitudes had worsened. Every fourth respondent (23 per cent) said that his/her perception of the Chinese people was worse than 10 years ago, and 15 per cent of the respondents said that their perceptions had improved.[35]

The survey also brought out some cultural antagonisms towards the Chinese in the Russian Far East. Every third respondent (34 per cent) admitted that he/she felt like rejecting the Chinese while communicating with them; another third (32 per cent) had never thought about it. About 29 per cent of the Russian respondents felt superior to the Chinese, but every fourth respondent had not noticed this feeling. About 38–39 per cent of the people tried to assure the interviewers and themselves that they did not harbour such feelings towards the Chinese, although their sincerity might be questioned. Numerous talks and interviews with people of different levels of education and economic status, professional qualification, age, social status and political view convinced the author that rejection of the Chinese is fairly prevalent among them. Most Russian citizens can tolerate the Chinese working in their country and those employed by Russians. However, some Russians would find it humiliating to work for Chinese. Even on Sakhalin Island, far removed from the Russian–Chinese border, where only a few hundred Chinese are present, the attitudes of the local population towards the Chinese are mostly negative, although people do not have grounds for talking about "Beijing expansion" or "Chinese penetration" into their region.

Most of the Chinese working in the Russian Far East do not find the region very attractive and promising for long-term settlement. The unfavourable atmosphere they experience is one of the main reasons why they see their stay there as temporary. Thus "Chinatowns", seen in many other parts of the world, have not emerged in the region. Nor do the extant Chinese communities in the RFE serve as a magnet to all the Chinese there. These communities are small in number and have limited influence among the Chinese, but there are efforts under way to change this. For example, the Khabarovsk Chinese Society tries to unite Chinese in Khabarovsk. This organization was established in 1994 and includes Chinese citizens of both the Russian Federation and the Peoples' Republic of China.[36]

The Chinese in Vladivostok established the Union of Chinese and Huaqiao (overseas Chinese). The group hosted a Great Patriotic War celebration and a reception for war veterans on 9 May 2002.[37] The Chinese–Russian Industry and Commerce Union, founded in 2002, unites and coordinates the activities of Chinese businessmen and traders in the southern areas of the RFE. Its charter states that the organization's major goals are "to protect the legal rights of its members through legal means; to facilitate matching up of Chinese businessmen who permanently reside in the Russian Far East and *huaqiao* with Russian businessmen; and to strengthen exchange and cooperation; to encourage business development". The Union also works to establish mutual understanding and dialogue between Chinese and Russian local authorities, public organizations and economic establishments and bodies; to stimulate trading, technical and economic cooperation between Chinese and Russian regions; and to strengthen exchange and coordination between local societies. Finally, it seeks to contribute to the development of the local economy and society and to help Chinese businessmen and *huaqiao* to generate high incomes and improve their personal skills and abilities.[38]

However, Chinese students from Dalian and Harbin studying at Far Eastern State University in Vladivostok informed this author that they knew nothing about the activities of the Union. They do not have any relationship with traders and businessmen or with the students of other universities in the city.

The perception of China and the Chinese in the Russian Far East

In the past decade, there were more Chinese visitors to the southern territories of the Russian Far East than from any other country. Primorskii Krai and Amur Oblast were the main destinations for Chinese, and consequently experienced the greatest influence from China. In Primorye, the Chinese constituted 70–75 per cent of foreigners visiting the territory in 1996–2003. The percentage of Chinese who visited Amur Oblast each year exceeded 99.9 per cent of all foreign visitors. Only 2 per cent of the Primorskii Krai respondents to the 2003 survey mentioned earlier stated that they had never interacted with a Chinese person. The remaining 98 per cent had interacted with Chinese, mainly in Russia. Hundreds of thousands of Russian Far East residents had had opportunities to go to China as tourists and shuttle traders.[39] Most of them formed personal images of China, its people and its culture through the skewed prism of the border cities they visited, such as Heihe, Suifenhe, Dongning and Harbin. None of these cities could be said to provide a representative picture of Chinese society. The largest part of the RFE's population drew their impressions of China from the local media, whose depiction of contemporary China was unfavourable, full of anti-Chinese sentiments.

That skewed and often unflattering information about China helped to create misunderstandings and suspicions, as well as enmity and sinophobia. Many people in the Russian Far East also feared possible Chinese expansion into their territories. There is a strong perception in the RFE that the Chinese are out to take advantage of the Russians, to steal from them and perhaps to take over their territory. In spite of many official statements from both sides that the border disputes between China and Russia are basically resolved, many local residents continue to fear that China will claim territories from Russia in the future.

There are two main reasons for these fears. The first is the huge demographic disparity along the border, including asymmetries in population size and rates of employment. Second, the fears are based on the history of the two countries' territorial disputes and earlier Chinese statements that the border treaties signed by them in the nineteenth century were unfair.[40] Weakened ties between the Russian Far East and the rest of Russia, as well as lack of faith in Moscow's willingness to protect and fight for these territories, fuel the local population's rekindled sense of a "yellow peril".

Although other sources of information based on deeper knowledge of the subject, such as official statistics and some scientific analyses, disagree with the existence of a "Chinese threat", their influence on the local population is not as strong as that of the alarmists. As a result, a substantial part of the population of the southern frontier of the Russian Far East agrees with the theme of the "Chinese threat" and accepts the possibility of Chinese expansion into their territories.[41] There is a general consensus on the Russian side that the present-day "Chinese threat" is not militaristic in nature but economic and political. Thus, many believe that the best way to resist this threat is through the economic development of the RFE. It should be noted, however, that the level of fear is different in different territories of the region. People in Khabarovsk, several of whose islands are under dispute with China, appear to be the most anxious. The residents of Amur Oblast seem equally divided between optimists and pessimists (see figure 2.4).

The aforementioned 2003 survey shows that only 20 per cent of the population of Primorskii Krai estimated the number of Chinese to be less than 5 per cent of the region's population (i.e. less than 100,000 people).[42] Every fifth interviewee stated that he/she had no idea of the number of Chinese in their region. The remaining 60 per cent of the respondents guessed the Chinese presence to be from 5 to 30 per cent, without taking a moment to consider that these figures would imply that several hundred thousand Chinese lived there.

A substantial part of the RFE's population views China through the prism of various real and perceived threats, such as "ethnic" and economic aggression, political pressure and criminal activities. They take this view instead of competing for the vast Chinese market and employing Chinese labour for regional industrial development and agriculture,

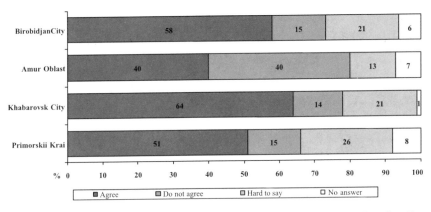

Figure 2.4 Attitudes towards the idea of "Chinese expansion" in the Russian Far East, summer 2003 (*Sources*: Victor Larin, "Kitaiskii factor v obschestvennom soznanii rossiiskogo prigranichiya: srez 2003 goda" ["Chinese factor in Russia's border regions public opinion: 2003 outlook"], *Far East Affairs* 4, 2004, p. 77).

which would improve their own well-being and prosperity. Anti-Chinese sentiments are particularly extreme among the political and military elites and the population along the Russian–Chinese border. Officially, people call for Russian–Chinese friendship and use slogans prophesying the inevitability of collaboration, but in reality fear and disappointment rule the hearts of a majority of politicians and ordinary citizens. Many of them still harbour the old, "yellow peril" way of thinking.[43] Also, the perception of different categories of Chinese is not uniform. According to the 2003 poll, a majority of respondents (83 per cent) in the Russian Far East were against the illegal presence of Chinese in Russia, while three-fourths of them welcomed tourists from China. Their attitudes towards Chinese workers, businessmen and traders also varied (see figure 2.5).

Despite their opposition to a mass Chinese presence on Russian territory and their fear of "Chinese expansion", the local people are for the most part interested in friendly relations with the Chinese and optimistic about the future of Russia–China relations (see figure 2.6).

The majority of Russians living in the border regions evaluate the prospects of Russian–Chinese relations as positive, although they are concerned about Chinese migration, the RFE's growing economic dependence on China and unresolved territorial problems. However, the real dangers – the continuing depopulation of the RFE, its industrial degradation and growing economic dependence on neighbouring countries, as well as corruption and a generally unfavourable political climate – are connected not to China's policies but to the actions of Russia itself. They are tied to the calculated and serious policies of the Russian gov-

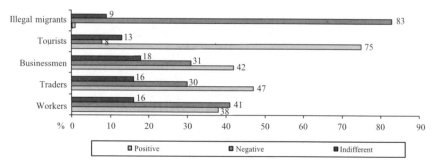

Figure 2.5 RFE residents' attitudes towards different categories of Chinese people in Russia, 2003 (*Sources*: Victor Larin, "Kitaiskii factor v obshestvennom soznanii rossiiskogo prigranichya: srez 2003 goda" ["Chinese factor in Russia's border regions public opinion: 2003 outlook"], *Far East Affairs* 4, 2004, p. 78).

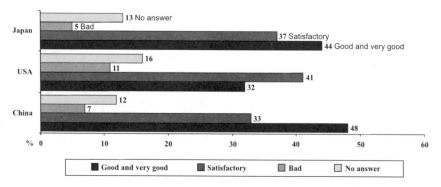

Figure 2.6 Future developments in Russia's relations with Asia-Pacific countries: Views of the southern RFE, summer 2003 (*Sources*: Victor Larin, "Kitaiskii factor v obshestvennom soznanii rossiiskogo prigranichiya: srez 2003 goda" ["Chinese factor in Russia's border regions public opinion: 2003 outlook"], *Far East Affairs* 4, 2004, p. 79).

ernment in the RFE and to its ability to develop and protect its Far Eastern territories.

Conclusion

Its contiguity to China and the growing Chinese presence in Russia have become very important factors in the ongoing social, political and economic transformations of the Russian Far East. Since the beginning of the 1990s, most residents of the RFE have perceived China as a threat to the national security, sovereignty and territorial integrity of their country. This multifaceted threat perception has led to the absence of a unified Russian strategy towards China, of an understanding of China's importance to Russia's national interests and national security and of an adequate migration policy in Russia. As a result, the regional perception is that the Russian–Chinese border has been poorly regulated and ineffectively developed for nearly a decade. Beijing's policy towards Russia has been consistent with developments in the north-eastern provinces of China, but Moscow's policy has been out of harmony with the interests and concerns of the Russian Far East.

A number of reasons mentioned in this analysis explain why the Chinese issue in the RFE has developed such a strong and negative character. First, there is a lack of reliable information on China's foreign policy (including its Russia policy). Second, there is great ignorance about the number of Chinese in Russia and about what their interests there are. The closed nature of Chinese communities in Russia and some legal problems related to them (the illegal status and semi-legal entrepreneurship of some of the Chinese, their involvement in illegal export-import operations, the smuggling of natural resources and drugs, extortion, robbery, murder and other criminal offences among them) also contribute to the problem. Moscow's unwillingness to pay enough attention to the problems of the RFE has allowed the problem to worsen. Moreover, some regional bureaucrats and politicians have tried to use the so-called threat of Chinese expansion as a trump card in their political game with the federal centre.

So far, Russia's approach to Chinese migration to the RFE has been based on the predominantly negative sentiments found in the region. This approach is mostly restrictive and results in partly effective measures to regulate the presence of Chinese migrants. But at the same time, such measures have invited corruption and produced strong anti-Chinese feelings among the residents of the RFE. As a result, the Chinese do not feel secure there. They are forced to live and act in a limited space in order to protect their lives.

Although China is perceived as a possible threat to Russia's national integrity and the Chinese are viewed as a threat to the identity of Russian society, Russians do not yet associate the Chinese presence in Russia with a threat to their human security or their cultural identity. First and foremost, Russians understand Chinese migration in terms of their own current economic conditions and the future of the region.

There are at present very few applications by foreign labourers for work in the Russian Far East. The minor scale and limited effectiveness of foreign labour is determined by several factors. The region's small and declining population limits the size of the consumer market. The investment climate is still unfavourable and industries continue to stagnate. General anxiety over a rising China and a sense of vulnerability fuels the prevailing negative attitudes towards the Chinese in Russia. It would be naive to believe that the regional mood towards China and the Chinese will change in the near future.

Although the authorities and businessmen understand that the local labour supply is not sufficient to provide for regional economic development and that they will have to employ labour from other territories (but mainly from abroad), a fear of China's domination causes them to take a cautious approach with regard to foreign workers. Primorskii Krai's governor Sergei Darkin, in his message to the citizens of the territory on 24 April 2004, compared the consequences of employing foreign labour to taking medicine and stated, "Both are useful in small amounts, but overdose can lead to death."[44]

It is quite evident that Russia needs a clear and consistent policy towards China, one that is well coordinated between Moscow and the RFE. Russia's national migration policy needs to take into account the specific character of its regions. Regional programmes must be developed within the framework of national migration policy so that there is a clear understanding of the power that the regional authorities have in dealing with migration issues in their territories.

Notes

1. Since 1993, many conferences, round tables and field surveys have been dedicated to the study of the phenomenon of Chinese migration in Russia. They have resulted in countless publications on the topic in Russia and abroad.
2. Alexander Gol'bakh, "Pogranichnaya bezopasnost' i sovremenniyie aspecti okhrani gosudarstvennoi granitsi RF v dal'nevostochnom regionye" ["Border Security and Contemporary Issues of the Russian Federation Border Guard in the Far East Region"], in *Pogranichnaia politika: praktika i osobennosti eio realizatsii v regionakh Dal'nego Vostoka. Materialy mezhregional'noi nauchno–prakticheskoi konferentsii 23 aprelia 1998 g. Khabarovsk: Dal'nevostochnaia akademiia gosudarstvennoi sluzhby* [Border Security: The Practice and Its Regional Peculiarities in the Far East Regions. Papers from the Interregional Conference, Khabarovsk, 1998], p. 11.
3. There is no need to enumerate the long list of publications devoted to the subject. It is worth mentioning the two most recent books: Alexander Larin, *Kitaitsi v Rossii vchera i segodnia: istoricheskii ocherk* [The Chinese in Russia: Yesterday and Today. A Historical Survey], Moscow: Muravei, 2003 and Alexander Petrov, *Istoriia kitaitsev v Rossii 1856–1917 gody* [A History of the Chinese in Russia. 1856–1917], Saint Petersburg: Beresta, 2003.
4. Li Jingjie, "Sino-Russian Relations in Asia Pacific", in Koji Watanabe, ed., *Engaging Russia in Asia Pacific*, Tokyo: Japan Center for International Exchange, 1999, p. 63.
5. Gao Yuhai, Feng Pengfei and Deng Peng, "Guanyui Heilongjiang sheng dui e laowu hezuo de yanju" ["Heilongjiang Province Labor Cooperation with Russia"], *Sibolia Yanjiu* 3, 2002, pp. 17–18.

6. *Heilongjiang Province Social and Economic Development. Statistical Reports, 2001, 2002, 2003*, available at http://www.hlj.stats.gov.cn, http://www.stats.gov.cn.

7. By the end of the 1990s, Jilin Province estimated that there were as many as 215,000 would-be workers looking for employment. See *Jilin tognji ninjian 2000* [Jilin Province Statistical Yearbook 2000], Beijing: Zhongguo tongji chubanshe, 2000, p. 25.

8. The opinion survey conducted among the Chinese in the Russian Far East in 1999 showed that only 2 per cent of them in Vladivostok, 3.9 per cent in Khabarovsk and 8 per cent in Ussuriisk could not find work at home. Most of them mentioned an "opportunity to make profits" or a "desire to work in Russia" as the main reasons for coming. See Vilya Gelbras, *Kitaiskaia real'nost' Rossii* [Russia's China Reality], Moscow: Muravei, 2001, p. 65.

9. According to this agreement, tourist groups of no less than five people, headed by a representative of a given tourist company (initially the tourist companies were owned by the state), had a right to cross the border without a visa. A visa, on the other hand, remained relatively expensive, with a single-entry visa costing US$50, an expedited visa (provided the same day) costing US$100 and a triple-entry visa costing US$150.

10. Three executive orders by Primorskii Krai governors, dated 1997, 1999 and 2000, favoured better control of foreigners. The orders are respectively No. 429, Concerning the Measures of Control over Employment and Use of Foreign Labor in the Sphere of Service and Trade; No. 202, On the Establishing of Protocols for Foreign Citizens' Work in Trade and Consumer Services in the Territory of Primorskii Krai; and No. 598, On the Measures to Prevent Foreign Citizens and People without Citizenship from Illegally Migrating into Primorskii Krai. In October 1995, Amur Oblast passed the decree On the Residence of Foreign Citizens in the Oblast. In 1997 and 1998, local legislation was amended to toughen the rules for foreigners' entry and movement in the territory. The rules for foreigners and persons without Russian citizenship in Khabarovsk Krai were implemented by Governor Victor Ishaev's executive order of March 1997. Sakhalin Oblast has its own decree, of March 1996: On the Measures to Prevent and Decrease Uncontrolled Foreign Migration in the Territory of Sakhalin Oblast and the decree of January 1998: On the Measures to Prevent Illegal Foreign Migration in the Territory of Sakhalin Oblast. In early 1998, the Sakhalin Oblast administration signed with Heilongjiang Province the agreement On the Procedure for Employing PRC Citizens for Organized Trade in the Wholesale Markets of Sakhalin Oblast.

11. "Foreigner operations", some of them conducted by Primorskii authorities since the mid-1990s, gave rise to criticisms because of strict measures applied towards violators of the passport regime in Russia, but they were rather effective in improving the situation concerning illegal migrants in the territory.

12. Available at www.vostokmedia.ru/news.details.php?id=3405 (accessed 18 March 2004).

13. Sometimes migration statistics mechanically sum up the figures of various Far Eastern territories, misrepresenting the real number of Chinese that visit the RFE. Most of the Chinese who come to Magadan, Kamchatka and Sakhalin oblasts (for example, about 700 Chinese visited Sakhalin Island in 2000 and 1,700 in 2001) arrive by domestic flights from Vladivostok and Khabarovsk and have already been included in the statistics of local migration and border guards.

14. Vilya Gelbras, "Kitaiskiie zemliachestva i kitaiskaia migratsiia v Rossiiu" ["Chinese Communities and Chinese Migration in Russia"], presented at the 18th Symposium of History Researchers and Economists of the Far Eastern Branch of the Russian Academy of Sciences and the Kansai Region, Kyoto, Japan, 23 December 2002, pp. 10–11, unpublished.

15. *Vladivostok*, 29 May 2003.

16. *Collection of Russian-Chinese Agreements, 1949–1999*, Moscow: Terra-Sport, 1999, pp. 145–149.
17. According to the migration service of Primorye, during the first nine months of 2003 administrative charges were brought against 14,696 foreigners for violation of the passport regime. Seventy per cent of them were Chinese. *Vladivostok*, 20 October 2003.
18. Sergei Goncharov, "Kitaitsi v Rossii – kto oni?" ["The Chinese in Russia – Who Are They?"], *Far East Affairs* 4, 2003, pp. 17–18.
19. Natalia Ostrovskaya, "Pozhelteli nashi nivy" ["Our Fields Have Yellowed"], *Komsomolskaya Pravda*, 15 July 1999 and Yuri Avdeev, Sergei Pushkarev and Valentina Ushakova, "Migratsionnaya situatsiya i rynki truda v Primorskom krae: problemy trudovoi immigratsii" ["Migration situation and labor markets in Primorye territory: the problems of working immigration"], in Galina Vitkovskaya and Dmitri Trenin, eds, *Perspectives of the Far East Region: Population, Migration, Markets*, Moscow: Gendalf, 1999, p. 65.
20. *Vladivostok*, 6 January 1996 and *Pul's planety*, 25 December 1996, p. AK-2.
21. *Komsomolskaya Pravda*, 9 September 1999.
22. Tatiana Yaropolova, "Regulirovaniie protsessov vneshnei trudovoi migratsii: sostoyanie i perspektivy" ["Regulating Processes of External Labor Migration: Conditions and Perspectives"], in Petr Baklanov, ed., *Istoricheskii opyt osvoyeniia Dal'nego Vostoka. Vypusk pervyi. Ekonomicheskie i sotsial'no–demographicheskieproblemy* [Historical Experiences of Far East Exploration. Issue 1: Economic and Socio-demographic Problems], Blagoveshchensk: Amurskii gosudarsvennyi universitet, 2000, p. 193.
23. Lyudmila Ponkratova, "Mezhdunarodnye trudovye migratsii v Amurskoi oblasti: otsenka i tendentsii" ["International Labour Migration in Amur Oblast: Assessment and Tendencies"], in Nikolay Shindyalov, ed., *From the History of Russian-Chinese Relations*, Blagoveshchensk: Amurskii gosudarsvennyi universitet, 1999, p. 140.
24. *Vladivostok*, 21 January 2003.
25. Elizabeth Wishnick, *Mending Fences: The Evolution of Moscow's China Policy from Brezhnev to Yeltsin*, Seattle and London: University of Washington Press, 2001, p. 169. See also Wishnick, chap. 3, in this volume.
26. See "Analiticheskii otchet ob osnovnykh napravleniiakh deyatel'nosti territorial'nogo organa Minfederatsii Rossii v Sakhalinskoi oblasti za 2001 god" ["Analytical Report on Basic Directions of Activities of the Territorial Unit of the Ministry of the Russian Federation in Sakhalin Oblast in 2001"], p. 11, unpublished.
27. Anatolii Shkurkin, "Dal'nevostochnyi rynok truda kak faktor kitaiskoi trudovoi migratsii" ["The Far Eastern Labour Market as a Factor of Chinese Labour Migration"], in Galina Vitkovskaya and Dmitri Trenin, eds, *Perspectives of the Far East Region*, p. 41.
28. Alexander Zhuravlev, "Kushat' podano! Kitaiskii ris s ephedrinom – samoie modnoie bliudo sezona?" ["Dinner is Served! Is Chinese Rice with Ephedrine the Most Popular Dish of the Season?"], *Moskovskii Komsomolets in Vladivostok*, 3–10 August 2000 and Vladimir Syrtsov, "Inostrantsy v zakone" ["Foreigners in the Law"], *Vladivostok*, 5 March 1999, p. 12.
29. Igor Naumov, "Mafia – khorosho? Eto bol'shoi vopros" ["Is the Mafia Good? A big question"], *Parlamentskaya Gazeta*, 11 August 1999, pp. 1 and 4.
30. *Rossyiskaya Gazeta*, 30 October 1999.
31. *Vladivostok*, 21 January 2003.
32. Dmitrii Korobov, "Utro publichnoi kazni. Kitaiskie triady vovsiu oruduiut v Primorye" ["The Morning of Public Execution. The Chinese Triads are at Work in Primorye"], *Vladivostok*, 25 October 2002, p. 2.
33. The last one was committed in Vladivostok on 9 April 2004. Su Lei, the owner of the well-known Golden Pheasant restaurant and woodworking workshop and vice-president

of the Vladivostok Association of Chinese Businessmen, was robbed and beaten to death near his office. The regional edition of *Komsomol'skaya Pravda* gave the following title to its article: "The Chinese will Search for the Murderer by Themselves". *Komsomol'skaya Pravda*, regional edition, 17 April 2004.

34. Nikolai Romanov, "Nekotorye aspekty prebyvaniia grazhdan KNR v Primorskom krae" ["Some Issues Related to the Chinese Stay in Primorskii Krai"], in Galina Vitkovskaya and Dmitri Trenin, eds, *Perspectives of the Far East Region*, p. 92.

35. In both cases, 40 per cent of respondents said that their position had not changed.

36. Judging from the opinion of Chairperson Wan Baoling, the Society was quite influential among Chinese businessmen and has been economically sustainable. *Tikhookeanskaya zvezda*, 16 February 1999.

37. *Donfang qiaobao*, May 2002, p. 3.

38. *Donfang qiaobao*, June 2002, p. 5.

39. The 2003 opinion poll shows that every third adult citizen of Primorye has visited China at least once. The poll results have not yet been published, but are available from the author.

40. It should be mentioned that the Chinese side understands and tries to dispel these fears. Chen Qimao writes:

[T]his is a misunderstanding. It is true that in border negotiations in the 1960s China said that the border treaties signed by Qing China and tsarist Russia in the 19th century, including the 1858 Ai Hui Treaty, the 1860 Beijing Treaty, the 1864 Treaty of Demarcation of the Northwest Border and the 1881 Yi Li Treaty, were unequal treaties imposed on China by Russia. However, at the same time China declared: "Considering the reality, China is willing, through peaceful negotiations, to resolve the border disputes between the two countries comprehensively and to redefine the whole demarcation line on the basis of those treaties. China is not demanding back the territories seized by tsarist Russia.

Chen Qimao, "Sino-Russian Relations after the Break-up of the Soviet Union", in Gennady Chufrin, ed., *Russia and Asia: The Emerging Security Agenda*, Oxford: Oxford University Press, 1999, p. 295.

41. In 2003, more than half of all respondents (54 per cent) in the southern part of the Russian Far East approved. Only 18 per cent did not believe in the expansion; the others did not answer. Ten years ago, the popular mood was the same.

42. According to local statistics, the entire population of Primorskii Krai at the beginning of the twenty-first century was 2.1 million people.

43. The "yellow peril" syndrome first became apparent in Russia more than 130 years ago. Superficially, the feeling of "yellow peril" looks to be produced by Russians' fear of all Eastern countries, but in fact it is associated exclusively with China, not Korea or Japan. Different sources have been nourishing this syndrome ever since. During the past decade, the long-standing understanding of the vulnerability of Russia's position in East Asia as determined by its history, geography, traditions of foreign policy and subconscious realization of Russians' status as outsiders in the region has become stronger and more acute because of the growing economic and military power of China and the activities of the Chinese in Russia. For the history and present-day condition of the "yellow peril" syndrome in Far Eastern Russia, see Victor Larin, "Ershi shiji chuqi he moqi elosi yuandong zhengqede 'huanghuo' zonghezheng" ["'Yellow Peril' Syndrome in Russia Far Eastern Policy at the Beginning and at the End of the 20th Century"], *Dongou Zhongya yanjiu*, No. 1, 1996, pp. 87–96.

44. *Vladivostok*, 27 April 2004, p. 6.

3

Migration and economic security: Chinese labour migrants in the Russian Far East

Elizabeth Wishnick

Left on the sidelines of economic globalization and trailing behind other regions in their respective countries, the Chinese Northeast (*dongbei*) and the Russian Far East have turned instead to each other and sought to develop regional economic cooperation. On the surface, *dongbei*'s underemployed labour force, cheap consumer products and need for natural resources would seem to be a good fit for the Russian Far East, which is plagued by labour shortages, dependent on imported consumer goods and blessed with abundant land, energy and mineral resources. Nevertheless, the issue of Chinese migration to the RFE has proved to be an intractable obstacle to the development of mutually beneficial regional economic ties, despite the decade-long Sino-Russian partnership, codified in the 16 July 2001 Treaty on Good-Neighborliness, Friendship and Cooperation.

This chapter examines the relationship between migration and economic security, focusing on the political, economic and social factors inducing Chinese people's migration to the Russian Far East and on Russian reactions to their presence. It is argued that inadequate economic security in *dongbei* motivates Chinese traders to try to improve their circumstances by seeking temporary employment across the border. Residents in the Russian Far East, however, interpret the steps that Chinese traders take to enhance their economic security as a threat to their own economic security, creating an economic "security dilemma"[1] with potentially adverse implications for Sino-Russian relations. This analysis attempts to identify the "push" and "pull" factors, i.e. the economic security causes, of Chinese migration to Russia. It notes that the perception that Chinese migration flows put Russian jobs at risk, increase crime and exacerbate an already bleak demographic picture for the shrinking local Russian population has implications for Russian national security and Sino-Russian bilateral relations.

Despite the rapid expansion of global and interregional labour flows, nation-states still play an important role in regulating migration, particularly as global governance in this area is relatively undeveloped.[2] Typically, receiving states seek to limit migration, but this is very difficult, because for regulation to be effective, it needs to be combined with their national labour policy.[3] Communities have different reactions to migrant labour flows: some may seek to regularize illegal migration in order to minimize associated social problems; others opt for punitive measures so as to deter would-be illegals from entering and competing with locals for jobs.[4] Although migrants may create jobs, by opening new businesses for example, recipient communities may perceive the newcomers as a threat to their livelihoods. Sending states, on the other hand, focus on increasing access to employment opportunities and the rights of migrant workers, especially family reunification. Thus migration may raise economic security concerns for both sending and receiving states.[5]

Economic security is a component of human security, a concept that emerged from late Cold War-era debates about the interconnection between development and national security. The 1994 Human Development Program of the United Nations Development Program elaborated a broad conception of human security, including economic security (basic income), food security (access to food), health security (freedom from disease), environmental security (a non-degraded ecosystem), personal security (protection from physical violence and threats), community security (ability to pursue one's cultural identity) and political security (basic rights and freedoms). Although the concept of human security has been criticized for its excessive breadth, the main contribution of this approach has been to highlight the importance of the security of people and to shift the level of analysis in security studies from the nation-state to the individual.[6]

Despite the efforts of political scientists to create distinct analytical categories, some phenomena, such as migration flows, defy neat categorization. Migration may adversely affect the security of individuals (both of migrants and of individuals in receiving states), communities (migrants' home communities and host societies) and states (through conflict between the migrants' home country and the host country).[7]

Background: The history of Chinese economic migrants in the Russian Far East

Concern about the economic security implications of Chinese migration to the Russian Far East is far from new. Although the issue became a flashpoint in regional relations right after the collapse of the USSR, when visa-free travel between Russia and China was instituted between 1991 and 1993, Chinese migration has been a sore point in relations for more than a century.

In the mid-nineteenth century, Chinese traders, workers and farmers began playing an important role in the economy of the region now known as the Russian Far East.[8] Like today, Chinese migrants travelled north for a variety of reasons. Some were fleeing economic hardship in Manchuria; others saw opportunity in gathering resources such as ginseng, sea cucumber and deer antlers in the Priamur *guberniya* (governorship), established in 1884.[9] As Priamur developed, the construction of the trans-Siberian railway and the development of gold mining required an influx of new workers, many of them from China.[10]

Merchants from Shandong were especially successful in establishing trade and shipping networks throughout the Amur and Maritime districts, part of which then was the Priamur governor-generalship.[11] Chinese traders shipped tea, flour and soybeans to Priamur, a key export destination for north-eastern China. From 1911 to 1917, China exported 20 million pounds of soy and 37 million pounds of grain (more than 64 per cent of its total national grain production) via Vladivostok.[12] Russia began shipping seaweed to China, a new export for the RFE. Once the trans-Siberian railway became operational, Russians and Chinese cooperated in an unusual form of transit trade. Owing to poor rail connections in China, products from southern China were shipped by sea to ports in Priamur and then by rail to the Chinese border, from where they were exported to north-eastern China.[13]

Nevertheless, officials in Russia's eastern territories in the nineteenth century were ambivalent about the region opening up to foreign trade. Like today, these territories depended on foreign imports of food and consumer products as a result of the unfavourable climate and the high cost of shipping these goods from European Russia. For example, in the late nineteenth century, flour from Odessa cost four times the price of Chinese flour.[14] But Russian officials were concerned that the sparseness of the Russian population in the Far East and weak lines of communication would invite foreign control. Prior to the completion of the trans-Siberian railway, it could take almost a year to travel from Moscow to Vladivostok by land.

Russia's concern about the security of its Pacific borders served as a rationale for expansion into Chinese territory. Taking advantage of China's weakness after its defeat in the Opium Wars, Russia gained the Qing government's acquiescence to the Treaty of Aigun (1858), according to which the Russian empire extended its territory southwards to the north bank of the Amur River, all the way to the Tatar Strait. In exchange for Russian assistance in accomplishing a withdrawal of British and French forces from China, two years later the Chinese signed the Treaty of Beijing (1860). This granted Russia control over the Primor'e territory, from the Ussuri River to the Tumen River, thereby ending Chinese access to the Sea of Japan.[15] By allowing Manchu subjects residing north of the Amur and Ussuri rivers to remain and by providing for a free-trade zone along the Amur River,[16] these treaties codified the existence of a Chinese diaspora within the Russian empire and opened up new possibilities for economic cooperation along the Sino-Russian border.

To forestall Russian expansion into Manchuria, the Chinese government had accelerated Han settlement there in the latter half of the nineteenth century.[17] St Petersburg in turn became worried about the demographic imbalance along the Sino-Russian border. The census of 1897 reported that there were 213,287 Russians living in the Amur and Maritime districts. During that year, 43,000 Chinese and 26,000 Koreans resided in these districts and comprised 32 per cent of the population.[18] Across the border there were 300 million Chinese, including 6 million in neighbouring Manchuria.[19]

The changing demographic picture in the Russian Far East fed into an underlying fear that the Chinese would seek to regain their lost territories; but in St Petersburg, officials held fast to their conception of Russia as a unitary state rather than a multinational federation.[20] Tensions also erupted periodically between the Chinese residing in Priamur and local officials over taxation issues. At the societal level, resentment over the presence of the Chinese occasionally elicited racist reactions and incidents, and concepts of a "yellow peril" emerged among the population at large.[21] Despite such problems, the importance of labour from China and Korea for the regional economy enabled these national populations to remain in the Russian Far East until Stalin's concern about the possibility of Russia's infiltration by Japanese spies led to the expulsion from the RFE in 1937 of some 19,000 of the 25,000 Chinese and the exile of 135,000 of the 165,000 Koreans to Central Asia.[22] Chinese began appearing once again in the Khabarovsk area as of 1950, although their entry into Vladivostok remained prohibited.[23]

Chinese labour migration to the Russian Far East: Push and pull factors

Underdevelopment and underemployment

Russian concern about illegal Chinese immigration today is fuelled by a perception of demographic pressure from China. The Russian Far East constitutes 36.4 per cent of Russian territory and has a population of 6,680,000. Owing to the high cost of living and to underemployment, the RFE had lost 7 per cent of its population by the mid-1990s. Although its northern areas experienced the most substantial outflows, the population of Primorskii Krai and Khabarovsk Krai declined by 1.5 per cent and 3.3 per cent respectively.[24]

Although the Chinese Northeast is less populated than central and southern China, it has been disproportionately affected by adverse economic trends. Its three provinces hold just 8 per cent of China's population (see table 3.1) but receive 22 per cent of the country's poverty relief.[25] According to Hu Angang, a renowned Chinese economist, layoffs from state-owned enterprises (SOEs) in the north-eastern provinces are nearly twice the national average of 18.3 per cent: 31.3 per cent in Heilongjiang, 31.9 per cent in Jilin and 37.3 per cent in Liaoning.[26] As workers in SOEs account for more than 73 per cent of industrial labour in *dongbei*, the region faces severe unemployment and underemployment problems.[27] Moreover, food-producing regions such as Heilongjiang have been adversely affected by China's entry into the World Trade Organization (WTO), because the province's main crop, soy, now faces competition.[28] But even before China joined the WTO, farmers had experienced continually diminishing revenues owing to falling prices for their output, which had dropped by 22 per cent between 1997 and 2000, and the burden of illegal taxes.[29]

With the number of new entrants into the urban workforce not peaking until 2005, Zhang Zuoji, the Chinese Labour Minister, characterized the employment situation in the Northeast as "very grim".[30] It is quite

Table 3.1 Population of the Chinese Northeast, 2002

Province	Population	Natural growth rate (%)
Heilongjiang	38,130,000	2.54
Jilin	26,990,000	3.19
Liaoning	42,030,000	1.34
Total	107,150,000	–

Source: *China Statistical Yearbook*, Beijing: China Statistics Press, 2003, p. 98.

Table 3.2 Full-time employment in north-eastern Chinese provincial capitals compared to other Chinese cities, 2002

City	Total population (m)	Number of fully employed staff and workers (m)
Beijing	11.36	4.35
Changchun	**7.12**	**0.91**
Guangzhou	7.20	1.70
Harbin	**9.48**	**1.73**
Shanghai	13.34	2.92
Shenyang	**6.88**	**1.10**

Source: *China Statistical Yearbook*, Beijing: China Statistics Press, 2003, pp. 390–391.

Table 3.3 Reasons for Chinese workers to go to Russian Far East for work

Reason	Number of respondents	Percentage of respondents
I was unemployed	123	49.2
My work unit sent me there	54	21.6
I was looking for a better job	40	16.0
The standard of living is higher in Russia	13	5.2
To marry a Russian	7	2.8
To become a Russian citizen	4	1.6
To emigrate to a third country	4	1.6
To buy property in Russia	3	1.2
To become a permanent resident of Russia	2	0.8

Source: findings of author's survey, July 2004.

difficult to find accurate unemployment statistics, because the available ones measure the number of jobless but do not include the large number of laid-off (*xia gang*) workers. Although still on the books, they are not working and may not receive salaries or other benefits. Table 3.2 presents the issue from the other direction: it compares the number of fully employed staff and workers in the three north-eastern capitals, Harbin, Changchun and Shenyang. Beijing, Shanghai and Guangzhou are included for comparative purposes in order to highlight the relatively lower levels of full-time employment in *dongbei*.[31]

My July 2004 survey of 250 Chinese workers – in Harbin (40) and three border cities in Heilongjiang Province: Suifenhe (90), Dongning (60) and Heihe (60) – who work in the Russian Far East shows that unemployment is the primary factor motivating respondents to seek employment there.[32] (See table 3.3.)

Decreasing industrial employment opportunities in the Northeast and inadequate government compensation have already led to large-scale strikes. From March to April 2002, thousands of laid-off workers in three north-eastern cities, Liaoyang (Liaoning Province), Daqing (Heilong-jiang Province) and Fushun (Liaoning Province) took to the streets to protest non-payment of wages and benefits.[33] Recognizing the economic situation as a threat to social stability, Chinese leaders now assert that revitalizing the Northeast is a key priority. After the strikes, Premier of the State Council Wen Jiabao visited Daqing and Fushun, and in early 2004 the Chinese leadership announced a new programme to rejuvenate the north-eastern industrial base, which targets key sectors.[34] As of this writing (August 2004), it remains unclear what impact the new pro-gramme will have on *dongbei*'s substantial structural economic problems.

Opportunity

Chinese shuttle traders who work in the Russian Far East come for the most part from the Northeast, primarily Heilongjiang Province.[35] Workers in construction and the restaurant business as well as in trade can earn significantly more money in the RFE than at home.[36] By con-trast to China's minimum wage, which does not exceed 600 yuan per month,[37] most Chinese workers in the RFE report a much higher in-come, with 37.2 per cent earning more than five times the Chinese mini-mum and 14.4 per cent exceeding it by ten times. (See tables 3.4 and 3.5.)

Labour export

Chinese labour export (*laowu shuchu*) originated as a component of the PRC's development assistance for third world countries such as Bangladesh and Tanzania.[38] With the onset of economic reform in the 1980s, companies that obtained licences to work on projects overseas were given the right to hire Chinese workers. There were 211 such firms by 1992.[39] Specialized labour-supply firms began to develop in the 1990s, and there were 48 by 2001. Some of these firms are subordinate to the Ministry of Economics and Trade and others are affiliated with provincial labour ministries, but most are in the non-state sector. Many companies integrate labour export with other business activities, such as construc-tion.[40] By 2001, more than 475,000 Chinese workers had participated in labour export programmes since those opportunities had begun.[41] Most of those workers (approximately 400,000) were involved in projects oper-ated by provincial authorities or non-state companies. China's southern provinces provide the largest number of workers for overseas projects.[42] Nevertheless, workers from Heilongjiang Province account for 65 per cent of Chinese contract labourers in the Russian Far East, with Jilin Province making up 10–25 per cent. The rest come from Liaoning, Shan-dong and Jiangxi provinces.[43]

Table 3.4 Monthly salary of Chinese workers in Russian Far East, 2004

Monthly salary (Chinese yuan)	Number of respondents	Percentage of respondents
Less than 1,000	9	3.6
1,000–2,999	91	36.4
3,000–4,999	93	37.2
5,000–7,999	17	6.8
8,000–9,999	1	0.4
More than 10,000	36	14.4
No answer	3	1.2

Source: findings of author's survey, July 2004.

Table 3.5 Occupation of Chinese workers in Russian Far East, 2004

Occupation	Number of respondents	Percentage of respondents
Individual trader	119	47.6
Business person	39	15.6
Construction worker	34	13.6
Restaurant worker	21	8.4
Forestry worker	11	4.4
Official	10	4.0
Student	6	2.4
Farmer	2	0.8
Other	8	3.2

Source: findings of author's survey, July 2004.

Chinese policy-makers view labour exchanges with other states as mutually beneficial, but those countries' fundamentally different approaches to the use of foreign workers have hindered China's labour cooperation with them. Although Japan, South Korea and Russia all face varying degrees of worker shortages, they tend to have more closed immigration policies, thereby limiting opportunities for China's surplus workforce.[44] For example, as a part of Sino-Russian discussions about Russia's entry into the WTO, China has urged Russian leaders to open the Russian market completely to Chinese labour and service providers as a part of its accession, a move that has met with opposition in Moscow.[45]

Moscow now allocates an annual number of foreign workers for each region. For example, in 2004 Primorskii Krai was entitled to bring in 15,000 foreign workers, although its labour needs are much greater. Despite being one of the first Chinese provinces to start sending workers to Russia (beginning in 1988), currently Heilongjiang Province sends just 3,000–5,000 workers each year. These are mostly farmers and workers in construction and forestry who are sent to participate in projects in Amur Oblast, Khabarovsk Krai and Jewish Autonomous Oblast, although smaller numbers also go to Chita Oblast and Krasnoyarsk Krai.[46] Chinese officials recognize that despite the need for foreign labour in the Russian Far East, its areas often prefer to bring in labour from North Korea, Vietnam and the CIS states.[47]

China's labour export to Russia is relatively small, and constitutes less than 3 per cent of its total labour export.[48] For example, Heilongjiang Province and Inner Mongolia saw their labour exports fall by an average of 10 per cent between 1992 and 2001.[49] Since 2001, the number of Chinese contract workers sent to Russia has declined because of a rise in the cost of obtaining the required permits. Moreover, in an effort to promote regional cooperation, some Chinese companies are compromising with Russian firms by acceding to their demands to use Russian labour and technology instead of their Chinese equivalents.[50]

Although Chinese scholars assert that boosting Sino-Russian labour cooperation would be mutually beneficial, they note that China's export of labour has many shortcomings that should be addressed. Problems arise when inexperienced small firms send poorly trained workers to the Russian Far East. Chinese scholars suggest that the two sides' labour cooperation would benefit from the involvement of larger, more established Chinese firms, which could bring in competitive technology and highly qualified workers. This would of course require greater communication between Chinese and Russian firms regarding their labour and technology needs.[51] However, Chinese analysts acknowledge that it may be difficult to attract highly qualified workers for positions in Russia, because they have better opportunities elsewhere.[52]

While admitting that there is much room for improvement on the Chinese side, Chinese analysts complain about unscrupulous Russian partners and the necessity of paying bribes to navigate through onerous Russian administrative procedures.[53] According to them, Chinese workers often are paid in goods, which they take home to sell. But in order to do so, these workers must first obtain an export permit and pay customs duties, thereby increasing the cost and inconvenience to the Chinese side.[54] On the other hand, when they are paid in cash, they have difficulty in repatriating the money and often resort to the black market.[55]

Tourism and trade

Since entering the WTO, China has been simplifying its border control procedures, to harmonize them with international practice. Previously, ordinary Chinese required an invitation from a foreign sponsor in order to obtain a passport and then needed an exit permit for first-time travel.

But now PRC citizens can apply to their local public security bureau (*gonganbu*) for a private passport by presenting their identity card and residence document. These passports can be used for five years, and provide greater mobility for Chinese citizens. Although easier access to private passports may increase the opportunity for Chinese to overstay their visas while overseas, the new process also provides an opportunity for the public security bureau and the customs and border authorities to track the movements of passport holders.[56]

In addition to loosening up the administrative requirements for passport issuance to Chinese citizens, the Chinese government is trying to make it easier for Russians to visit border trade zones on Chinese territory. Frustrated with the slow pace of cross-border cooperation, it appears to have changed tactics, and is now offering to pay for the infrastructure necessary to boost trade. It has reportedly offered to finance the entire cost of the bridge between Heihe and Blagoveshchensk,[57] proposed over a decade ago, and is planning to invest US$36 million to build a 1,380 km rail link from Dalian to Pogranichnyi.[58] On 16 January 2004, the Chinese government declared the entire city of Heihe, the city across the Amur River from Blagoveshchensk, to be a free-trade area, enabling Russians to spend up to 30 days in the city without a visa and even to purchase their own cars and real estate.[59] Previously, visa-free travel had been limited to Heihe Island on the Amur River, located between Heihe city and Blagoveshchensk.

Despite the liberalization of China's passport issuance and increased opportunities for trade and travel in free-trade zones along the Sino-Russian border, efforts to regulate cross-border activities have led to a criminalization of legitimate business activity, while criminal activities proceed unimpeded. Because of the time, cost and travel involved in obtaining a work visa, Chinese business people opt to travel as tourists to Russia, thereby circumventing the visa requirement, as tourists travel visa-free. Workers on contracts also complain that difficulties in obtaining the necessary papers lead them to return to Russia many times on tourist visas in order to complete projects.[60]

Business visas for Chinese citizens wishing to travel to Russia cost 700 yuan (US$84.50) for a regular, two-week processing and 1,200 yuan (US$145) for a rush job. The only Russian consulate in the Chinese Northeast is in Shenyang in Liaoning Province. A personal interview is sometimes required, adding to the cost and inconvenience of the application process. Participation in a tour group costs less, approximately 600–700 yuan, and does not involve any onerous procedures.[61] Respondents to my July 2004 survey expressed a clear preference for this form of travel: 40.8 per cent replied that they travelled with a tour group although their purpose was business. Consequently, cross-border tourism has been expanding rapidly, a testimony to the growth of cross-border trade, because few of the participants are actually engaging in tourism. According to figures from the Heilongjiang provincial government, in 2002 there were 630,000 border crossings by tourists travelling from Heilongjiang Province to Russia (mainly to the Russian Far East), a 21 per cent increase over 2001. In 2003, there was a decline in these crossings, to 568,626.[62] Chinese tourists from Heilongjiang Province accounted for 160,000 of the 630,000 crossings in 2002, or 25.3 per cent of the total.[63]

Russia and China have never signed an agreement on promoting tourism, so that major travel agencies in Beijing are unable to advertise tours for legitimate tourists.[64] Only border tourism is promoted, enabling travel agencies in the border posts of *dongbei* to organize group travel to the Russian Far East. Some of these tour groups are sex tours housing Chinese male tourists in brothels in cities in the RFE, a practice involving the cooperation of Chinese tour organizers with Russian prostitution rings. Similar arrangements are reportedly available for Russian tourists in China. Although purchasing the services of a prostitute is illegal in China, Chinese authorities turn a blind eye to these tours, and typically neither the organizers nor the participants on the tours are prosecuted on either the Chinese or the Russian side. Ironically, legitimate business people are obliged to circumvent visa rules in order to carry out legal activities by posing as tourists while sex tourism flourishes without restriction, despite being illegal.

Inadequate regulation and corruption

The misuse of tourist status has led in turn to a strengthening of restrictions on tourism between Russia and China. Tourists are limited to a 30-day stay and are restricted to cities specified in the tour agenda. Tour group leaders retain the passports of all group members and must present a list of all participants to Russian customs. If any tourist fails to return with the rest of the group, then Russian customs fine the tour organizer 5,000 roubles and the company risks losing its right to engage in border tourism.[65] As in the case of Chinese tour groups to Southeast Asia, organizers who are concerned about tourists failing to return to China may charge a "deposit" of 15,000 yuan (US$1,811), to be repaid upon return to China.[66]

According to a former official in the Chinese consulate in Khabarovsk,[67] Russia's enforcement of the time limits for Chinese travellers is lax. Instead of requiring Chinese who overstay to leave Russia immediately, local officials demand regular "payments", thereby creating a mutually beneficial criminal situation: Chinese are allowed to remain beyond their allowed time limit and Russian officials are provided with a regular illegal income. Chinese visitors who travel to Russia legally also complain of being harassed by Russian authorities, taken to the police station to show their documents and charged "fees" as high as 500 roubles to be left alone, even if they hold valid passports and visas.[68]

According to one tour group official, although in principle Chinese tour groups are fined for failing to bring back the original number of tourists, in practice the penalties incurred depend on the relationship between the tour group organizer and the Russian and Chinese authorities. This would explain why Russian officials claim that 99 per cent of foreign tourists (the majority of whom come from China) now return within their allowable time frame while continuing to warn about the threat posed by illegal Chinese migrants.[69]

Chinese labour migration in perspective

Chinese policy-makers have taken steps to encourage legal labour exchanges, but consistently deny Russian allegations that China is promoting illegal migration. During Jiang Zemin's first visit to Moscow, in September 1994, he defended China's policies in the border regions and expressed the hope that Russia "would protect the legitimate rights and interests of Chinese citizens who are engaged in normal trade and other activities". The Chinese leader stated his opposition to illegal migration and attributed concern over the issue to inadequate preparation by both sides for the opening of the border.[70] Jiang noted that he and President Boris Yeltsin had agreed to continue to develop regional cooperation despite these problems "rather than [to give] up eating for fear of choking, as the Chinese saying goes".[71]

The issue of Chinese migration to the Russian Far East has remained on the bilateral agenda, although both Russian and Chinese leaders have done their best to minimize its impact. The 16 July 2001 Sino-Russian Treaty of Friendship, Good-Neighborliness and Cooperation commits both parties to create an atmosphere of trust and cooperation in the border regions and to cooperate in combating illegal immigration.[72] In a 23 March 2004 article in *Izvestiya*, Sergei Prikhod'ko, the Russian president's deputy chief of administration, stated that there are no more than 150,000 to 200,000 Chinese living in Russia on a permanent basis and that the most recent census found an even smaller number – 35,000. He stated unequivocally that "there is no basis for saying that the government of the PRC 'promotes' its citizens to resettle in Russia, especially not illegally".[73]

A key question in understanding Chinese labour migration to the Russian Far East is, what is its overall purpose? Do Chinese economic migrants intend to settle permanently in Russia, as many Russians fear, or do they plan to stay temporarily in the RFE and then return home to their families in China?

Until the mid-1990s, the Chinese government distinguished between Chinese nationals living abroad (*huaqiao*, or sojourners) and ethnic Chinese with permanent residence rights or foreign nationality (*huaren*, or people of Chinese descent).[74] The *huaqiao*, by maintaining ties with their home villages, became key links in migration chains, facilitating the migration of their compatriots.[75] Whether or not they became *huaren* depended on the citizenship rules of the host country as well as their prospects back in China should they have chosen to return. For the millions who settled in Southeast Asia prior to 1950, for example, return was not an option, despite pervasive discrimination, because the PRC government treated returnees harshly during the Cultural Revolution.

Since the mid-1990s, the Chinese government has referred to all Chinese who have left the country as *xin yimin* (new migrants), without making distinctions based on their citizenship.[76] The blurring of these distinctions reflects an increased effort by officials responsible for foreign economic relations to reach out to overseas Chinese investors, whom they see as an important potential source of investment in high-tech industries. Some provinces promise the *xin yimin* special investment privileges, and their children may benefit from a special quota in the highly competitive university admissions process.[77] The *xin yimin* are also encouraged to return home, and many do so given the right job opportunities.

All the same, Chinese scholars object to using the term "migrants" (*yimin*) to refer to Chinese working in the Russian Far East. They typically refer to these workers as overseas workers (*waipai laowu*). Regarding the intentions of Chinese working in Russia, my July 2004 survey shows that family ties and attachment to China are significant factors for a majority of these workers. Previous surveys of Chinese showed a population interested in putting down roots in Russia,[78] but these respondents were Chinese residing in Russia; they represent the views of a minority of Chinese workers, most of whom return home. According to my July 2004 survey of Chinese workers in Heilongjiang Province, a majority (61.2 per cent) claim that they have successfully integrated their Russian work experience into their lives in China, as table 3.6 demonstrates.

A majority of respondents were married but were unaccompanied by family members, especially children, who typically remain in China.[79] When asked why they returned to China, 32 per cent complained of too much competition from other Chinese in their industry and 22.8 per cent mentioned completion of their project or contract. These results show a working population temporarily residing in Russia for work purposes

Table 3.6 Influence of Chinese workers' experience in RFE on their life in China

Influence	Number of respondents	Percentage of respondents
I learned to appreciate my life in China more	92	36.8
My experience in Russia had limited impact on my life in China	82	32.8
I gained valuable experience for my job/studies	61	24.4
I found it difficult to readjust to life in China	13	5.2
No answer	2	0.8

Source: Findings of author's survey, July 2004.

but retaining family and cultural ties with China. Moreover, they suggest that properly enforced contracts help to ensure that temporary workers will return to China once their projects are completed.

Despite efforts by both Russian and Chinese officials to downplay the migration problem in Sino-Russian regional and bilateral relations, many Russian analysts continue to assert that as a reflection of its great power aspirations, the Chinese government's migration policy is directed towards resettling the Russian Far East and integrating it within the Chinese economy.[80] Viewing the behaviour of others "as more centralized, planned, and coordinated than it is" is a common misperception, as Robert Jervis noted in his study of perceptions in international politics.[81] Indeed, Beijing's *lack* of a national migration policy has made it more difficult for the central authorities to regulate provincial-level efforts to promote the export of labour.

Although the Chinese government maintains contact with overseas Chinese worldwide through a variety of associations as well as through embassies and consulates, these are largely devoted to generating trade and investment among the *xin yimin* communities.[82] However, after the Chinese leadership's brutal crackdown on peaceful demonstrators in Tiananmen Square in June 1989 resulted in sanctions by Western countries and demonstrations by overseas Chinese residing there, the Chinese government sought to win back the political support of the overseas Chinese. It also endeavoured to mobilize them in support of Beijing's position on various foreign policy issues, for example to participate in protests against NATO's bombing of the Chinese embassy in Belgrade in 1999.

It is the provincial governments in *dongbei* that have been promoting labour cooperation with the Russian Far East. This has not always proceeded smoothly, particularly in the early and mid-1990s when Heilongjiang officials were subject to Beijing's wrath for lax supervision of cross-border trade.[83] At the provincial level, push factors such as underemployment create incentives for officials to expand labour export opportunities, by organizing official exchanges or supporting the activities of non-state labour export agencies. Provincial officials benefit economically more directly from such exchanges, in contrast to national policy towards migration, which is more opportunistic, seeking to use labour cooperation as a way of boosting Sino-Russian economic relations. Nevertheless, in the past decade Beijing's main policy interest, as is generally true of central governments in labour exporting countries, has been to minimize the political fallout from Russian criticism of Chinese migration.[84]

Russian perceptions of Chinese migrants

As the RFE was reopened to regional economic cooperation with Russia's Northeast Asian neighbours in the 1990s, the migration of Asian populations to its territories once again became an important matter for national and regional officials. However, integrating the Russian Far East into the Asian economy has turned out to involve a delicate balancing act. Although openness is necessary to encourage trans-border economic flows, the unintended consequences of these exchanges, such as increased migration, require greater regulation, which could stifle regional economic cooperation.

Since the mid-1990s, Chinese migration to the Russian Far East has become a controversial issue in centre–region relations in Russia and China alike, as well as in Sino-Russian bilateral and regional relations. Unlike their colleagues in Moscow, who have made the Sino-Russian partnership a priority, officials in the RFE currently view China as Russia's main competitor in the short term and as a potential threat in the long term. Divergent priorities, assessments of the regional balance of power and understandings of the costs and benefits of cooperation are at the root of differences in views in Moscow and the RFE.

Complementary economies and regional economic cooperation

Officials in the RFE believe that Russian and Chinese policy-makers overstate the potential for economic cooperation with China. Although initially, in 1992 and 1993, the Russian border areas showed enthusiasm for trade with China, this was more a reflection of the collapse of the Russian economy and the dependence of the Russian Far East on imported low-cost consumer goods and food products now that they could no longer be purchased from European Russia at affordable prices.

Policy-makers in Moscow and Beijing like to emphasize the economic complementarities underlying economic cooperation between their two countries. But to officials in the Russian Far East, these are political anathema.[85] The Russian border areas are not very interested in taking advantage of China's main asset, an unlimited supply of cheap labour, owing to concern about illegal migration and the dwindling Russian population in the RFE. Politicians there especially resent the role of their region as resource supplier to Asian states, and hope to secure investment capital to develop processing industries. China, which has its own processing industries, has little interest in facilitating the growth of this sector in Russia. Nor has it made significant investments in the RFE, with the exception of short-term trade ventures and the service sector.

As the market in the Russian Far East has become more differentiated, consumers have expressed a preference for higher-quality goods from South Korea, Japan and the United States. The August 1998 Russian financial crisis raised the cost of imports from those countries and led Russian consumers to turn once again to more reasonably priced Chinese goods. Nonetheless, officials in the RFE continue to see their economic future as linked to their ability to expand economic relations with those countries, which have the investment capital that the region desperately needs.[86]

Border relations and perceptions of the regional balance of power

More than economic strategy is at stake in the divergence of views about China in Moscow and the RFE. Their respective policy-makers also have very different views about the regional balance of power. For politicians in Moscow, the strategic partnership with China provides a respite against Western pressure, ensures a peaceful border and provides a rationale for substantial arms sales. In the Russian Far East, on the other hand, China represents the main potential threat to areas weakened by economic decline and population outflow.

Although policy-makers in Moscow still focus on Russia's standing vis-à-vis the West, the long-term impact of a rising China worries regional officials. And even though the "rise" of China is often overstated and the Chinese regions across the border actually share many of the same structural impediments to reform that are present in the RFE, regional officials still fear that an increasingly prosperous and populous neighbour with unclear intentions will overshadow it.

For this reason, policy-makers in Moscow and the Russian Far East perceive the consequences of cooperation with China quite differently. In Moscow, the Putin administration stresses the mutually beneficial political and economic results of partnership. And as national policy-makers emphasize the absolute gains of Sino-Russian cooperation, so regional leaders see only relative gains: China's gain inevitably will be Russia's loss.[87] This logic has posed obstacles to regional cooperation projects such as the Tumen River Area Development Program (and to some extent the inter-Korean railway project), as regional officials have opposed any region-wide infrastructure projects with potential benefits for China. In their view, even if Russia also benefited, the incremental gains for China would offset any gain for the RFE and put it at a disadvantage in economic competition with an even stronger neighbour. Consequently, even though officials in the RFE recognize the necessity of cooperating with China, they express a distinct preference for expanding cooperation with the United States, Japan and the Koreas.

As Victor Larin shows in chapter 2 of this volume, there is widespread fear among communities in the RFE about negative consequences of Chinese immigration for their economic well-being. However, by highlighting that Russian cities with high unemployment rates tend not to attract significant numbers of foreign migrants, Vilya Gelbras demonstrates that Russian concern about competition for jobs from Chinese workers is largely unfounded.[88] Perceptions in the RFE of the detrimental impact of Chinese migrants on the region's economic security may depend less on the general economic situation there and reflect more communities' assessments of the net gains or losses incurred by the activities of Chinese in their locality or the degree to which local leaders and media have succeeded in portraying the Chinese migration problem as a security threat (i.e. in "securitizing" the Chinese presence).[89]

China and Russia's migration policy

Many Russians fear that Chinese workers will entrench themselves in Russian society by buying property and marrying local women, thereby retaking Chinese territory lost to the Russian tsars in the nineteenth century by "peaceful expansion". This raises the question of the Russian government's ability to control its extended peripheries and regulate population flows across its lengthy border with China. Does Russia in fact have control? Does Chinese migration occur because of forces that cannot be regulated or because of Russian policies? Russia's role in regulating Chinese migration is at issue here.[90] How Russian policy-makers address the problem depends on their appreciation of the Sino-Russian balance of power, global economic forces, the interplay of regional and national migration policies, and cultural factors.

Political realist explanations argue that 1) migration policy is a matter of state security and that potential host countries such as Russia will open their borders if it is in their national interest to do so. They contend that 2) the distribution of power in the international system and the relative position of states will affect the dynamics of migration.[91] At the root of some Russian anxieties about Chinese migration is the potential asymmetry in the Russian–Chinese balance of economic power as China continues to boom economically while continued Russian economic growth appears less secure. Nevertheless, it is the economic *weakness* of the north-eastern regions of China, where migrants originate, that prompts them to seek opportunities in Russia.

Scholars who study globalization see a contradiction between the trend in most states towards lifting controls on flows of capital, information and services while strictly controlling national borders to limit migration.[92] According to Nestor Rodriguez, migration flows challenge the relevance of national boundaries. Using the United States–Mexico border as an example, Rodriguez describes a process of "autonomous international migration", the development of migration networks that make national boundaries irrelevant. Motivated by economic survival, Mexican workers and peasants form extra-legal transnational networks facilitating migration. Thanks to progress in telecommunications, members of transnational communities maintain constant contact with their former homes.[93] It is the development of Chinese networks of this kind in Russia that increasingly concerns Russian observers, although this is not a phenomenon unique to Russia.[94] For centuries, overseas Chinese have formed similar communities worldwide, particularly where their presence has met with hostility.[95]

It is true that the formation of transnational networks of migrant communities facilitates migration by reducing its costs (providing a hospitable environment for newcomers, financial support, information etc.). Also, the easing of travel restrictions within and from China makes it easier for migrants to leave their home communities. Nevertheless, other conditions must be present for migration to Russia to occur: 1) employers must be willing to hire migrants or to persuade the authorities to tolerate the presence of the Chinese; 2) historic ties must predispose Russia to allow Chinese to settle in the RFE; and 3) Russia must allow the families of Chinese migrants to join them.[96] The first condition is easily satisfied: many employers in the Russian Far East will hire Chinese. But historical patterns of Chinese settlement in the RFE serve as a disincentive for regional political leaders, who fear a loss of sovereignty to China, to allow migrants to establish residence. They are unlikely to encourage family reunification because that would be tantamount to promoting Chinese resettlement in the Russian border areas.

The impact of Chinese migrants on the RFE economy is not the only consideration for regional policy-makers, however. According to Myron

Weiner, security and stability considerations may become paramount in determining how a state deals with migration. He notes that the admission of migrants into a community may be perceived as a threat to national security if the host perceives the newcomers as violating existing norms or threatening cultural values.[97] For the underpopulated Russian Far East, isolated from Asian communities for more than 50 years but situated on China's northern border, the formation of Chinese migrant communities is perceived as a threat to its Russian identity. Nevertheless, as Saskia Sassen concludes from her historical research, migrations cannot be likened to invasions because they are rooted in economic, political and social systems that limit the flow of migrants, even when border controls are inadequate, as was the case in nineteenth-century Europe.[98]

The economic security dilemma in China–Russia regional relations: Policy recommendations

The economic security dilemma that has arisen regarding Chinese migration to the Russian Far East has proved to be intractable because its resolution is contingent upon the independent actions of Russian and Chinese authorities to address domestic problems, such as regional underdevelopment and corruption. Both the Chinese and Russian governments have outlined plans to revitalize their ailing border regions, but rapid progress is unlikely given the structural economic problems in the RFE and the Chinese Northeast. Moreover, at present neither the Russian government nor the Chinese government is giving high priority to funding the development of these border regions, making it likely that factors promoting Chinese migration and Russian hostility to it will persist in the near future. All the same, the Chinese and Russian central authorities could do more to improve the administration of cross-border labour exchanges so as to reduce tensions and expand mutually beneficial regional economic cooperation.

First, the Chinese government should develop a national labour export policy with standards for participating firms and workers. Generally, the resolution of a security dilemma involves accentuating defensive actions and reducing behaviour that can be seen as offensive. For Chinese policy-makers, this would involve further efforts to regulate cross-border interaction. Ironically, although Russians allege that the Chinese authorities have a migration policy aimed at resettling the Russian Far East, the problem is exactly the opposite: China lacks a national labour export policy. Decentralization to the provincial level of responsibility for labour export enables small, poorly qualified firms to provide inadequately trained contract labourers to the RFE. National guidance regarding standards for labour export would improve administration and the quality of workers sent abroad, thereby reducing some of the problems associated with contract labour.

Second, instead of focusing exclusively on restricting entry, the Russian and Chinese governments should work together to facilitate legal travel. According to Chinese analysts, the absence of a Russian migration policy is at fault. The Putin government has tried to take steps to address the issue. Since May 2002, the Ministry of the Interior has been given responsibility for migration issues, with the Federal Migration Service now integrated within it. According to new legislation that came into force on 1 November 2002, a quota of approximately 500,000 foreign migrant workers will be set annually, and these workers will be awarded special permits, in this way instituting a system similar to the admittedly imperfect American "green card".

If successful, the new Russian migration permits will improve the information available regarding the number of Chinese migrants working in Russia and reduce fears about massive migration, although the Deputy Interior Minister conceded that the quota figure would not cover those Chinese registered in Russia prior to the new regime.[99] The Ministry is trying to reduce the opportunity for bribe taking (by requiring that half the foreign migrant's permit stub be numbered and left with the authorities), but proper enforcement will still be necessary. Although it expects to weed out illegal migrants over time by establishing who lacks a proper permit, this process still provides ample opportunity for bribery and circumvention.

The Russian government's emphasis on restricting the entry of Chinese migrants, despite the Russian Far East's growing need for labour, creates incentives for illegal behaviour on both sides of the border. The Russian and Chinese governments should work together to simplify procedures for business travellers so that Chinese seeking to work in Russia can do so legally. This would involve expanding the number of cities in the Chinese Northeast and the RFE where a business visa could be applied for and also reducing fees and processing time. These measures would ensure that only legitimate sightseers would have access to visa-free tourist travel. They would contribute greatly to the reduction of corruption on both sides because there would be fewer incentives to travel illegally or under a false pretext.

Notes

1. Robert Jervis first developed the concept of the security dilemma in "Cooperation under the Security Dilemma", *World Politics* 30 (2), January 1978, pp. 167–174.

2. UN Commission on Human Security, *Human Security Now*, New York: United Nations Publications, 2003, p. 46. For example, few countries have signed the 2002 treaty regulating the treatment of migrant workers.

3. Stephen Castles and Mark J. Miller, *The Age of Migration: International Population Movements in the Modern World*, Basingstoke: Macmillan, 1993, pp. 268–270; David Held, Anthony McGrew et al., *Global Transformations: Politics, Economics, and Culture*, Stanford: Stanford University Press, 1999, p. 323.

4. Saskia Sassen, *Guests and Aliens*, New York: The Free Press, 1999, p. 104.

5. David T. Graham, "The People Paradox: Human Movements and Human Security in a Globilising World", in David T. Graham and Nana K. Poku, eds, *Migration, Globalisation, and Human Security*, London: Routledge, 2000, pp. 186, 193.

6. Amitav Acharya, "Human Security: East Versus West?", Working Paper No. 17, Institute of Defence and Strategic Studies, September 2001, pp. 3–4, 8; Kanti Bajpal, "Human Security: Concept and Measurement", Kroc Institute Occasional Paper #19, August 2000, pp. 36–38; and Roland Paris, "Human Security: Paradigm Shift or Hot Air?", *International Security* 26 (2), Fall 2001, p. 100.

7. Anatoly Vishnevsky, "Migratsiia i bezopasnost': analiz aspektov vzaimodeistvii" ["Migration and Security: Analysis of Interactive Aspects"], *Migratsia i bezopasnost' v Rossii* [Migration and Security in Russia], Moscow: Moscow Carnegie Center, 2000, p. 36.

8. Several scholars have studied the impact of Chinese migration on the Russian Far East economy in the late nineteenth and early twentieth centuries. See, for example, Igor R. Saveliev, "Chinese Migration to Russia in Space and Time", in Pal Nyiri and Igor R. Saveliev, eds, *Globalizing Chinese Migration: Trends in Europe and Asia*, Aldershot, UK: Ashgate Publishing, 2002, pp. 34–73 and John J. Stephan, *The Russian Far East: A History*, Stanford: Stanford University Press, 1994.

9. A Priamur governorship was established in 1884, including much of what are now the Chita, Amur, Khabarovsk, Sakhalin, Magadan and Kamchatka *oblasts* (regions), the Primorskii and Khabarovsk *krais* (territories) and the Chukotka Autonomous Okrug (district). Stephan, *The Russian Far East*, pp. 55–56.

10. For example, in 1910 more than 80 per cent of the workers in the gold mine in the Priamur region were Chinese. Saveliev, "Chinese Migration to Russia in Space and Time", p. 39. On the patterns of Chinese labour migration in the late nineteenth and early twentieth centuries, see also Anatolii M. Shukrin, "Chinese in the Labor Market of the Russian Far East: Past, Present, Future", in Nyri and Saveliev, eds, *Globalizing Chinese Migration*, pp. 75–85.

11. Saveliev, "Chinese Migration to Russia in Space and Time", p. 39.

12. Go Yanchun, "Vzaimovygodnye svyazi" ["Mutually Beneficial Ties"] *Rossiia i ATR* [Russia and the Asia-Pacific] No. 1, 1994, pp. 120–121.

13. N.A. Troitskaia, "Russkaia dal'nevostochnaia burzhuaziia i severo–vostochnyi Kitai. O vlianii prigranichnogo polozheniia na predrpinimatel'skuiu deiatel'nost'" ["The Russian Far East Bourgeoisie and Northeast China. On the Influence of the Border Location on Entrepreneurial Activity"], paper prepared for the conference on "Russia in Asia: Past and Present", Khabarovsk, 26–28 August 1995, pp. 6–8, unpublished.

14. Ibid., p. 8.

15. Stephan, *The Russian Far East*, pp. 48–49 and S.C.M. Paine, *Imperial Rivals*, Armonk: M.E. Sharpe, 1996, pp. 69 and 89.

16. Paine, *Imperial Rivals*, p. 89. The trade zone was confirmed by the Treaty of St Petersburg (1881). See Paine, ibid., p. 162. See also R.K.I. Quested, *Sino-Russian Relations: A Short History*, Sydney: George Allen & Unwin, 1984, pp. 74–77.

17. Paine, *Imperial Rivals*, pp. 180–181.

18. Steven G. Marks, "Conquering the Great East", in Stephen Kotkin and David Wolff,

eds, *Rediscovering Russia in Asia: Siberia and the Russian Far East*, Armonk: M.E. Sharpe, 1995, p. 27.

19. Paine, *Imperial Rivals*, p. 196.
20. Marks, "Conquering the Great East", p. 24.
21. One of the most serious anti-Chinese incidents took place in Blagoveshchensk in 1900, when 3,000 Chinese were killed during a bungled forced evacuation effort by the Amur district military governor. Saveliev, "Chinese Migration to Russia in Space and Time", p. 54.
22. Stephan, *The Russian Far East*, pp. 212–213.
23. Saveliev, "Chinese Migration to Russia in Space and Time", p. 43.
24. Galina Vitkovskaiia, Zhanna Zayonchkovskaia and Kathleen Newland, "Chinese Migration into Russia", in Sherman Garnett, ed., *Rapprochement or Rivalry? Russia-China Relations in a Changing Asia*, Washington, DC: Carnegie Endowment for International Peace, 2000, p. 351.
25. "Special Report: The Other China", *The Economist*, 10 January 2004, p. 59.
26. Cited in Dorothy J. Solinger, "Jobs and Joining: What's the Effect of the WTO for China's Urban Employment", paper prepared for the conference on "The Political and Economic Reforms of Mainland China in a Changing Global Society", National Taiwan University, Taipei, Taiwan, 25–27 April 2002.
27. "Special Report: The Other China", p. 60.
28. "Chinese Experience Gains, Pressure from WTO Membership", *Renmin Ribao*, 8 March 2002.
29. Wang Shaoguang, Hu Angang and Ding Yuanzhu, "Behind China's Wealth Gap", *South China Morning Post*, 31 October 2002, p. 22.
30. David Murphy, "Nothing to Lose", *Far Eastern Economic Review*, 7 November 2002, p. 3.
31. Guangzhou and Changchun have similar population figures, but the southern capital has nearly double the number of fully employed workers. Although Harbin has 3 million more people than Guangzhou, the two have similar numbers of fully employed workers. Shenyang has half the population of Shanghai but one-third the number of fully employed. Although there are over 2 million more people in Beijing than in Harbin, the Chinese capital still has more than double the number of fully employed. One in four Beijing residents is fully employed, but approximately 1 in 5 in Harbin has a full-time job and nearly 1 in 7 in Changchun and Shenyang has a full-time job.
32. This survey was carried out in cooperation with Xia Huanqin, Director, Institute for Northeast Asia, Harbin Academy of Social Sciences.
33. Human Rights Watch, *Paying the Price: Worker Unrest in Northeast China* 14 (6), August 2002, pp. 15–35.
34. Tang Qinghua, interview with Chen Xiaoguang, Vice Governor of Jilin Province, "Northeast Plans Rejuvenation", *Beijing Review*, 18 March 2004, p. 29.
35. According to the results of my July 2004 survey, 62.4 per cent of respondents came from Heilongjiang Province, compared to 18 per cent from Jilin Province, 17.2 per cent from Liaoning Province and 4 per cent from Inner Mongolia. 2.4 per cent were from other parts of China. Of the 250 surveyed in Heilongjiang Province, 76.4 per cent rated their experience as satisfactory (this was 56 per cent of those surveyed in all places), 14 per cent rated it as positive overall despite problems and 6.4 per cent rated it as very positive. Respondents rated good living conditions (37.6 per cent) and salary (25.6 per cent) as the most positive aspects of their experience in the Russian Far East.
36. "If the Chinese in Russia Are Driven Away, It Would Cause Inconveniences to Many Local People in Their Daily Lives", *Global Times*, 28 November 2003, available at ⟨http://www.english.peopledaily.com.cn/data/russia/html⟩.

37. *Xinhua*, 26 July 2004.
38. Xiang Biao, "Emigration from China: A Sending Country Perspective", *International Migration* 41 (3), September 2003, p. 32.
39. Idem.
40. Zhao Jinping, "Zhongguo dui Eluosi touze de fazhan qushi jiqi tedian" ["The Development Trends and Characteristics of China's Investment in Russia"], in Deng Peng, ed., *Mianshang mulai de ZhongE jingmao guanxi* [Sino-Russian Economic Relations: Review and Prospects], Beijing: Zhongguo Fazhan Chubanshe, 2003, p. 140.
41. Yin Hao, "International Labor Migration from China: Policy and Trends", in Yasuko Akase, ed., *A Study on Trade, Investment and International Labor Migration in the APEC Member Economies*, APEC Study Center, Institute of Developing Economies, JETRO, March 2002, p. 104.
42. Ibid., p. 117. Fujian Province accounted for 17 per cent of total labour exports and Jiangsu Province for 15.9 per cent, compared to 17.6 per cent for all three north-eastern provinces together. Liaoning sent 32,073 (8 per cent of the total personnel sent overseas), Jilin 30,255 (7.5 per cent of that total) and Heilongjiang 8,262 (2.1 per cent of it).
43. Li Chuanxun, "Jin nian lai ZhongE pilin diqu zhengzhi jingji guanxi zoushi" ["Trends in Current Sino-Russian Border Regional Political and Economic Relations"], in Hokkaido Slavic Research Center Seminar Report, "The Sino-Russian Strategic Partnership: Current Views from the Border and Beijing", Sapporo, Hokkaido, April 2003, p. 28.
44. Wang Shengjin, "Dongbeiya laodongyuan kaifa yanjiu" ["Research on Use of Labor Resources"], *Northeast Asian Research Center Report*, Changchun: Jilin University, 2001, p. 23.
45. China Eases Its Stand on Russia's Accession to the WTO, *Vedomosti*, 10 June 2002.
46. Interview, Harbin, 25 March 2004.
47. Interview, Harbin, 25 March 2004.
48. Zhao Jinping, "Zhongguo dui Eluosi touze de fazhan qushi jiqi tedian", p. 140.
49. The two provinces sent a total of 29,789 workers to Russia in 1993, the peak year for labour exchanges, but just 6,980 in 2001. Ibid., p. 141.
50. Interview, Beijing, 2 April 2004.
51. Chen Yingqi, "ZhongE laowu hezuo de xingli, qianjing ji zhanlue" ["Sino-Russian Labor Cooperation: Characteristics, Prospects, and Strategy"], in Li Chuanxun and Mei Zhenjun, eds, *ZhongE quyu hezuo yanjiu* [Research on Sino-Russian Regional Cooperation], Harbin: Heilongjiang Remin Chubanshe, 2003, pp. 167–169. Interview, Harbin, 26 March 2004.
52. Interviews, Beijing, 30 March 2004 and 2 April 2004.
53. Idem.
54. Li Chuanxun, "Jin nian lai ZhongE pilin diqu zhengzhi jingji guanxi zoushi", p. 28 and Deng Peng, "Xiang Heilongjiang shen fazhan dui E laowu hezuo de zhuyao wenti" ["Key Questions Regarding the Development of Labor Cooperation between Heilongjiang Province and Russia"], in Deng Peng, ed., *Mianshang mulai de ZhongE jingmao guanxi*, pp. 240–241.
55. Interview, Harbin, 23 March 2004.
56. Xiang Biao, "Emigration from China", pp. 26–27.
57. Chinese investment would be repaid with revenue from bridge tolls. Interview, Harbin, March 2004.
58. AFX-ASIA, 4 February 2004.
59. James Brooke, "Asia's New Trade: Siberia Warms to China", *International Herald Tribune*, 31 March 2004, p. 6.
60. Deng Peng, "Xiang Heilongjiang shen fazhan dui E laowu hezuo de zhuyao wenti", p. 241.

61. Interview, Harbin, 23 March 2004.
62. Information Office, Peoples' Government of Heilongjiang Province, *Heilongjiang Today*, Harbin, 2003, p. 44.
63. As of this writing (August 2004), the number of Chinese who crossed from Heilongjiang to Russia in 2003 had not been published.
64. Interviews, Beijing, 1 April 2004 and 2 April 2004.
65. Interview, Harbin, 26 March 2004.
66. James K. Chin, "Reducing Irregular Migration from China", *International Migration* 41 (3), 2003, p. 56. Interview with a tourism official in Beijing, 2 April 2004.
67. Interview, Beijing, October 2002.
68. Interviews, Beijing, 31 March 2004 and Harbin, 25 March 2004.
69. According to Russian regional Interior Ministry data, in 1994 just 64 per cent of foreign visitors to Primorskii Krai left the region within the time allotted by their visas; but between 1997 and 2000, more than 99 per cent left on schedule. Igor Verba, "Polzuchaia ekspansiia velikogo soseda" ["The Great Neighbor's Creeping Expansion"], *Nezavisimaya Gazeta* [Independent Newspaper], 17 February 2001, available at ⟨http://www.securities.com⟩.
70. Text of speech by PRC President Jiang Zemin at the Institute of International Relations of Russia, 3 September 1994, in *FBIS* (PRC), 6 September 1994, p. 18.
71. Idem.
72. Text of the Sino-Russian Treaty, *Xinhua*, 17 July 2001.
73. Sergei Prikhod'ko, "My ne dolzhny boiat'sia Kitaia" ["We shouldn't be afraid of China"], *Izvestiya*, 23 March 2004. Higher "semi-official estimates" abound in the Russian media, as Larin notes in chap. 2 of this book.
74. Wang Gungwu, *Don't Leave Home: Migration and the Chinese*, Singapore: Times Academic Press, 2001, p. 145.
75. David S.G. Goodman, "Are Asia's 'Ethnic Chinese' a Regional Security Threat?", *Survival* 39 (4), Winter 1997–1998, p. 142.
76. Pal Nyiri, "Expatriating is Patriotic? The Discourse on 'New Migrants' in the People's Republic of China", in Roy Starrs, ed., *Asian Nationalism in an Age of Globalization*, Richmond, UK: Japan Library, 2001, p. 145.
77. Ibid., p. 152.
78. Vilya Gelbras concludes on the basis of his 2002 survey of Chinese in Khabarovk, Vladivostok, Irkutsk and Moscow that a majority of Chinese have no interest in returning home and that the longer they stay in Russia, the harder it will be for them to reintegrate into Chinese society. Vilya Gelbras, *Rossiia v usloviiakh global'noi kitaiskoi migratsii* [Russia under the conditions of global Chinese migration], Moscow: Muravei, 2004, pp. 29 and 88.
79. Most respondents were married (79.2 per cent). Of those, 48.4 per cent were accompanied by a spouse; their children remained in China. Only 3.6 per cent lived in the Russian Far East with both spouse and children. A majority of respondents lived in temporary housing (56.8 per cent in dormitories and 14 per cent in hotels), although some rented apartments (22 per cent) or stayed with friends or relatives (4.4 per cent). A few (1.6 per cent) owned housing.
80. For example, Gelbras, *Rossiia v usloviiakh global'noi kitaiskoi migratsii*, p. 146.
81. Robert Jervis, *Perception and Misperception in International Politics*, Princeton: Princeton University Press, 1976, p. 319.
82. Pal Nyiri, "From Class Enemies to Patriots: Overseas Chinese and Emigration Policy and Discourse in the People's Republic of China", in Nyiri and Saveliev, eds, *Globalizing Chinese Migration*, p. 212.
83. Elizabeth Wishnick, "Chinese Perspectives on Cross-Border Relations", in Sherman W. Garnett, ed., *Rapprochement or Rivalry? Russia-China Relations in a Changing Asia*,

Washington, DC: The Carnegie Endowment for International Peace, 2000, pp. 240–241.

84. Nyiri, "From Class Enemies to Patriots", pp. 232–233.

85. Nationalists and liberal democrats in Moscow share the concern of officials in the Russian Far East about the potential threat from China. For a detailed exploration of the different views on China among the foreign policy elite in Moscow, see Elizabeth Wishnick, *Mending Fences: Moscow's China Policy from Brezhnev to Yeltsin*, Seattle: University of Washington Press, 2001, chap. 9.

86. Interviews with officials in Blagoveshchesnk, Khabarovsk, Vladivostok and Yuzhno-Sakhalinsk, October 1999.

87. Joseph Grieco has found that "relative disparities" in capabilities may lead a state to resist economic cooperation for fear of strengthening a stronger partner. See Joseph Grieco, "Systematic Variation in Regional Institutionalization in Western Europe, East Asia, and the Americas", in Edward W. Mansfield and Helen V. Milner, eds, *The Political Economy of Regionalism*, New York: Columbia University Press, 1997, p. 176.

88. Vilya G. Gelbras, *Kitaiskaya real'nost' Rossii* [Russia's Chinese Reality], Moscow: Muravei, 2001, pp. 144–145.

89. For a discussion of securitization dynamics, see Elizabeth Wishnick, "The Securitization of Chinese Migration to the Russian Far East", forthcoming. Also see Mikhail A. Alexseev, "Economic Valuations and Inter-ethnic Fears: Perceptions of Chinese Migration in the Russian Far East", *Journal of Peace Research* 40 (1), January 2003, p. 95.

90. James F. Hollifield, "The Politics of International Migration: How Can We Bring the State Back In?", in Caroline B. Brettell and James F. Hollifield, eds, *Migration Theory: Talking across Disciplines*, New York: Routledge, 2000, p. 137.

91. Ibid., p. 154.

92. Saskia Sassen, "Beyond Sovereignty: Immigration Policy Making Today", *Social Justice* 23 (3), 1996, p. 9.

93. Nestor Rodriguez, "The Battle for the Border: Notes on Autonomous Migration, Transnational Communities, and the State", *Social Justice* 23 (3), 1996, pp. 22–25.

94. Gelbras, *Rossiia v usloviiakh global'noi kitaiskoi migratsii*, p. 44.

95. Darryl Crawford, "Chinese Capitalism: Cultures, the Southeast Asian Region and Economic Globalisation", *Third World Quarterly* 21 (1), p. 78.

96. Aristide Zolberg, "Introduction: Beyond the Crisis", in Aristide R. Zolberg and Peter M. Benda, eds, *Global Migrants, Global Refugees*, New York: Berghahn Books, 2001, pp. 10–11.

97. Myron Weiner, "Security, Stability, and International Migration", *International Security* 17 (3), Winter 1992–1993, p. 110.

98. Sassen, *Guests and Aliens*, p. 155.

99. Press Conference with Andrei Chernenko, Deputy Interior Minister and Chief of the Federal Migration Service regarding the Law on the Legal Status of Foreign Citizens in the Territory of the Russian Federation, *Federal News Service*, 31 October 2002.

Part III

Russian, Chinese and Korean communities in Japan

4

The Russian presence in contemporary Japan: Case studies in Hokkaido and Niigata

Tsuneo Akaha and Anna Vassilieva

Introduction

Globalization is challenging societies around the world, along with technological revolutions and population and demographic changes. Japan and its Northeast Asian neighbours are no exception. Japan is well equipped to adapt to technological revolutions. In fact, as the world's second-largest economy, it is a principal source of technology-induced changes worldwide. There is serious concern, however, about its ability to adjust to population and demographic changes domestically and in neighbouring countries. A fast-ageing population and an influx of foreign migrants into Japan are forcing the Japanese to redefine their identity and their relationship with the growing number of non-Japanese members of their communities. This is a formidable task, as the Japanese are accustomed to viewing themselves as a homogeneous people.

Japan is in the middle of a debate over how widely it should open its doors to foreigners seeking opportunities there. Some Japanese argue that the country's rapidly greying population, which is at a near-zero growth rate, and the consequent labour shortages in some sectors will severely limit its future economic growth. They maintain, therefore, that Japan must open its job market more widely to foreign workers, including unskilled labourers who are currently not allowed to work in the country. Others advocate that Japan should maintain its current restrictive immigration policy in order to protect its assumed ethnic homogeneity and its long-cherished social order, even if such a policy may mean

95

reducing the country's global economic profile.[1] Even though the Japanese government's official policy is designed to control the import of foreign labour, private companies and the government itself often violate the principles upon which the restrictive policy is based.[2] Although the Japanese as a whole are increasingly accepting of foreigners in their country, there is evidence that their respect for the basic rights of aliens may be waning.[3] The dilemmas presented by the influx of foreign nationals, with their own cultural identities and social customs, are challenging the *sakoku* (national seclusion) mentality of the Japanese people and stimulating the age-old debate, known as *Nihonjinron*, on what it is to be Japanese.[4] The outcome of the national discussion is far from certain.[5]

Increasing numbers of foreign nationals are entering Japan and more and more Japanese are going overseas, raising the spectre of a third *kaikoku* (opening of the country) in Japan's modern history.[6] The number of foreigners coming to Japan has nearly doubled since the end of the 1980s – from 2,985,764 in 1989 to 5,771,975 in 2002.[7] Arguably, the most "foreign" of all foreign ethnic communities in contemporary Japan are the Russians, most of whom have come since the end of the Cold War. They are a relatively small presence in the country, particularly in comparison with South Korean, Chinese and other Asian nationals. As such, their presence has not attracted serious academic attention.[8] However, the Russian presence is quite significant in present-day Japan. In fact, Russian residents represent the largest of the European communities in Hokkaido Prefecture and the city of Niigata in north-western Honshu.

There are several reasons why our study of Russians in contemporary Japan is both important and timely. First, as noted, they represent a fairly recent presence, catching many host communities unprepared and causing some social and cultural friction. Second, there are for the most part no serious studies of Russians in contemporary Japan, although there are some fine studies about them in nineteenth- and early twentieth-century Japan.[9] Third, Russians are absent from contemporary discourse on Japanese immigration policy and minority communities in the country. Virtually all studies of immigration to Japan place the Russians into the undifferentiated category of "others" and focus instead on larger ethnic groups, such as Koreans, Chinese, Japanese Brazilians and Filipinos.[10] Fourth, the wide cultural gap between Japanese and Russians poses interesting questions about social accommodation and cultural assimilation in Japan. We are reminded that Japan's uneasy and at times violent encounters with Russians in the nineteenth and early twentieth centuries did much to awaken Japanese nationalism and contributed to the consolidation of its national identity.[11]

In the post-war era, the Cold War hostility between East and West and the United States–Japan security alliance against the Soviet Union solidified Japanese people's antipathy towards their northern neighbour.[12] The vast majority of Japanese have never met Russians; but they stubbornly maintained negative views of Russians throughout the Cold War, and their unfavourable views remain largely unchanged to this day.[13] Less known, at least in Japan, is the fact that a majority of contemporary Russians hold favourable views of Japan.[14]

What is the impact of the growing Russian presence in Japan on the Japanese public's views of Russia and Russians? What opportunities and problems do the Russians in Japan present in those communities where their presence is visible? How do the Russian residents evaluate their experience of living in Japan? Do they encounter serious ethnic, cultural or social problems? What steps might be taken to solve the problems that Russian–Japanese interactions may be creating?

We shall examine the above questions through case studies in Hokkaido and Niigata prefectures. These prefectures present particularly interesting cases because of the significance their leaders attach to their ties to Russia. The study uses mainly three sources of information. First, we use publications and statistics supplied by prefecture and city administrations that inform us about the two prefectures' ties to Russia. Second, we conducted surveys of Japanese and Russian residents in Sapporo in 2001 and 2003, in Wakkanai in 2001, in Nemuro in 2003 and in Niigata City in 2001 and 2003,[15] and they provide valuable information on the perceptions of Russian and Japanese residents of each other. Although the survey samples are not large and are by no means representative of the entire local citizenry, they do allow us to canvass the range of views that exist in the communities. Many of the views expressed in these surveys are corroborated by a series of interviews we conducted in Niigata City in 2001 and several cities in Hokkaido in 2001 and 2003.[16] These interviews constitute the third source of information employed in this study.

Before we discuss our findings from the surveys and interviews in Hokkaido and Niigata, we shall take a brief look at national statistics. They indicate the level of the Russian presence in Japan and how it compares with the presence of other foreign nationals.

The growing Russian presence in Japan

Of the 5,771,975 foreign nationals who entered the country in 2002, the largest number came from South Korea (1,472,096, or 25.5 per cent of the total), followed by Chinese from Taiwan (Republic of China) (909,654, or 15.8 per cent), Chinese from the People's Republic of China (527,796, or 9.1 per cent) and Filipinos (197,136, or 3.4 per cent). In comparison, far fewer Russian nationals (36,693, or 0.6 per cent) entered

Japan.[17] Nevertheless, the number of Russians coming to Japan has steadily grown since the mid-1990s. (See table 4.1.)

What brings Russians to Japan? Government statistics show that "entertainment" is by far the main purpose of longer-term Russian visitors to Japan, with 5,068 Russians (nearly 16 per cent) entering Japan on an entertainment visa in 2002.[18] (See table 4.2.) Some criminal elements inside and outside Japan are taking advantage of the rather loose definition of "entertainment"[19] and bringing into the country tens of thousands of young women from around the world, including Russia, for the lucrative business of "entertainment", including prostitution. This visa category has contributed to human trafficking into Japan, and has come under growing criticism by human rights organizations in the country and the US State Department. In response to the mounting criticism, the Japanese government has begun a review of the entertainment visa.[20]

Among the 25,124 temporary Russian visitors to Japan in 2002, the largest segment (10,435 people) came as sightseers, followed by 9,978 who came on business and 2,472 who visited the country for cultural and study activities (see table 4.3). The number of Russian tourists had nearly doubled since 1999. The number of businessmen had also increased. These numbers did not include the tens of thousands of Russians who, then and now, visit various port cities in northern Japan on a special landing permit while their ships are anchored in the ports.

In 2003, there were 6,734 Russian residents in the country, compared with 613,791 Koreans (from both North Korea and South Korea), 462,396 Chinese and 185,237 Filipinos. Among the Europeans, the Russians constituted the second-largest resident foreign community in Japan, after British citizens (18,230).[21] It is the long-term residents and short-term visitors from Russia and their impact on local communities that we are going to examine in the following analysis.

The Russian presence in Hokkaido and Niigata

Among the 47 prefectures of Japan, Hokkaido and Niigata are the seventh and the fourteenth most populous respectively. Sapporo, the capital city of Hokkaido, has a population of over 1.8 million people, making it the fifth-largest city in Japan. Niigata City is Niigata Prefecture's capital, and has a population of around 530,000. Most Russians from Siberia and the Russian Far East come to Hokkaido, Niigata and other northern provinces of the country. By contrast, most Russians from the European part of Russia look for opportunities in the culturally and economically more vibrant metropolitan areas of the country, such as Tokyo, Yokohama and Osaka.

Table 4.1 The number of Russian nationals entering Japan, 1995–2002

Year	1995	1996	1997	1998	1999	2000	2001	2002
Number	24,232	26,349	30,120	26,896	23,064	30,290	33,772	36,693
% change from previous year	–	8.70	14.30	−10.70	−14.20	31.30	11.50	8.60
% of total foreigners	0.65	0.62	0.65	0.59	0.47	0.57	0.64	0.6

Source: Japan Immigration Association, *Statistics on Immigration Control 1999*, Tokyo: Japan Immigration Association, 2000, p. 14; Judicial System Department, Minister's Secretariat, Ministry of Justice, ed., *Annual Report of Statistics on Legal Migrants, 2003*, Tokyo: Kokuritsu Insatsukyoku, Tokyo, 2003, p. v.

Table 4.2 The number of new Russian visitors to Japan by purpose of entry, 2002

Total	Diplomats	Government officials	Professors	Artists	Journalists
31,707	267	321	103	42	2
Business investors/ managers	Researchers	Instructors	Engineers	Specialists in humanities/ international services	Intra-firm transfers
4	34	4	18	30	6
Entertainers	Skilled labourers	Cultural activities	Temporary visitors[a]	College students	Pre-college students
5,068	23	90	25,124	152	24
Trainee	Visiting family	Designated activities[b]	Dependants of Japanese nationals	Dependants of permanent residents	Long-term residents
93	185	8	82	1	26

Source: Judicial System Department, Minister's Secretariat, Ministry of Justice, ed., *Annual Report of Statistics on Legal Migrants, 2003*, Tokyo: Kokuritsu Insatsukyoku, Tokyo, 2003, pp. 54 and 57.
[a] See table 4.3 below for a breakdown of their activities.
[b] Includes working holidays and other activities.

Table 4.3 The number of new temporary Russian visitors in Japan, 2002

Total	Sightseeing	Business	Cultural, study activities	Visiting relatives	Other
25,124	10,435	9,978	2,472	654	3,202

Source: Judicial System Department, Minister's Secretariat, Ministry of Justice, ed., *Annual Report of Statistics on Legal Migrants, 2003*, Tokyo: Kokuritsu Insatsukyoku, 2003, pp. 100–101.

Foreign nationals residing in Japan for 90 days or longer are required to register with the local administration. As of the end of 2003, there were 444 Russians officially registered in Hokkaido, an increase of 21 from 2001 but a decrease of 3 from 2002. There were 278 Russians in Niigata Prefecture in 2003, an increase of 29 from 2001 and an increase of 59 from 2002.[22] They represented 6.6 per cent and 4.1 per cent respectively of the total number of Russians registered in Japan in 2003. The Russians in Hokkaido constituted the third-largest Russian community in Japan, after Tokyo (1,627) and Kanagawa (539). Niigata was the fifth most popular place of residence for Russians in Japan. (See table 4.4.) As

Table 4.4 The number of registered Russians in Japan by prefecture, end-2003

Total	**Hokkaido**	Aomori	Iwate	Miyagi	Akita	Yamagata	Fukushima
6,734	444	83	62	152	31	19	62
Ibaraki	Tochigi	Gunma	Saitama	Chiba	Tokyo	Kanagawa	**Niigata**
242	55	73	269	369	1,627	539	278
Toyama	Ishikawa	Fukui	Yamanashi	Nagano	Gifu	Shizuoka	Aichi
154	87	139	11	30	108	173	264
Mie	Shiga	Kyoto	Osaka	Hyogo	Nara	Wakayama	Tottori
39	20	180	256	153	13	32	3
Shimane	Okayama	Hiroshima	Yamaguchi	Tokushima	Kagawa	Ehime	Kochi
32	52	108	41	35	20	18	7
Fukuoka	Saga	Nagasaki	Kumamoto	Oita	Miyazaki	Kagoshima	Okinawa
205	37	107	25	25	8	14	33

Source: Japan Immigration Association, *Statistics on the Foreigners Registered in Japan*, Tokyo: Japan Immigration Association, 2004, p. 53.

Table 4.5 The number of Russians registered in Hokkaido, 1991–2003 (at year-end)

1991	1992	1993	1994	1995	1996	1997	1998	1999	2000	2001	2002	2003
54	126	190	217	272	332	345	352	440	475	423	447	444

Sources: Hokkaido Somubu Chijishitsu Kokusaika, ed., *Hokkaido no Kokusaika no Genjo* [The present situation of Hokkaido's internationalization], Sapporo: Hokkaido Somubu Chijishitsu Kokusaika, 2001, p. 78; Judicial System Department, Minister's Secretariat, Ministry of Justice, ed., *Annual Report of Statistics on Legal Migrants, 2002*, Tokyo: Zaimusho Insatsukyoku, Tokyo, 2002, p. 166; Judicial System Department, Minister's Secretariat, Ministry of Justice, ed., *Annual Report of Statistics on Legal Migrants, 2003*, Tokyo: Kokuritsu Insatsukyoku, 2003, p. 167; and Japan Immigration Association, *Statistics on the Foreigners Registered in Japan*, Tokyo: Japan Immigration Association, 2004, p. 53.

of the end of September 2001, there were 233 and 105 Russian nationals registered as residents in the cities of Sapporo and Niigata respectively.[23]

The number of Russian citizens registered in Hokkaido is rising steadily, as shown by table 4.5. They represented about 2.5 per cent of all foreign citizens (17,852) registered in the prefecture in 2003. They were surpassed by four other groups: Chinese (6,056), Koreans (5,687), Filipinos (1,021) and US citizens (936).[24] The Russians were the largest group among the Europeans in Hokkaido.

Because of the nature of the special landing permit, not one of the tens of thousands of Russians coming ashore at the small northern ports of the country appears on the "radar screen" of the Japanese bureaucratic system of border control.[25] While their ships are at anchor, Russian visitors go shopping and eating and otherwise spend time in nearby towns. In 2001, as many as 58,723 foreign nationals came to Wakkanai in northern Hokkaido this way; 27,771 came to Otaru in western Hokkaido and 22,693 to Hanasaki, close to Nemuro in eastern Hokkaido. Most of these foreigners were Russian.[26] When the city officials presented statistics, we were amazed to discover that in one year, more Russian citizens came to Wakkanai than the entire population of the city.[27] In addition, Wakkanai, Nemuro and Otaru serve as entry and transit points for many Russians (505 and 214 and 2,030 respectively in 2001) who go elsewhere in Japan.[28]

Local administrators are excited about Russians coming to their hometowns. The growing number of Russian visitors to Hokkaido means increasing economic benefits to the local communities. During the 1990s, the number of Russian ships calling at Hokkaido ports increased twelvefold, from 731 in 1990 to 9,181 in 1999. This represented a doubling of trade turnover, to 88.6 billion yen (US$738 million).[29] Russian ships call at local ports, bringing mainly marine and forestry products, and members of Russian crews purchase used and new cars, office equipment,

Table 4.6 The number of Russians registered in Niigata 1991–2003

1991	1992	1993	1994	1995	1996	1997	1998	1999	2000	2001	2002	2003
7	20	37	51	80	69	97	104	107	180	190	219	278

Sources: Niigataken Kokusaikoryuka for 1991–2000 data; Judicial System Department, Minister's Secretariat, Ministry of Justice, ed., *Annual Report of Statistics on Legal Migrants, 2003*, Tokyo: Kokuritsu Insatsukyoku, Tokyo, 2003, p. 167 for 2001–2002 data; and Japan Immigration Association, *Statistics on the Foreigners Registered in Japan*, Tokyo: Japan Immigration Association, 2004, p. 53 for 2003 data.

household appliances, furniture, medicine and food. According to one estimate, Russian ships coming to the port of Nemuro in 1999 represented an estimated 9.39 billion yen (about US$78 million) in economic benefits for this provincial city.[30] The comparable figure for Wakkanai was 27.9 billion yen (US$232.5 million).[31]

The Russian community in Niigata Prefecture is much smaller than that in Hokkaido. The 278 Russian citizens registered in the prefecture in 2003 represented the eighth-largest foreign community in the prefecture but the largest among the European groups.[32] As indicated by table 4.6, the number of Russians in the prefecture is rising steadily. Niigata boasts several international ports, but far fewer Russian ships visit Niigata ports than Hokkaido ports. In 2001, of the 1,369 foreign-registered ships that called at the port of Niigata, just 154 were Russian-flag carriers. Of the 1,075 foreign ships that anchored in Niigata Higashi port, only 124 were Russian; and only 30 of the 294 foreign ships visiting Niigata Nishi port were Russian-registered.[33] These ships bring timber, finished wood, paper and pulp products, and produce to Niigata and take automobiles, other transportation equipment and metal products to RFE destinations. There is also a passenger ship service between Niigata and Vladivostok four times a year. Niigata airport serves as an important regional airport, with regular services to destinations in Russia, such as Khabarovsk, Irkutsk and Vladivostok. In 2000, a total of 225,391 Japanese and foreign passengers used this airport for international travel. Of these, 19,196 travelled to and from Vladivostok, 17,001 to and from Khabarovsk and 1,784 to and from Irkutsk.[34]

Factors behind the growing Russian presence in Hokkaido and Niigata

Hokkaido and Niigata could be considered political mavericks in terms of expanding relations with Russia, and we did not hear much Cold Warstyle rhetoric in their administrations. That was not only because of the close proximity of the two prefectures to the Russian Far East. Hokkaido and Niigata were forced to look north because their distance from Tokyo disadvantaged them during Japan's post-war industrialization, which was focused largely on the Pacific Ocean side of the country. Those prefectures facing the Sea of Japan had to look for economic opportunities in neighbouring countries even though the Cold War climate severely constrained relations between Japan and its communist neighbours.

When Hokkaido and Niigata sought opportunities to develop ties with their counterparts in the RFE during the Cold War era, the public sector, namely the provincial administrations, led the way, building air and sea transportation infrastructure. The governors of Hokkaido and Niigata encouraged municipalities in their prefectures to establish sister-city and other ties in Russia, South Korea and China and also supported people-to-people diplomacy.[35] To date, 16 formal partnerships have been established between municipalities in Hokkaido and Russia. This equals all other municipal partnerships between Japan and Russia combined. By contrast, there are only three formal partnerships between municipalities in Niigata and Russia: Niigata City with Khabarovsk and Vladivostok, and Toyosaka with Birobidzhan. The interest of Niigata municipalities lies more with China and South Korea, with whom they have nine and five sister-city and friendship ties respectively; and there are also relationships between Niigata Prefecture and Heilongjiang Province in China.[36]

The collapse of the Soviet Union and communism raised the Japanese prefectures' interest in developing business opportunities in the Russian Far East. A good number of Japanese companies sought business partners in forestry, fisheries, tourism and trade, some of them establishing joint ventures and other cooperative arrangements. We met a number of business owners from Hokkaido and Niigata who had failed in their rush to take advantage of the seemingly lucrative opportunities in the chaos of the post–Soviet Russian Far East. Most of them lost money and withdrew their investment. However, the provincial administrations continue to encourage local business communities not to lose interest the RFE.[37]

Historically, Hokkaido has played an important role in defining Japan's territorial, security, political and economic interests vis-à-vis Russia (and the Soviet Union).[38] One of the most notable developments in recent times is the bilateral arrangement known as "no-visa visits", which since 1991 has allowed Japanese citizens to visit the Northern Territories (the southern Kuriles)* and Russian citizens from the disputed islands to

---

* In the waning days of World War II, Soviet troops seized the islands – the Habomais, Shikotan, Kunashiri and Etorofu – and the Soviet Union/Russia has since controlled the territories. Tokyo and Moscow both claim the islands, and have been unable to resolve the dispute. Japan insists that the conflict must be resolved before it will conclude a peace treaty with Russia.

visit Japan without a visa. By 2001, the arrangement had involved 109 Russian delegations comprising 4,724 individuals and 187 Japanese delegations consisting of 8,836 people.[39] Another element in the growing contacts between Hokkaido and the Russian Far East is the development of oil and gas off the eastern coast of Sakhalin Island.[40] The energy development projects have attracted the attention of power, construction, transportation, trade and service companies in Hokkaido.

Niigata Prefecture is a pioneer in the internationalization (*kokusaika*) movement that has been sweeping Japan in recent decades. Since the 1960s, the public sector has played a pivotal role in the prefecture's growth as a regional hub for international transportation. Its efforts to develop ties with Russia have focused on Nakhodka, Vladivostok, Khabarovsk and, more recently, Irkutsk. Since 1990, Niigata has adopted formal action programmes with Primorskii Krai and with Khabarovsk Krai designed to promote various exchanges involving administrative personnel, students, technical experts and representatives of port authorities. The provincial administration and the business community in Niigata are also exchanging trade missions in an effort to promote business opportunities, but so far their impact has been very limited.[41] We heard frequent references to the uneven sharing of the financial burden in support of the exchange programmes. As enthusiastic as both sides are about those programmes, only the Japanese side seems to be able to come up with the necessary financial support.

The above factors have contributed to an expansion of human flows between Hokkaido and Niigata and the Russian Far East. Our field research was designed to capture one aspect of the impact of this development – the growing presence of Russians in these areas of Japan.

Japanese views of the Russian presence in their communities

In 2001 and 2003, in order to assess Russian–Japanese mutual perceptions, we conducted interviews and surveys of Japanese and Russian residents in four cities in Hokkaido and in the city of Niigata.[42] Table 4.7 shows the number of Japanese and Russian citizens in our samples, including 162 Japanese and 43 Russians, for a total of 205 subjects. The Japanese subjects included prefectural and municipal administrators, journalists, researchers, business people and representatives of non-governmental organizations (NGOs). They also represented different age groups, ranging from the late teens to the 70s. The Russian subjects also varied in age, from the early 20s to the late 60s. They included technical school students, university students, business people, housewives and representatives of NGOs.

Table 4.7 The number of Japanese and Russian interviewees and survey subjects in Hokkaido and Niigata City, 2001 and 2003

	Sapporo	Wakkanai	Kushiro	Nemuro	Niigata	Total
Japanese interviewees						
2001	7	14	–	–	5	26
2003	3	–	4	4	–	11
Subtotal	10	14	4	4	5	37
Survey subjects						
2001	33	28	–	–	–	61
2003	–	–	–	–	64	64
Total	43	42	4	4	69	162
Russian interviewees						
2001	3	–	–	–	3	6
2003	1	–	1	1	–	3
Subtotal	4	–	1	1	3	9
Survey subjects						
2003	16	–	–	–	18	34
Total	20	–	1	1	21	43
Grand total	63	42	5	5	90	205

Source: authors' own figures.

Views in Sapporo

Sapporo is the largest city north of Tokyo. It boasts a very modern and vibrant community offering business, educational and cultural opportunities. It is also home to a Russian consulate-general. We interviewed both Russian and Japanese residents of the city, including city administrators. Our Japanese interlocutors all agreed that their neighbour Russia, particularly Sakhalin and the RFE, had a special importance for Hokkaido. They were proud that Hokkaido was ahead of all other Japanese prefectures in developing relations with Russia, notably Sakhalin, although some admitted that the general public's interest in and understanding of Russia was still limited. They agreed that the dispute over the Northern Territories was an obstacle to the improvement of state-level relations between Japan and Russia but noted that the problem should not and did not seriously affect local- and regional-level contacts, including those between the citizens of Hokkaido and Sakhalin. Most of them said that the expanding contacts between Japanese and Russian people in Hokkaido were a good thing, but they also pointed out that the local mass media tended to highlight negative incidents involving Russian citizens.[43]

In October 2001, we received completed surveys from Japanese residents in Sapporo and Wakkanai. Generally, they showed that those who had direct contact with Russians had more positive impressions of Russians in general than those who had little or no contact. Our Sapporo respondents were clearly more favourably inclined towards Russia than the general public in Japan. They were for the most part receptive to the idea of more Russians coming to their community, and favoured more active promotion of ties with their city's Russian partner cities. On the question of how to improve Russian–Japanese relations, slightly more than half of the respondents said that bilateral exchanges should be expanded, including information, economic and cultural ones.

Views in Wakkanai

Wakkanai is a port city located at the northern end of Hokkaido. Directly across the Soya (La Perouse) Strait from the city lies the island of Sakhalin. There is a regular ferry service between Wakkanai and Korsakov when the Sea of Okhotsk is not frozen. In 2001, it was used by 4,205 passengers. Russian visitors are very visible in Wakkanai, on the streets and in restaurants, bars and consumer goods stores. Some retailers cater specifically for Russian customers. Wakkanai is home to an active but dwindling fishing industry. City leaders see the expansion of relations with Russia, particularly Sakhalin, as crucial to Wakkanai's economic vitality, indeed its future survival. They actively promote city-level contacts, business ties and people-to-people diplomacy with Sakhalin. The city established friendship-city (*yukotoshi*) ties with Nevel'sk in 1972, with Korsakov in 1991 and with Yuzhno-Sakhalinsk in 2001. The permanent Russian presence is very small, however. In 2001, only 59 Russians were registered in the city, but they constituted over one-fourth of the foreign resident population in Wakkanai.[44]

Everyday life in Japanese provincial towns is woven of predictability and convention. The rumour mill of the townsfolk is busy. The "intrusion" of visitors from the north with their "strange" language and "unconventional" behaviour easily disturbs the tranquillity of the local scene.

Our interviews and surveys in this provincial town revealed that most respondents had very limited contact with Russians but that, as in Sapporo, direct contact with Russians appeared to improve their impressions of them. Many subjects said that the impact of the Russian presence on their community was negative, citing public safety as a major concern. Residents were very disturbed by the growing number of incidents of shoplifting, bicycle thefts and violent crimes in the city, and tended to blame them on Russians. Even though more crimes were committed by Japanese, the locals tended to emphasize those committed by foreigners, including Russians. Perceptions of Russians tended to be rather negative among our survey respondents, most of whom were college students with no personal contact with them.[45] About half the respondents were aware of the friendship-city relationship between their city and Yuzhno-

Sakhalinsk, and a slightly smaller proportion of the respondents correctly named Nevel'sk and Korsakov as Wakkanai's friendship partners. Most survey respondents and interviewees agreed that Japan and Russia should improve relations by either concluding a peace treaty or expanding contacts and building mutual trust.

It was disconcerting that Russian visitors give a distinctly negative impression to many local residents, particularly young people. The big challenge for the city, therefore, is how to promote closer ties with Sakhalin for economic reasons while controlling the negative fallout of the visible presence of Russian visitors.

Views in Kushiro and Nemuro

Kushiro and Nemuro are important in considering Japanese–Russian relations, for several reasons, which came out clearly in our interviews in the two cities. First, the disputed territories were part of Nemuro district before the Soviet occupation of the islands in autumn 1945; second, most former Japanese residents there settled in Nemuro; and, third, the economies of the two cities depend heavily on fishing and commercial ties with the Northern Territories. Also, the economy of the disputed islands has become tied to Hokkaido, a mere 3.3 km away at its closest point.[46]

Kushiro's economic mainstay, fishing and fish processing industries, has experienced a continuous decline since the late 1970s, when the Soviet Union and the United States established 200-mile exclusive economic zones off their coasts in order to protect coastal fisheries from Japanese and other foreign fishing. The fishing industry of Kushiro was hit hard by those developments. The decline continued in the 1980s and 1990s, shaking the city's economic foundations. In the aftermath of the break-up of the Soviet Union, poaching became a widespread phenomenon in the waters of the Russian Far East, encouraged by criminal elements in both Russia and Japan. The Russian and Japanese authorities' efforts in recent years to curb poaching and other illegal fishing in Russian waters, and also in waters surrounding the disputed islands, exacerbated the problem of the shrinking amount of marine products shipped to Kushiro and Nemuro. Fishing industry representatives in Kushiro informed us that in order to make up for the dwindling access to fishery resources in Russian waters and to sustain their heavily invested fish processing industry, they were eager to develop closer ties with Kamchatka. They also said that they were very interested in the return of the Northern Territories to Japan, believing that both Kushiro and Nemuro would benefit from access to the rich fishing grounds around the islands.

Our interviews in Nemuro revealed the symbolic and material importance of the Northern Territories to the city.[47] The presence of many former Japanese residents of the Northern Territories gave the city a distinct perspective on relations with Russia. We interviewed a former Japanese resident of one of the Habomai islands, who headed the Nemuro branch of the League of Chishima-Habomai Island Residents, an association devoted to the return of the Russian-controlled islands to Japan. According to him, the reversion of the islands should be a prerequisite for normalizing Japanese–Russian relations, and the Second World War was not over until the islands were returned to Japan.[48] The importance of this issue was not lost on other residents of Nemuro. One businessman stated, "People in Wakkanai often complain that we in Nemuro are dragging them down with our staunch, ideological position on the territorial issue. We are indeed concerned about the Northern Territories as an issue of importance to our national identity."[49]

Nemuro's strategic vision contrasted sharply with that of the other cities we visited in Hokkaido. Although the city administrators of Wakkanai, Kushiro and even Sapporo were prepared to forge ahead with economic ties with Russia, the leaders of Nemuro viewed the resolution of the territorial dispute as a major precondition for closer ties. When Nemuro became a city in 1957, there were 36,813 residents. At its peak (in 1990), the population stood at 49,607, but it had dropped to 33,510 in 2003.[50] For the city leaders, the reintegration of the Northern Territories into their administrative district is an intrinsic part of their future planning. At the present time, conducting business with Russian residents of the disputed islands is illegal, although some locals do engage in business ventures with Russian islanders.[51] In these circumstances, Russian visitors to the city present virtually the only legitimate opportunity offering material benefits to the Nemuro citizens who are not in fisheries. (As noted above, many businesses cater to Russian visitors from the disputed islands.)

Rather than viewing them as adversaries, the residents of Nemuro were making the best of the opportunities that Russian visitors offered. They reminded us that many locals were studying Russian in order to be able to communicate with their neighbours. They also attributed their positive attitudes towards Russian visitors to the fact that many of them were coming back. They had learned how to conduct themselves in Japan, unlike the many first-timers in other parts of Hokkaido, who were causing cultural friction with local Japanese. The fact that most of the population of Nemuro were traditionally fishermen made its residents more understanding and accommodating towards the behaviour of Russian visitors.

In summary, it is noteworthy that growing contact with Russia is accompanied by somewhat different perspectives in different parts of Hokkaido, with residents of Kushiro and Nemuro expressing more complex views than their counterparts in Sapporo and Wakkanai. In addition, negative stereotypes of Russians appear to be more of a problem in Sapporo and Wakkanai than in Kushiro and Nemuro. On the other hand, there is a near-consensus among the citizens of Hokkaido that expanding ties with Sakhalin and the Northern Territories is in the interest of the local economy.

Japanese views of the Russian presence in Niigata

Our interviews in Niigata City in October 2001 and a survey there in August 2003 revealed several aspects of local Japanese views of Russia and Russians. There was much interest in Russia, particularly the Russian Far East. The interviewees were very proud of their city's long history of active diplomacy towards the RFE. The Niigata city administration had devoted, and continued to devote, a good amount of resources to the development of ties with it.[52] The interviewees agreed that there was a sustained, if not overwhelming interest among Niigata residents in expanding opportunities for experiences abroad for themselves and their children and that Russia was a prominent part of that interest. They concurred that the local media were much more positive about relations with Russia than the national media and that too much attention was paid to crimes involving Russians.

The interviewees' contacts with Russian residents or visitors were limited. In our view, this further accentuated the importance of mass media reports in the formation of local people's images of Russians. There was no uniform view of Russians in the community, but the interviewees did note some stereotyping by Niigata citizens. Many locals had the impression, as a result of the Russian visitors they saw, that most Russians were poor. They assumed that very rich Russians went to Tokyo and other places in Japan. Regular contacts with Russians were limited to those who lived or worked near the entertainment establishments in the city, which employed young Russian women (many supposedly working as hostesses or prostitutes), or near Higashi port, where many Russian sailors could be seen strolling in the streets. In the eyes of the residents, the casual and often unruly manners of the Russian seamen were offensive and unacceptable. This reinforced the rather negative impressions many locals had of Russians. There was disagreement about whether the territorial dispute had any impact on the interaction between Russians and Japanese at the local and regional levels. We detected little emotional engagement with the issues among the Niigata residents whom we met.

Our general finding was that the growing contact between Russians and Japanese in Niigata is generally welcome. But lack of genuine communication between local Japanese and Russian residents/visitors, Japanese residents' reliance on the mass media for information on Russia and Russians, and the resulting stereotypes they hold about Russians contribute to their limited understanding of Russia and Russians.

Views of Russian residents in Hokkaido and Niigata about the local Japanese

Interviews in Sapporo and Niigata

The absence of interaction between Russian and Japanese residents and the prevalence of negative stereotypes about Russians were the two most common themes that emerged from our interviews with Russian residents in Sapporo and Niigata. Russians undergoing training in Sapporo said they were so busy that they had little or no time to socialize outside their business office. They were nevertheless very appreciative of the opportunity to learn new information and skills (in banking and tourism) and said that they planned to use them when they returned home to Yuzhno-Sakhalinsk. Another Russian said that her Japanese husband worked in the Sapporo city administration and that she had only limited opportunities to socialize with other Japanese.

We should mention a lawsuit filed by a former US citizen, now a Japanese citizen married to a Japanese woman, against the city of Otaru, a large port city west of Sapporo, for allowing a public bathhouse to discriminate against non-Japanese customers. The business owner posted a sign reading *"Gaijin okotowari"* (No foreigners allowed) after its customers complained that Russians were disturbing them by using the facility in a culturally offensive manner. The American-turned-Japanese citizen won the lawsuit and the discriminatory sign was removed. The episode had become well known throughout the country. Many of our interviewees, both Russians and Japanese, brought it up as an example of the wide cultural gap that existed between Russians and Japanese. The Japanese we interviewed recognized the fact of discrimination but also acknowledged that it might be unavoidable owing to cultural differences.

From interviews with a Russian researcher and Russian consular officers in Niigata City, we learned that there was very little that the Russian residents did together as a community. Most of them preferred to lead an independent life and to come together only when there were official functions, such as those organized by the consulate-general. The interviewees confirmed that Russians and Japanese had very limited contact outside the work environment. According to them, the local Japanese people did not show any outward sign of discrimination against Russians; but in Higashi port, where many Russian ships and sailors come in, local authorities tended to look at Russians with suspicion. Local shopkeepers were also less than friendly towards Russians, fearing the possibility of theft. Some restaurants even displayed signs indicating that Russians were not welcome, presumably because of worry on the part of the owners about unfamiliar, thus unwelcome conduct. Our interviewees, both Japanese and Russians, attributed these problems to media reports of thefts and other incidents involving Russians. Russian interviewees added, however, that the reluctance to accept Russian customers was not totally groundless because some Russian sailors had indeed committed crimes, such as drug smuggling and petty theft.

We also learned that the number of Russian residents in Niigata, particularly Russian women, had increased in recent years. Many Russian women married Japanese men, often for the benefit of long-term residence and work rights that inter-racial matrimony afforded them.[53] We were told that it was typical for the Russian women to feel isolated or rejected by their Japanese husbands because of conflicting expectations regarding their role in marriage and other cultural differences. When relationships soured, our interviewees told us, a typical Japanese man would want a divorce. However, his Russian wife would prefer a separation rather than a divorce so that she could continue to live in Japan. According to the interviewees, a child born to a Japanese–Russian couple would typically adopt Japanese citizenship because there was no bilateral treaty allowing dual citizenship. We were also told that there was a public perception that many Russian women in Niigata were engaged in illegal or semi-legal activities, among them prostitution.

Surveys in Sapporo and Niigata

Most of the Russian residents in Sapporo and Niigata who responded to our surveys in spring and summer 2003 said that they interacted with Japanese people at work or at school on a daily basis. The frequency of interaction with Japanese outside work or school was somewhat less, but a good many respondents still socialized with Japanese on a daily basis. The respondents thought that their Japanese co-workers or schoolmates were hard-working, punctual, kind, sympathetic, well meaning and responsible. They had equally favourable impressions of the Japanese whom they had met in social settings.[54] Most of the respondents considered themselves either very knowledgeable or somewhat knowledgeable about Japan, and more than half of them rated their Japanese-language ability as either good or excellent. The vast majority said that they relied on their personal experience more than anything else for information about Japan.

The Russian respondents in the two cities were evenly divided between those who thought that Russian people's presence in their respective communities had a positive impact and those who thought that it had little or no effect. Our respondents in Sapporo offered a variety of views on the impact (or absence thereof) of the Russian presence on the local communities. On the positive side, they thought that they were contributing to a better understanding of and greater interest in Russia and Russian culture. On the negative side, however, most Russian respondents in Sapporo said that Japanese people did not seem to be particularly interested in Russia. We were reminded that the number of Russians in the city of 1.8 million people was too small to have any significant impact. Most respondents in Niigata also thought that they were promoting mutual understanding between Russians and Japanese. Some of them noted the limitations of their influence in terms of the small number of Russians living in Niigata and the limited scope of social interaction between Russian and Japanese residents. But some respondents noted that a few criminal or misbehaving Russians were having a negative impact on the local Japanese image of Russians.

Not surprisingly, most of the Russian respondents in the two cities expressed affinity towards Japan; not one of them felt unfriendly towards it. Their positive feelings spilled over into their assessment of contemporary Russian–Japanese relations, with more than half of them believing bilateral relations to be good. Many comments offered by Russians in Niigata reflected a sense of frustration and resignation that the two countries were not genuinely interested in each other and thus that their relations were rather superficial. Some Russians in Niigata noted the one-sided nature of exchanges, in which the Japanese side carries most of the burden and the Russian side benefits more.

Most Russians were aware of their communities' sister-city partnerships with Russian cities – Niigata with Khabarovsk and Vladivostok, and Sapporo with Novosibirsk. They agreed that these ties were good but they gave mixed assessments of their impact on bilateral relations at the national level.

The Russian respondents' personal experience of living in Japan and interacting with Japanese people professionally or socially was the most important source of their generally favourable views of Japan and Japanese. The mass media seemed to play a much less important, if not negligible role in shaping their attitudes towards Japan. We should note that everywhere we met with Russians living in Japan, there was a common complaint that their Japanese colleagues and neighbours did not take a personal interest in them. However, we were told of exceptions to the rule – the Japanese who would go out of their way to be friendly and supportive. Fortunately for those Russians, such Japanese friends could be found in most places.

At the end of the questionnaire, the respondents were asked to offer any comments that they wished to make. Most respondents in Sapporo had a fairly elaborate appreciation and sophisticated understanding of the Japan they had come to know, several expressing love and admiration for the country. Most of these individuals emphasized Japan's social and cultural traditions, its particularly sympathetic and caring human relations, hard-working people, aesthetic and well-maintained infrastructure and the quality of services available to ordinary citizens. Many of them expressed admiration as well for Japan's modern economy and technology.

Russian respondents in Niigata offered candid comments. One theme ran through those comments: the formality and superficiality of relations with the Japanese as they saw them. They experienced a sense of estrangement and distance from Japanese people. They attributed the problem to the busy lifestyle, the rigid social rules and the frustratingly formal interpersonal relations that they were experiencing in Japan.

Conclusion

Our case studies in Hokkaido and Niigata indicate that the growing presence of Russians is having a visible impact on local Japanese views of Russia and Russians. In the two prefectures, local initiatives have helped to expand ties between the two countries and to promote contacts between ordinary Russians and Japanese. It can be said too that a sense of geographical proximity to Russia has become a part of the identity of the people of the two prefectures, particularly Hokkaido.

The dispute over the sovereignty of the Northern Territories has been a focal point of efforts in Hokkaido to change the nature of Japanese–Russian relations, and these undertakings have borne some fruit, particularly in promoting human contacts between Japanese and Russians. But this finding does not apply uniformly throughout Hokkaido. Residents of Nemuro are by far the most focused on the resolution of the territorial dispute, for symbolic and material reasons. Even there, however, pragmatic attitudes have developed among the population, such that the dispute has not disrupted local initiatives to develop closer ties with the Russians now living in the Northern Territories. Pragmatism is even more pronounced in the other areas of Hokkaido that we have examined.

In our opinion, the Japanese and Russian governments should encourage these and other efforts to bring the two peoples closer, to overcome the centuries of suspicion and animosity. After all, in earlier periods Japanese intellectuals saw Russia not only as a power to defend against but also as a source of learning and a people with whom they shared a common interest, particularly in the search for a national identity in the face of the forces of Westernization and modernization.[55]

The cases of Hokkaido and Niigata demonstrate that Japanese people's views of Russia can change significantly as a result of local-level contacts between the two countries. The direction of change is not uniform, however. On the one hand, those who are predisposed towards international exchanges and intercultural experiences generally seek out opportunities to meet Russians and develop more nuanced and balanced views of Russians. On the other hand, those with little or no interest in Russia who do not seek contact with Russians are unlikely to change their views of Russia. In recent decades, Japanese people's views of Russia have tended to be negative. Their unfavourable impressions are bound to solidify when they observe the culturally offensive behaviour of some Russian visitors and when they receive mass media reports on crimes committed by some Russians in Japan.

As our study shows, the best way to improve public perceptions of Russia and Russians is to increase the amount of personal interaction between Russians and Japanese. Local initiatives for cultural and social exchanges and interactions are important, and they should be expanded. Public agencies, educational institutions and NGOs should organize workshops, training programmes and other educational opportunities for Russian residents and visitors, as well as members of the local communities, to learn about each other. These programmes should go beyond the conventional "cultural exchange" and deal with real-life issues, such as education, health, marriage, childrearing, ageing, environment and employment, which are of immediate concern to all. The ingenuity of individual citizens should be explored for creative solutions to common problems they face in Japan and Russia. Moreover, considering the heavy impact that short-term Russian visitors have on the local population's views, prefectural and municipal governments should support efforts by voluntary organizations to help Russian visitors to learn about culturally acceptable and unacceptable manners in Japan.

Acknowledgements

We are grateful to the Freeman Foundation and the US Institute of Peace for providing grants that partially funded the research for and writing of this project. We also thank the United Nations University, Tokyo, for supporting conferences in Tokyo in 2002 and 2003 and in Monterey, California, in 2004 in which earlier versions of this chapter were presented. Thanks are also due to numerous individuals in Hokkaido and Niigata who assisted us by providing information, being interviewed, completing surveys and administering surveys. Finally, the authors thank Richard Sedgwick, a research assistant at the Center for East Asian Studies, Monterey Institute of International Studies, for administering the survey in Niigata. Needless to say, the authors alone are responsible for the contents of the chapter.

Notes

1. Sakanaka Hidenori, "21-seiki no Gaikokujin Seisaku: Jinkogensho Jidai no Nihon no Sentaku to Shutsunyukoku Kanri" ["Policy toward foreigners in the 21st century: Alternatives for Japan and immigration control in the age of population decline"], in Sakanaka, *Nihon no Gaikokujin Seisaku no Koso* [A plan for Japanese policy toward foreigners], Tokyo: Nihon Kajo Shuppan, 2001, pp. 3–21.
2. Wayne A. Cornelius, "Japan: The Illusion of Immigration Control", in Wayne A. Cornelius, Philip L. Martin and James F. Hollifield, eds, *Controlling Immigration: A Global Perspective*, Stanford: Stanford University Press, 1994, p. 387.
3. For instance, the Cabinet Office's survey in January–February 2003 showed that the proportion of Japanese who believed the rights of foreigners living in Japan should be protected to the same extent as the rights of Japanese citizens had declined from two-thirds in 1997 to around one-half in 2003. Less than one-third acknowledged that such treatment was outright discrimination against foreigners. *Asahi Shimbun*, electronic version available at ⟨http://www.asahi.com/national/update/0412/018.html⟩ (accessed 12 April 2003).
4. For "*sakoku* mentality", see Mayumi Itoh, *Globalization of Japan: Japanese Sakoku Mentality and U.S. Efforts to Open Japan*, New York: St Martin's Press, 1998.
5. Demetrios G. Papademetriou and Kimberly A. Hamilton, *Reinventing Japan: Immigration's Role in Shaping Japan's Future*, Washington, DC: Carnegie Endowment for International Peace, 2000, pp. 46–51.
6. The first opening of Japan was the Meiji Restoration and the second opening was the US occupation of the country following defeat in World War II.
7. Japan Immigration Association, *Statistics on Immigration Control 2002*, Tokyo: Japan Immigration Association, 2003, p. 6.
8. Akaha's correspondence with Professor Takashi Murakami, Director (at the time of correspondence), Slavic Research Center, Hokkaido University, Sapporo, September 2001.
9. The few recent publications that include studies of Russians in Japan relate to pre-war periods. Examples include Naganawa Mitsuo and Sawada Katsuhiko, eds, *Ikyo ni Ikiru: Rainichi Roshiyajin no Ashiato* [Life in a foreign country: Footprints of Russians in Japan], Tokyo: Seibunsha, 2001; J. Thomas Rimer, ed., *A Hidden Fire: Russian and Japanese Cultural Encounters, 1868–1926*, Stanford, CA: Stanford University and Washington, DC: Woodrow Wilson Center, 1995, pp. 1–14; and Wada Haruki, *Hopporyodo Mondai: Rekishi to Mirai* [The northern territories problem: history and the future], Tokyo: Asahi Shimbunsha, 1999.

10. See Sakanaka, *Nihon no Gaikokujin Seisaku no Koso* and Papademetriou and Hamilton, *Reinventing Japan*. See also Atsushi Kondo, "The Development of Immigration Policy in Japan", *Asian and Pacific Migration Journal* 11 (4), 2002, pp. 415–436; Vera Mackie, ed., *Japan's Minorities: The Illusion of Homogeneity*, London: Routledge, 1997; Komai Hiroshi, ed., *Kokusaika no Naka no Imin Seisaku no Kadai* [Immigration policy issues amidst internationalisation], Tokyo: Akashi Shoten, 2002; and David Bartram, "Japan and Labor Migration: Theoretical and Methodological Implications", *The International Migration Review* 34 (1), Spring 2000, pp. 5–32.

11. For insightful essays on the impact of cultural encounters between Russia and Japan on the development of Japan's national identity, see Marius B. Jansen, "On Foreign Borrowing", in Albert M. Craig, ed., *Japan: A Comparative View*, Princeton, NJ: Princeton University Press, 1979, pp. 18–48; J. Thomas Rimer, ed., *A Hidden Fire*; David Wells and Sandra Wilson, eds, *The Russo-Japanese War in Cultural Perspective, 1904–05*, New York: St Martin's Press, 1999; Tadashi Anno, "Nihonjinron and Russkaia Ideia: Transformation of Japanese and Russian Nationalism in the Postwar Era and Beyond", in Gilbert Rozman, ed., *Japan and Russia: The Tortuous Path to Normalization, 1949–1999*, New York: St Martin's Press, 2000, pp. 329–356; and Yulia Mikhailova, "Japan and Russia: Mutual Images, 1904–05", in Bert Edstrom, ed., *The Japanese and Europe: Images and Perceptions*, Richmond, Surrey, UK: Japan Library (Curzon Press), pp. 10–171.

12. See, for example, Tsuyoshi Hasegawa, *The Northern Territories Dispute and Russo-Japanese Relations*, 2 volumes, Berkeley, CA: University of California, 1998.

13. For example, a 2003 opinion survey conducted by the Japanese Cabinet Office (Naikakufu) revealed that 74.1 per cent of the Japanese polled did not feel friendly towards Russia, as compared with 20.0 per cent who did feel friendly. Naikakufu Daijin-kanbo Seifukohoshitsu, ed., *Gekkan Seronchosa_Gaiko* [Monthly public opinion__ diplomacy], Tokyo: Zaimusho Insatsukyoku, 2004, p. 11. For Japanese views of the Soviet Union during the Cold War, see Hasegawa, *The Northern Territories Dispute and Russo-Japanese Relations*.

14. A 2001 survey in Russia showed that 45 per cent of those polled said that they liked Japan, and another 24 per cent stated that they had both likes and dislikes about Japan, with only 2 per cent indicating that they disliked Japan. Foreign Ministry, "Roshia ni okeru Tainichi Seron Chosa" ["Public opinion survey in Russia regarding Japan"], 2 August 2001, available at ⟨http://www.mofa.go.jp/mofaj/area/russia/chosa02/index.html⟩ (accessed 15 September 2002).

15. The surveys were conducted in Sapporo, Wakkanai and Niigata City in October 2001, in Sapporo in March 2003, in Nemuro in June 2003 and in Niigata City in August 2003.

16. The interviews were conducted in Niigata City in October 2001, in Sapporo, Otaru and Wakkanai in October 2001, in Sapporo in March 2003 and in Nemuro and Kushiro in June 2003. See table 4.7 for the numbers of interview and survey subjects.

17. These statistics are from Judicial System Department, Minister's Secretariat, Ministry of Justice, ed., *Annual Report of Statistics on Legal Migrants, 2003*, Tokyo: Kokuritsu Insatsukyoku, 2003, p. v.

18. Ibid., pp. 52 and 54.

19. The immigration law defines "entertainment" as "activities related to entertainment such as theater, variety entertainment, music performance, and sports". Sakanaka, *Nihon no Gaikokujin Seisaku no Koso*, p. 264.

20. *Asahi Shimbun online*, 4 December 2004, available at http://www.asahi.com/national/update/1205/024.html (accessed 5 December 2004).

21. Japan Immigration Association, *Statistics on the Foreigners Registered in Japan*, Tokyo: Japan Immigration Association, 2004, pp. 2 and 8.

22. Ibid., p. 53.
23. These numbers compare with 1,000 Koreans and 1,042 Chinese living in Niigata and 2,710 Koreans (from both North Korea and South Korea) and 2,332 Chinese registered in Sapporo. City administrators of Niigata and Sapporo supplied this information.
24. Japan Immigration Association, *Statistics on the Foreigners Registered in Japan*, pp. 49–50, 53 and 61.
25. "Special permits" are issued to passengers and crew members who wish to come ashore while their ships are calling at Japanese ports, to those who use these ports as transit points, to those requiring emergency landing and to others rescued by Japanese coastal authorities. Hokkaido Prefecture administrators supplied this information.
26. Hokkaido Prefecture administrators supplied these statistics.
27. Wakkanai's population in 2001 was 43,000 people, including 40 Russian residents.
28. Judicial System Department, Minister's Secretariat, Ministry of Justice, ed., *Annual Report of Statistics on Legal Migrants, 2002*, Tokyo: Zaimusho Insatsukyoku, 2002, p. 7.
29. These statistics were provided by the Hokkaido Governor's Office. Relevant statistics are also found in Hokkaido, *Hokkaido to Roshia Kyokuto: Koryu Jisseki to Roshia Kyokuto no Gaiyo* [Hokkaido and the Russian Far East: an outline of exchange and outline of the Russian Far East], Sapporo: Hokkaido, 2001.
30. Suzuki Shin'ichi, "Nemuro to Tai-Roshia Koryu: Jimoto Minkan Kigyo no Kokoromi" ["Nemuro and its interaction with Russia: The efforts of local private enterprises"], *Charivari*, No. 223, September 2000, p. 33.
31. The estimate for Wakkanai is for 1997. *Hokkaido Shimbun*, 1 June 2000, p. 22 and 19 January 2000, p. 10.
32. The larger foreign groups in Niigata included 4,481 Chinese; 2,580 Filipinos; 2,399 Koreans (both North Korean and South Korean); 1,373 Brazilians; 395 Indonesians; 354 US citizens; and 336 Thais. Japan Immigration Association, *Statistics on the Foreigners Registered in Japan*, pp. 46, 51, 52 and 61.
33. Niigataken Niigata Kowan Jimusho, *Heisei 13-nen, Niigatako Tokei Nenpo* [Annual report on Niigata port statistics, 2001], Niigata: Niigataken Niigata Kowan Jimusho, 2002, pp. 32, 34 and 36.
34. Niigata City officials supplied the information on Niigata airport.
35. These initiatives are known as "*jichitai gaiko*", or diplomacy by local autonomous bodies. For a study of Niigata's diplomacy, see Ichioka Masao, *Jichitai Gaiko: Niigata no Jissen-Yuko kara Kyoryoku e* [Local autonomous bodies' diplomacy: From practice-friendship to cooperation in Niigata], Tokyo: Nihon Keizaihyoronsha, 2000.
36. Niigataken Kokusaikoryuka, *Heisei 14-nendo Kokusai Koryu Gaiyo*, pp. 97–98.
37. See Tsuneo Akaha, "Despite the Northern Territories: Hokkaido's Courting of the Russian Far East", *Pacific Focus* 18 (1), Spring 2003, pp. 89–122.
38. Idem.
39. The no-visa regime has since been expanded to include not only past and present island residents but also other Japanese and Russians. Of the 4,724 Japanese participants in this programme, 3,069 were from Hokkaido. Hokkaido Somubu Chijishitsu Kokusaika Roshiashitsu, *Hokkaido to Roshia Kyokuto: Koryu Jisseki to Roshia Kyokuto no Gaiyo* [Hokkaido and the Russian Far East: a record of exchange and outline of the Russian Far East], Sapporo: Hokkaido Somubu Chijishitsu Kokusaika Roshiashitsu, 2002, p. 40.
40. For analyses of the Sakhalin offshore development and its environmental implications for Hokkaido, see Murakami Takashi, ed., *Saharin Tairikudana Sekiyu-Gasu Kaihatsu to Kankyo Hozen* [Sakhalin offshore oil and gas development and environmental protection], Sapporo: Hokkaido Daigaku Toshokankokai, 2003.
41. In 2000, Niigata's trade with Russia as a whole represented only 0.1 per cent of its total

international exports and 1.8 per cent of its imports. In the same year, there were only two Niigata-based companies with a presence in Russia. Niigataken Kokusaikoryuka, *Heisei 14-nendo, Kokusaikoryu Gaiyo*, pp. 15–19 and 27–31.

42. For a full report on the interviews and surveys, see Tsuneo Akaha and Anna Vassilieva, "Russian Migrants in Niigata and Hokkaido: A Research Update", in Tsuneo Akaha, ed., *Human Flows across National Borders in Northeast Asia, Seminar Proceedings*, United Nations University, Tokyo, Japan, 20–21 November 2002, Monterey, CA: Center for East Asian Studies, Monterey Institute of International Studies, 31 January 2003, pp. 71–95.

43. An official of the Hokkaido Governor's Office said, "At least one incident is reported daily in Otaru, Wakkanai, or Monbetsu."

44. A Wakkanai city administrator supplied this information.

45. The students were from Wakkanai Hokusei Gakuen University, a four-year college with a student population of around 360 and one major, in information media.

46. Kanako Takahara, "Russian-held Isles' Hokkaido Connections on Rise", *The Japan Times* online, 22 September 2004, available at ⟨http://www.japantimes.co.jp/cgi–bin/getarticle.pl5?nn20040922f1.htm⟩ (retrieved 5 December 2004).

47. On the important difference between the symbolic and material (instrumental) significance of the Russo-Japanese territorial dispute, see Masao Kimura and David A. Walsh, "Specifying 'Interests': Japan's Claim to the Northern Territories and Its Implications for International Relations Theory", *International Studies Quarterly* 42 (2), 1998, pp. 213–244.

48. The subject informed us that about one-half of the more than 17,000 Japanese who evacuated the Northern Territories in 1945 had passed away and that the average age of those still alive was 71. He was very concerned that younger generations of Japanese did not appreciate the importance of the territories in question. He admitted, however, that if the islands were returned to Japan, most of the survivors would find it difficult to resettle there because so many years had passed since they lived there and also because of the poor infrastructure on the islands.

49. The businessman was an active member of the Japan Junior Chamber of Commerce and was serving as Vice Chairman of the Chamber's commission on the Northern Territories and Japanese–Russian affairs.

50. Nemuro, *Nemuro: 2003 Shisei Yoran* [Nemuro: survey of the city, 2003], Nemuro: City of Nemuro, 2003, p. 2.

51. Interview with a local business person in Nemuro, June 2003.

52. The city employed five foreign nationals at a time as international interns, including Russians, for three years each. In the city's International Exchange and Cooperation Department, there were 21 staff members. Five of them spoke Russian, two had taught Japanese in Vladivostok and three worked directly on projects related to Russia. This was one more than the number of staff concerned with China projects.

53. In 2001, there were nearly 100 Russian residents registered in Niigata, about one-half of them married to Japanese locals. About 80 per cent of those married to Japanese were women. Interview with Russian consulate-general officials, October 2001.

54. The adjectives they used most frequently to characterize the Japanese whom they had met in social settings were "happy", "cheerful", "kind", "caring", "hospitable", "friendly" and "affable".

55. See Wada Haruki, "Nihonjin no Roshiakan: Sensei, Teki, Tomoni Kurushimu Mono" ["Japanese views of Russia: teacher, enemy, and those with whom to share pain"], in Fujiwara Akira, ed., *Roshia to Nihon: Nisso Rekishigaku Shimpojiumu* [Russia and Japan: symposium of Japan-Soviet historical studies], Tokyo: Sairyusha, 1985, pp. 11–32.

5

Chinese migrants in contemporary Japan: The case of Niigata

Daojiong Zha

Introduction

According to the latest Japanese immigration statistics, legal Chinese entrants into Japan in 2002 rose by 18.8 per cent from the previous year, reaching 527,000 in total.[1] In 2003, Chinese people made up the largest group (45 per cent of the total) of foreign residents arrested by Japanese law enforcement authorities.[2]

Since the late 1980s, when the Japanese government began to allow Chinese labourers into the Japanese market, the pattern has been a familiar one. On the one hand, the Japanese government finds it necessary to accommodate the market's needs for Chinese labourers by allowing Chinese to enter Japan for a long-term (over 90 days) stay. On the other hand, it is often at a loss at what to do concerning Japanese society's anxieties about the increasing Chinese presence and public anger over crimes committed by Chinese migrant workers and students.[3]

This chapter examines the Chinese presence in Japan by looking at how residents in a Japanese prefecture, Niigata, react to the presence of Chinese labourers. The questions addressed are: what impact do Chinese migrants, unskilled Chinese workers in particular, have on the local community? In what ways, if any, will relationships between Chinese migrants and local Japanese communities such as Niigata affect the relationship between Japan and China?

The chapter is based on findings from surveys of ordinary citizens and of prefectural and city government officials of Niigata.[4] The survey of the ordinary citizens was conducted during my time at the International University of Japan (IUJ), located in Niigata Prefecture. I sent a written questionnaire to Japanese individuals registered to participate in the University's volunteer conversation partners programme, created for assisting its foreign students to learn the Japanese language. I also tried to conduct follow-up interviews with some of the respondents who agreed to identify themselves; but I was not successful, mainly because they declined to be interviewed when they learned that the researcher was a Chinese.

The opinions in the completed surveys may not necessarily be representative of those of wider sections of Japanese society, as the survey respondents already demonstrated a degree of willingness to interact with foreign (including Chinese) students of the IUJ. Moreover, the sample size is small (24 individuals). But I tried to make up for these deficiencies by conducting a survey among employees of various departments of the Niigata prefectural government and the Niigata city government, including those who are involved in managing China-related affairs. In addition, I conducted interviews with Niigata Prefecture and city officials in charge of exchanges with Chinese provinces as well as with volunteers working for the Niigata International Association, an umbrella organization for various citizens' groups promoting exchanges between Japanese and foreign residents in the city.[5]

Niigata and China

Before the findings from the surveys and interviews are summarized, it is useful to review Niigata's ties with China. In historical terms, the port of Niigata, on the north-western coast of the main Japanese island Honshu, served as a main launching pad for the Japanese imperial army to march into Manchuria and for the subsequent Japanese project to establish Manchukuo as a puppet state. According to one account, until May 1945 a total of 12,641 "agricultural developers" and "young military volunteers" (involving 1,648 households in 14 groups) from Niigata Prefecture were sent to Manchukuo, making Niigata the fifth-largest Japanese prefecture in terms of organized wartime civilian migration to Manchuria.[6] Understandably, Niigata played its part in the effort to resettle "war-displaced" Japanese back in Japan. Partly because most of Niigata's "war-displaced" Japanese lived in Heilongjiang Province, Niigata and Heilongjiang established sister-city ties in the early 1980s, when Japanese public sentiment experienced a "China boom".[7] Indeed, Sano Tozaburo (1923–1994), a Manchurian war veteran, has become a local legend in building post-war friendship ties between Niigata and Heilongjiang. In his lifetime, Sano made over 30 trips to Heilongjiang, sharing his expertise in swampland treatment in Niigata and relentlessly lobbying the Japanese government to grant official development assistance for the specific purpose of flood control in Heilongjiang's Baoqing County, where the first Japanese family from Niigata settled.[8]

In the post-war era, beginning with the friendship/exchange programme between Niigata City and the Russian city of Khabarovsk in 1964, Niigata's city and prefectural governments and local business communities worked hard to restore economic ties across the Sea of Japan (known in Korea as the "East Sea").[9]

Since 1991, the Niigata prefectural administration has pursued an internationalization strategy aimed at transforming the Japan Sea rim region from one of Cold War-era confrontation to one of common prosperity and cooperation. The strategy has three purposes: building a national consensus within Japan about the importance of the concept of region-building in this part of the world; playing a leadership role in the Japan Sea rim movement through international collaborative research and publicity activities; and garnering international attention for the cause of Japan Sea rim cooperation.[10]

Heilongjiang's own economic ties with the outside world began to flourish in the late 1980s, about a decade later than other provinces in China. When it did begin integrating with the rest of the world economy, its primary focus was on promoting cross-border trade with Russia and other former Soviet economies.[11] Both in natural resources and in foreign economic policy orientation, Heilongjiang is a weaker partner in the emergence of a "natural economic territory" around the Sea of Japan. Nonetheless, Niigata Prefecture has continually cultivated economic ties with Heilongjiang, which itself holds annual trade and investment conventions for promoting economic ties across its border with Russia. Even so, Japanese businesses generally are still hesitant to invest there, largely because the local business environment is less developed than in other Chinese provinces.[12]

In 1998, Niigata successfully lobbied for the central governments of Japan and China to open a passenger airline service to Harbin, and thus increased the international use of Niigata airport. Also in 1998, Niigata Prefecture successfully launched an airline service to Xi'an (via Shanghai), in part by taking advantage of the symbolism of being home to the ibis birds the Chinese government gave to the emperor of Japan as a goodwill gift. In addition to air transportation connections, Niigata has since 1996 operated a weekly container sea line linking it to the Chinese ports of Dalian, Qingdao and Shanghai. And in 1997, the Niigata prefectural government established a trade office in Dalian.

Besides establishing formal business ties, the Niigata prefectural government worked to assist local businesses to recruit Chinese "trainees" by utilizing the sister-city arrangements it had established with local authorities in China. These otherwise largely symbolic ties serve an important function: to make sure that Chinese workers sent to Niigata are selected by accountable if not always reliable Chinese authorities.[13]

The Chinese presence in Niigata

As of 2001, there were 3,120 Chinese registered as staying in Niigata. Their status of residence ranged across all Japanese visa categories except those of artist, practitioner of religion, journalist, lawyer and accountant (see table 5.1).

Table 5.1 tells us several things. First, it informs us that Chinese come to Niigata primarily for jobs. Trainees are unskilled workers who are allowed to stay, under a designated employer's sponsorship, for up to three years at a time. It is possible that a good majority of those in the "designated activities" category are actually short-term employees of businesses in the prefecture. This is because in the Japanese system for registering foreign residents, those in the "designated activities" category are either on "working holidays" or simply listed as "others". As Japanese visa rules do not allow Chinese passport holders to enter and spend "working holidays" in Japan, it is possible for Japanese employers to sponsor the entry of Chinese workers under the broad "others" category.[14]

A total of 208 employers (organized into 21 groups) in Niigata had 496 Chinese trainees working for them in 2001. A variety of Chinese labour-exporting agencies, based mainly in north-eastern China but going as far south as Shanghai, Jiangsu Province (west of Shanghai) and Hubei Province (in central China) were responsible for dispatching unskilled Chinese to work in Niigata.[15] The Chinese agencies sending labour are almost identical with the agencies featuring in friendship agreements with administrative units in Niigata. In other words, friendship agreements below the prefectural level do seem to serve the labour needs of Japanese

Table 5.1 Registered Chinese in Niigata, 2001

Status	Students	Trainees	Dependants	Designated activities	Permanent residents	Japanese citizens' spouses	Long-term residents
	516	609	262	443	170	588	228

Source: Statistics on the Foreigners Registered in Japan, Tokyo: Japan Immigration Association, 2001, pp. 72–75.

employers, particularly those located in remote areas of the prefecture. Regrettably, my attempt to conduct a Chinese-language survey of Chinese trainees was not successful because their employers declined to cooperate. The employers preferred to keep the presence of Chinese working in their shops as low-key as possible, perhaps owing to the bad treatment Chinese trainees were getting in the Chinese-language press in Japan.

Second, table 5.1 shows that a fairly large number of Chinese residing in Niigata are Japanese citizens' spouses. Chinese–Japanese marriages deserve some discussion. On the demand side, Niigata, like other rural areas of Japan, sees its own marriageable female population moving to more prosperous parts of the country, creating the need to import foreign wives for its farming population. The phenomenon of international marriages in the farming communities of Niigata began in the mid-1970s. On the supply side, many Chinese women see marrying into a Japanese family, despite having to live in a rural area, as a great improvement in their standard of living.[16]

Third, although Niigata is not known in Japan for being a home to prestigious educational institutions, the relatively sizeable number of Chinese students is notable. It is indicative of the primary reason for Chinese to come to Niigata: to pursue a degree in an area where jobs are available to support their studies. In this regard, the difficulties I encountered in getting Chinese students enrolled in Niigata University (located in Niigata City) to participate in a Chinese-language version of the questionnaire survey are noteworthy. To begin with, it was not easy to gather them together and explain the project because, as I was informed, Chinese students usually do not show up on campus unless there are classes to attend. At other times, they concentrate on their part-time jobs off campus. Even the head of the Chinese student association of the university showed little interest in assisting with the survey: he knew that without some cash compensation for the time required to complete the survey, his fellow students would most likely just throw the survey sheets into the waste-paper basket.

It is important to note that a small number (12 in 2001) of Chinese students in Niigata are sponsored (with full funding) by the prefecture to pursue their degree studies. Niigata began to sponsor international students to study for degrees in universities in the prefecture in 1969 (beginning with students from Brazil), and has paid for students from China since 1984. As of 2002, 187 Chinese students had come to Niigata through this channel, including 34 who had been invited for training in the prefecture's cancer treatment centre. Chinese, eight per annum, are the largest national group to benefit from the prefecture's sponsorship scheme.[17] According to officials in its international affairs division, the primary purpose for funding these students – all from Heilongjiang Province – is to cultivate goodwill among a new generation of Chinese individuals; it is hoped that they will assist Niigata Prefecture's efforts to promote its interests in the Chinese province and, on a larger scale, to help increase trust between the Chinese and Japanese peoples. The result thus far, however, has been said to be less than satisfactory. In early 2002, a Niigata official commented, "When the Chinese students return to their home province, they act individually. Thus it is difficult for them to have tangible influence on policy-making in their home society. Why don't they even form an alumni group of their own?"[18]

Short-term exchanges

The number of registered Chinese in Niigata reflects only part of the dynamics of human movement from China, as Japanese law requires a foreigner to register his or her stay only if it is for longer than 90 days. Since Niigata Prefecture began formal friendship relations with Heilongjiang Province it has organized a variety of short-term exchange programmes bringing ordinary Chinese to experience interaction with Japanese people and everyday life in Japan. Such exchange programmes have included youth groups since 1986, sports groups since 1990 and high school student exchanges since 1991. Each of these groups averages 10 participants per annum. The prefecture's sponsorship, since 1993, of Chinese-language instructors to teach in the local women's college also helps to promote mutual understanding at the grass-roots level.[19]

The launching of direct air services between Niigata and cities in China opened another route for Chinese to come to Niigata on a tourist visa. Indeed, the number of passengers on the Niigata–Harbin route increased rapidly, from nearly 9,000 in the inaugural year (1998) to 31,000 in 2000; and the number of passengers using the Niigata–Shanghai route grew from 19,000 to 24,000 during the same period. Although the number of self-financed Chinese on those trips is not known, the numbers indicate the expanding opportunities for interactions between Chinese and Japanese.

To sum up, Niigata's promotion of local-level diplomacy and economic ties with Heilongjiang Province and other administrative units in China has directly affected the number of Chinese coming to Niigata. The prefecture's initial rationale, in the mid-1980s, was to promote grass-roots exchanges with north-eastern Chinese provinces. But since the early 1990s, it has moved on to meeting local economic needs, especially to securing cheap industrial and agricultural labour from rural China. How do Japanese residents in Niigata view the Chinese presence in their communities?

Questionnaire survey of ordinary Japanese residents in Niigata: Views on the Chinese presence

I distributed survey questionnaires to about 40 potential respondents in January 2002. Twenty-four completed surveys were returned by mail. The respondents lived in seven different administrative districts of Niigata Prefecture, including the cities of Niigata, Joetsu and Nagaoka (the three largest in the prefecture), as well as in towns and villages. Tables 5.2 to 5.4 summarize the background of the 24 respondents.

It should be noted that the respondents either have had experience (30 per cent had experienced direct contact with foreign residents in their neighbourhoods) or have shown an interest in interacting with foreign individuals living in the prefecture through language-exchange programmes. Those local residents who have less experience and/or interest in interacting with foreign residents in the prefecture may reply differently to the survey questions. This, as well as the small number of samples collected, presents only a limited picture of Niigata citizens' views about Chinese residents.

In terms of frequency of contact with Chinese on the job, only one of the respondents had daily contact with Chinese living in the prefecture. This respondent, an employee of a public healthcare provider, interacted with a Chinese trainee who was studying Japanese ways of caring for the

Table 5.2 Occupations/professions of Japanese survey respondents

Total	Company employees	Teachers*	Housewives	Unemployed	University students	Self-employed
24	7	5	4	4	3	1

Source: author.
* Includes two who offer private group language lessons for a living.

Table 5.3 Age of Japanese survey respondents

Total	20s	30s	40s	50s	60s
24	3	5	4	7	5

Source: author.

Table 5.4 Highest level of education obtained by Japanese survey respondents

Total	High school	Two-year college	University
24	6	9	9

Source: author.

elderly by assisting Japanese doctors. Six respondents recalled occasional encounters with Chinese, either through overhearing conversations in Chinese or observing their presence in neighbourhood grocery stores and at parent–teacher meetings in schools. Three respondents reported meeting Chinese on a weekly basis. One of them had a Chinese friend, and the other two simply knew that Chinese were around because they saw them come to the canteen where they worked. The remaining 14 respondents reported no contact with Chinese whatsoever.

Apart from at work, the survey respondents had only limited contacts with Chinese residents. For the five who reported interacting with Chinese on a monthly or weekly basis, conversations took place either in the Chinese-language courses they were enrolled in, which were organized by the local government, or in exchange teaching. In one case, a 38-year-old language instructor was teaching English to a Chinese, who in return was teaching her Chinese. Their meetings took place on a weekly basis.

Over half of the respondents described favourably their impressions of the Chinese individuals they knew or knew of. The most frequently mentioned adjective, used by nine respondents, was "diligent". Other positive terms included "open-minded", "big-hearted", "trustworthy", "good at socializing", "friendly" and "caring about details". Negative impressions included "aggressive", "selfish", "cunning" and "self-centred". There were some neutral characteristics as well, such as "full of personality" and "independent" – attributes that do not readily fit in with social norms in rural Japan but might be quite acceptable in urban areas of the country. As most of the respondents reported no regular contact with Chinese residents, their impressions may have come through secondary sources or the media.

When asked about their participation in any organized Japan–China exchange programmes in Niigata, only one respondent said that she had had such an experience: cooking Japanese food for an Asian cultural festival in Joetsu City in 2000. A young prefectural employee (in his early 20s) also noted the limited participation by the Japanese of his community in government-sponsored exchange programmes. He complained that this might reflect unfavourable attitudes towards such activities. On the other hand, as the Niigata International Association reports 60 voluntary groups formed for the explicit purpose of promoting exchange between Japanese and foreign residents of the city, the potential for wider Japanese participation in international or intercultural programmes cannot be ignored.

In recent years, Japanese news media have focused heavily on crimes committed by Chinese residents, so much so that the growing number of reported crimes by Chinese living in Japan has contributed to a general turn to the negative in Japanese views on China in the past decade.[20] Throughout Japan, there is concern about the continuous growth of the manufacturing sector in China and its "hollowing-out" effect on the Japanese economy, and this concern is another important source of "China threat" rhetoric in Japan. Would it be logical, then, for average Japanese to prefer to see a reduction of the Chinese presence in Japan?

Eleven of the respondents to the questionnaire expressed "no opinion" about the future Chinese presence in their neighbourhoods, but eight replied that they would like to see a modest increase. Three of the latter group referred to the lack of variety in rural life as a reason for desiring a larger Chinese presence in their community. One elementary school teacher wrote in separate comments that "internationalization through the Japan Exchange and Teaching Programme organized by the government should bring in many nationals, including Chinese, rather than being an exclusive venue for English-speaking natives from Europe and America". A housewife in her 50s noted that it is important for Chinese people to experience the life of Japanese farmers.[21] Two others pointed out that an increase in the international presence in their neighbourhoods ought not to be limited to Chinese or to any other nationality. Five respondents clearly stated their opposition to any increase in the Chinese presence in their communities. One mentioned possible job competition as a reason. Another respondent asked in his comments, "There is no problem around here; why do we need to see an increase [in the Chinese presence]?"

When asked about the impact that the Chinese presence has had on the local communities, 13 of the 24 respondents indicated "no knowledge" of any impact and said that they were simply not aware of any Chinese living or working in their neighbourhoods. As a further seven respondents reported "no impact", clearly an overwhelming majority did not have direct knowledge of how the Chinese in Niigata lived. Of the three who did think that the Chinese presence had a positive impact on their neighbourhoods, one gave the marriage of Chinese women to Japanese men as a merit. Another said that she enjoyed talking to her Chinese friend without reservations, and the third stated that it was important to have more opportunities for promoting mutual understanding between the Japanese and Chinese peoples.

In short, the size of the sample is too small to draw definitive conclusions about Niigata residents' views on the presence of Chinese in their areas. Overall, the residents I surveyed did not seem to see the Chinese presence in their communities as an important issue that needs to be dealt with. There are two explanations for such a state of affairs. First, by appearance alone many Chinese are not distinguishable from Japanese. Unless there is clear self-identification, it is quite possible for a Chinese to be mistaken for a Japanese. Alternatively, the Chinese population of some 3,000 in Niigata is quite small in view of the prefecture's population of 2.5 million people. Unless there is a drastic increase in the Chinese presence in the prefecture, which is unlikely owing to the relative lack of economic opportunities in comparison with Tokyo, Yokohama and other metropolitan areas, the current situation may well continue.

Views on Japan–China relations

Five of the survey questions had to do with the respondents' assessment of the current state of affairs in bilateral relations between Japan and China. In response to the question about their feelings towards China, over half replied that they felt "close" or "somewhat close" to China, but they did not provide an explanation of their reply. One observed that there are many areas of similarity between Chinese and Japanese societies. Another respondent simply noted that China once provided ibises and pandas to Japan. It seems that the majority of the respondents did not feel that they could relate to China because they had no direct experience of life across the Japan Sea. Nonetheless, the percentage of people with positive feelings towards China was much higher than that in surveys conducted country-wide. For example, according to an *Asahi Shimbum* opinion survey published in September 2002, only 19 per cent of the respondents had positive feelings about China. By contrast, 62 per cent said that they had no particular feelings about China, either positive or negative.[22]

What did the respondents to my questionnaire think about Japan–China relations? The answers varied widely. The largest group (six) reported having mixed feelings about relations between the two countries. What contributes to such a judgement? Surprisingly, only two of the 24 respondents referred to the Japan–China war experience and the need for genuine reconciliation as a major concern. The two respondents, both in their 60s, said Japan should repay the "benevolence" that the Chinese leader Zhou Enlai displayed in the 1970s in not asking Japan to pay war compensation.

Next, three respondents mentioned China's growing economic power. One of them noted the need for better cooperation, to make sure that the change in the value of the Chinese currency would not impact adversely on the value of the yen. The second remarked that Japan must think about better ways of dealing with its pressing economic problems rather than blame competition from cheap Chinese imports. The third respondent said that the intensifying economic competition between the two countries was an important but complex issue to be reckoned with.

Finally, three respondents said that there were differences between human-level contacts between Chinese and Japanese and government-to-government contacts and that it was much easier for there to be close relationships between Chinese and Japanese at the individual level than it was for the two governments to work together. The solution, according to one respondent, was to expand the role of local governments and individuals in Japan–China relations.

What did the respondents see as necessary means of improving Japan–China relations? The 20 respondents who answered this question were evenly split in their opinions. Ten, in their 40s and older, referred to the need to overcome differences in the understanding of the relevance of history to contemporary political relations. One respondent, whose sister experienced growing up in China during the final years of World War II, commented that it was regrettable that people no longer seemed to differentiate between the warmth Chinese and Japanese individuals displayed towards each other and the media-projected images of animosity between the two societies. She also observed that history should not be painted as either black or white. A man in his 60s remarked that "the only thing that can improve Japan–China relations is time, as all other means of reconciliation have been exhausted". The questionnaire did not ask the respondents to express their feelings about the Chinese government's demand for Japan to apologize for the war, but one respondent did mention that necessity. In general, the respondents felt resigned to the fact that the history issue* between Japan and China remained a complex one.

The other 10 respondents emphasized the need to intensify cultural exchanges and to improve mutual understanding between the Chinese people and the Japanese people at the grass-roots level. There was definite disappointment with how both the Chinese and Japanese governments had handled political ties between the two countries. Only one respondent mentioned careful handling of the Taiwan question as a means of maintaining positive political ties between Japan and China.

In general, the respondents' comments on the means of improving Japan–China relations provided a good reflection of the complex web of interdependence, cooperation and friction that was reflected by the media in Japan, the main source of information about Japan–China ties for the respondents. The results differed from the 2002 opinion poll conducted by the Japanese Foreign Ministry in which 47 per cent of the re-

---

* At the levels of government diplomacy, intellectual debate and societal feeling between China and Japan, there exists a wide gap over specific acts in the history of Japanese colonialism in China as well as over the acceptable measures taken to address them. The gap is so wide that no volume of literature, in Chinese, Japanese or another language, is considered to do the matter justice.

spondents said that government-level consultations should be expanded in order to improve bilateral relations and 27 per cent recommended that people-to-people exchanges should be increased.[23]

Views on the presence of foreign workers in Japan

My questionnaire survey included a separate section that dealt specifically with the issue of the presence of foreign labourers in Japan. The level of concern about this matter was high. A majority (13 of 24 respondents) replied that they were either somewhat or very concerned about the presence of foreign labourers in Japan. Another six respondents said that they were "not very concerned". Only one chose "I don't know" as an answer. The percentages correspond with a survey on the same topic conducted by the Japanese prime minister's office in November 2000. Nearly 50 per cent of the respondents to this national poll expressed concern about the presence of foreign workers in Japan.[24]

Contemporary discussion in Japan about foreign labourers is often closely associated with images of crime, including illegal entry into the country. Half the survey respondents were aware of the Japanese government's system of bringing foreign labourers to Japan under the categories of trainee and on-the-job technical trainee, and they were able to identify the 1980s or the 1990s as the beginning of its implementation.

As for the aim of the foreign trainee system, half the respondents thought that its most important purpose was to extend economic assistance to developing nations. Eleven saw serving as a means to help relieve Japanese industries of their labour shortage as its second-most important purpose. Interestingly, six respondents identified dealing with the labour shortage as its most important purpose. Five believed that the number one purpose was to promote Japan's internationalization. One respondent observed that the primary rationale was simply to ensure that foreign labourers could be hired cheaply. Only seven respondents thought that "helping people who are suffering a harsh economic life in their home countries" qualified as either the second- or the third-most important purpose of the trainee system.

These replies are interesting in that they point to a continuing feeling of pride among ordinary Japanese people about their country's economic power and about spreading the country's wealth to the developing world. The findings of the survey contrast with the national poll about foreign labour mentioned earlier. The national survey found economic assistance to be the third-most important rationale for continuing with the policy of allowing foreign workers into the Japanese labour market.[25]

The respondents to my survey had little difficulty in identifying where foreign labourers came from: China, Southeast Asia, South America and Korea. Indeed, these are the countries or the regions of the world that have supplied Japan with large numbers of unskilled workers. On further querying, however, it became clear that the respondents had little knowledge of the scale of the presence of foreign labour in their prefecture.

As to the purpose for which foreign trainees come to Japan, the respondents were almost unanimous in choosing as the most or the second-most important purpose learning Japanese manufacturing skills and management know-how or earning more money than they could in their home countries. The respondents thought that the third-most important purpose was to experience Japan's culture and way of life. Five respondents thought that foreign trainees came to Japan to have a chance of permanent settlement.

Only three of the 24 respondents had experience of working with foreign trainees on their jobs, and replies to questions about foreign trainees in respondents' local areas were necessarily speculative. Of the two who did work with foreign trainees, one had worked with (Chinese and Filipino) students (treated as trainees) for up to two years and remarked that their aptitude was no match for Japanese employees and that their attitude towards work was "ordinary". But a second respondent knew of Korean trainees in the same company and thought that they were diligent.

I specifically asked the survey participants to identify possible positive and negative impacts that foreign trainees might have on their local area. Seven respondents indicated the following as the most positive effects: trainees help local companies to save on labour costs; they contribute to the healthy development of Japan's relationship with their home countries; and they contribute to the internationalization of the respondents' communities. Six respondents specified the relief of labour shortages in local companies as the second-most important positive impact; another six thought that foreign trainees did jobs that many Japanese were unwilling to take on.

On the negative side, the respondents presented a range of views. The most serious worry for seven respondents was the worsening of the employment situation, that is trainees' competition for jobs with locals; the decline of wages for local workers concerned six respondents. Eight subjects thought that the presence of foreign trainees imposed additional costs on local communities in terms of support for education, social welfare and the construction of living accommodation for them. Five respondents thought that foreign trainees contributed to an increase in crime.

Should the Japanese government reform its policy regarding foreign trainees? A majority (14 respondents) indicated "I don't know". Six respondents expressed mixed feelings about this question. The additional observations that the respondents offered gave a clearer picture of what these feelings were. A 42-year-old piano teacher wrote, "These days, no matter how you look at it, employment for Japanese is serious. At the level of human feelings, foreign workers can be accepted. Nonetheless, would it not be better to admit them when the Japanese economy has turned around?" A 66-year-old housewife did not want to see more foreign trainees in Japan and remarked that Japan's superpower status was a thing of the past. She asked, "Why do we have illegal foreign workers? ... The government should focus on bringing in foreign workers through legal channels."

Other respondents were more receptive to the presence of foreign workers in Japan but were nonetheless concerned about some aspects of foreign labour. For example, a 47-year-old part-time worker wrote, "Many young Japanese are reluctant to take the 3-K jobs (*kitsui*, hard; *kiken*, dangerous; and *kitanai*, dirty). Foreigners come in and work hard, because they do it simply for money. But foreigners enter to take the entertainment jobs, which is an offence [to] the foreign women's dignity. The Japanese government should focus on creating jobs that have a positive influence on the Japanese society." An elementary school teacher, 47, remarked, "In our prefecture too, we often hear [of] foreigners committing crimes. It is sad that the image of all foreigners is tainted due to the behavior of a few. Both Japanese and foreigners should make an effort to increase mutual understanding and benefit from the better parts of their respective spheres of life." Another respondent, 41, who had once taught Japanese to an Indonesian trainee, echoed the same sentiment, stating, "It is true that the increase in foreign workers has contributed to the worsening of crimes. Viewed from outside, Japan is an attractive society. But the Japanese way of life is insular. Does that not also make it easy for foreigners to commit crimes?" A 48-year-old respondent wrote, "In the age of globalization, it is important for the government to devise programs that can promote serious exchange of technological learning and keep such exchanges going on a regular basis." She added, however, that a farm near her house was simply "making use of foreign trainees as manual labour under the disguise of 'training'" and warned that "At best, upon their return, the foreigners will have earned some money, and they can act as tour guides for Japanese."

On balance, the respondents expressed more negative than positive sentiments about the presence of foreign labourers. Many of them no longer see Japan as a proud source of learning for poorer countries of the world. They are unfamiliar with the details of the Japanese government's policies for importing foreign unskilled labour through the trainee programme. Still, they expressed a desire for a change in the government's policy towards the import of foreign labourers.

Niigata Prefecture and Niigata City officials' views of Niigata–China ties

In January 2002, I distributed the same questionnaire among Niigata Prefecture and Niigata City officials, including those who were in charge of managing their administration's relations with China. I received 30 replies a month later.

The first noticeable difference between the government officials and the ordinary citizens who responded to my survey was that the former group appeared to be far more reluctant to identify themselves. Only 13 officials did so, including seven males (three in their 30s and four in their 40s) and six females (two in their 40s, one in her 30s and three in their 20s). More significantly, most of the government officials were selective in answering questions. They either left some questions unanswered or chose answers from lists of alternatives provided without offering any explanation. Several possible reasons can be given for this: a lack of time in their busy schedules, a lack of familiarity with the questions asked and job rotation in the Japanese personnel system.[26]

The second noticeable difference between government officials and ordinary citizens was that the former were far more cautious in expressing their views. Those officials with no contacts at all with Chinese people simply skipped many questions. In contrast, most of the ordinary Niigata residents surveyed did not hesitate to comment on their images of Chinese people regardless of the amount of experience or knowledge that they could claim about China.

Half the 30 prefecture and city administration officials had regular contacts with Chinese citizens, seven of them on a daily basis, six on a weekly basis and two on a monthly basis. Most of the other respondents had no contact with Chinese. Outside the work environment, however, 18 respondents had no contact with Chinese, and another six reported only occasional contact. Only one official had daily contact with a Chinese citizen: he had a Chinese wife. There was also only one person who had weekly contact with Chinese. She had spent seven years in Shenyang studying Chinese, returning to Niigata in 2000. This respondent, a lady in her 20s, was the obvious exception. She said that she maintained regular contact with friends in China by e-mail and telephone and socialized with other Chinese living in Niigata.

How can the limited social interaction between Japanese and Chinese in Niigata be explained? Some interviewees indicated people's busy lives as a reason. Another, perhaps more important, reason may be that Japanese and Chinese people want to avoid having to discuss controversial issues in China–Japan relations, issues that permeate Japanese news reports on bilateral relations.[27] I went to a lunar New Year's party organized by the Niigata International Association for Chinese residents and found only one Chinese family and four other Chinese there. Also, half the Japanese people who came to the party were over 60. This was clearly a sign of lack of interest among younger Japanese in meeting Chinese people.

The Niigata government officials had a variety of impressions of the Chinese individuals they had met. The positive characteristics they attributed to the Chinese they had encountered at work included "broad-minded", "strong", "hard-working", "reasonable", "friendly", "cheerful", "smart", "well-mannered" and "honest". Among the negative features were "very quick to express opinions", "unwilling to admit his/her own error", "short-sighted", "stingy" and "rough". By contrast, the officials' impressions of the Chinese people they had met outside the work environment were very positive: "diligent", "friendly", "sociable" and "good at cooking".

How did the government officials assess their knowledge of China? Only two of them said that they were very knowledgeable; they had each spent over five years studying in China. Four officials considered themselves "somewhat knowledgeable" about China. Twenty respondents said that they were "not very knowledgeable" and two admitted to having no knowledge about China at all. Their self-acknowledged dearth of knowledge was related to their lack of interest in meeting Chinese people in Niigata. Only one-fifth of the respondents indicated some previous involvement in exchange activities organized by local governments, and only one respondent said that he had attended a party organized by Chinese college students in Niigata.

Only a few government respondents gave their views on the movement of people between China and Japan. Five officials believed that for a variety of reasons the status quo should continue. Their concerns included a possible increase in crime, competition for living space, Chinese migrants' lack of language proficiency, necessary to survive in Japanese society, and the possibility of many more Chinese families coming to Japan. Four respondents wanted more Japanese to visit China. They agreed that it was inevitable for Japan and China to engage in more economic exchanges and therefore that it was necessary for more Japanese to develop an understanding of Chinese society.

In contrast to the ordinary citizens, 67 per cent (20 of 30) of the government officials who responded to the survey were aware of the official exchanges between Niigata Prefecture and Heilongjiang Province and between Niigata City and Harbin. Did they think that these exchanges should be strengthened in the future? They were evenly divided in view. Half of them thought that there should be more exchanges, and referred to the need to develop economic exchanges and mutual understanding at the personal level. The other half thought that the status quo was satis-factory. Two officials cited the stubborn persistence of the history issue in Japan–China relations as the main obstacle to achieving better results in local-level diplomacy.

The government officials were rather hesitant to express their opinion about China and the future of bilateral relations between China and Ja-pan. Over half of them (18) thought that bilateral relations could be im-proved but they seemed to want to leave the task to others, presumably the central governments of the two countries.

In sum, it is difficult to generalize about the survey respondents' views on Chinese as individuals, China the country and Japan–China relations. What is clear is that their opinions are closely related to their job. No government official showed "pre-conceived notions" about the questions the survey asked. On the other hand, television and news reports played as important a role as personal experience dealing with Chinese people.

Reflections on the presence of foreign workers

A solid majority (18 of 30) of the local government officials who re-sponded to the questionnaire said that they were "concerned" or "some-what concerned" about the presence of foreign workers in the prefecture. Nearly half (13) had knowledge of the Japanese government's foreign trainee system and noted that the system had begun either in the 1980s or the 1990s. In addition, they were aware that most foreign labourers in the prefecture came from China, Russia and Southeast Asia.

The respondents were nearly unanimous in believing that the Japanese government's reasons for bringing foreign trainees to Japan were, first, to promote Japan's internationalization; second, to provide relief to Japan-ese industries experiencing labour shortages; and, third, to provide eco-nomic assistance to developing countries. They were also nearly unani-mous in their understanding of the reasons why foreign workers came to Niigata: to learn Japanese manufacturing skills and to earn higher wages than they could in their home counties. Finally, the respondents were also knowledgeable about the types of work that foreign workers were engaged in: engineering, entertainment and food services, and textile production.

Sixteen of the government respondents reported having worked with foreigners as part of their job, including Chinese, South Koreans, Ameri-cans, Indonesians, Brazilians and Mexicans. Among their phrases de-scribing foreign workers were "very diligent", "full of questions but basi-cally constructive", "different from person to person, with a few excellent ones" and "interesting". The officials had more experience of Chinese and South Koreans than of people from other countries, and this reflected the fact that Niigata has closer ties with these two countries through trade and investment than with other countries.

It should be noted that the foreigners with whom the government officials work as part of their job are different from the unskilled foreign workers in factories in the prefecture's industries even though they are both categorized as "trainees". Only one of the respondents to my survey had direct knowledge of foreign (Chinese) contract workers in the prefecture. This official expressed sympathy towards the Chinese she knew about. She was concerned that it would be difficult for contract workers to save any money unless they were willing to work for up to 14 hours a day. She also noted that the minor incidents in which she was asked to intervene often resulted from a Japanese floor manager's impatience with and authoritarian approach towards a Chinese worker who took more time than the manager allowed to learn the details of her assignment or her failure to fit in with the norms of factory floor management. The official also pointed out that the language barrier often contributed to further frustration on both sides.

There was convergence between the government officials' and the ordinary residents' assessments of the impact of the foreign labour presence on the local economy. On the positive side, the government administrators viewed the foreign workers as contributing to the internationalization of the local area and enabling local companies to save on labour costs. On the negative side, one official wrote, "All these foreigners are interested in is money; it is just too superficial to speak of 'technology transfer', 'mutual understanding' or anything else." Many officials also blamed the worsening of the local area's employment situation and declining wage levels on the presence of cheap foreign labour in the prefecture. Moreover, they attributed the increasing crime rate in the local communities to the presence of unskilled foreign labourers.

The local government officials were evenly divided in their assessment of the Japanese government's programme for importing unskilled foreign labour. A third of them felt that the government should overhaul the programme; another third said that it was difficult to express their view in one phrase; and the final third simply replied that they had no idea of what advice to give to the national government. Two officials were more frank. One Niigata City official wrote, "We should simply call them [foreign trainees] 'imported labourers'." A prefecture administrator thought that the national government's top priority should be to reduce the number of illegal foreign labourers. But in view of their replies to other parts of the survey, these two officials were not very knowledgeable about the actual situation of local foreign labour.

Conclusion

Several conclusions can be drawn from the above analysis. First, the review of the history of Niigata's internationalization efforts revealed that official contacts between Japan and China at the provincial and local levels facilitated the movement of people from China to Japan, including government officials, students and unskilled workers. The prefectural government's promotion of Niigata airport as a transportation hub for north-western Japan also made it easier for the movement of people and goods between north-eastern Chinese provinces and Niigata. In this sense, the pursuit of local-level internationalization should have a positive impact on the local economy.

However, that impact was not readily discernible in the limited surveys conducted for the present study. As far as the surveys were concerned, locally organized exchange programmes oriented towards China did not appear to have had an appreciable impact on the daily life of the people of Niigata or on the nature of their interaction with Chinese residents in their communities. For the government officials, there appeared to be few opportunities for direct interaction with Chinese residents unless they were assigned to organize or to participate in exchange programmes or events arranged by their government. There may be more rhetoric than real change in the locally driven internationalization movement.

In addition, contacts between the ordinary citizens of Niigata Prefecture and Chinese migrants there appeared to be rather limited. Although one must accept the reality that individuals move across national boundaries in order to pursue personal goals in life, the lack of individual contact noted by the survey respondents and interviewees raises questions about the societal and cultural impact (or lack thereof) of cross-border human flows in this prefecture. It implies too that Japanese and Chinese people's images of one another in Niigata may be affected more by mass media reports than by personal contacts.

In 2000, the Niigata prefectural government launched a lobbying effort to invite the Chinese government to install a consulate in the city of Niigata. (As of May 2005, Niigata appeared to have lost in the bidding for an additional Chinese consulate in Japan to the city of Nagoya.) The purported benefit would be an expansion of economic cooperation projects between Japanese and Chinese partners. On the Chinese side as well, facilitating the export of unskilled labour is a means of relieving pressure on the domestic labour market. The fact that Chinese are not easily distinguishable from the majority of the local population perhaps eases the import of unskilled Chinese labour. It is important, however, that in both countries social awareness should be raised concerning the complex issues associated with bringing foreign labour into rural areas of Japan, a glimpse of which has been presented in the present study. When the economies of the north-eastern Chinese provinces gain more momentum, in part as a result of the Chinese central government's "Revitalize the Northeast" campaign, there will be reduced pressure for Chinese to enter areas of rural Japan such as Niigata in search of jobs. And if there is less pressure, it is possible that Niigata's pursuit of internationalization will bring more benefits than agonies, real and/or perceived, in local communities.

Notes

1. I thank Tsuneo Akaha for providing me with the latest published Japanese statistics.
2. Jiji Press English News Service, "Crimes by Foreigners Hit Record in Japan in 2003", 11 March 2004, p. 1.
3. Daojiong Zha, "Chinese Migrant Workers in Japan: Policies, Institutions, and Civil Society," in Pal Nyiri and Igor Saveliev, eds, *Globalising Chinese Migration: Trends in Europe and Asia*, London: Ashgate, 2002, pp. 129–157.
4. For the survey, I modified the questionnaire developed by Akaha and Vassilieva for their study of Russians in Hokkaido and Niigata, which is discussed in chap. 4 of this volume.
5. See the association's website at http://www.niigata-ia.or.jp.
6. Oshima Mitsuko, *Niigata-ken no Hyakunen* [One Hundred Years of Niigata Prefecture], Tokyo: Yamakawa Shuppansha, 1990, pp. 268–269.
7. In 1983, two years after the first group of Niigata's "war displaced" Japanese returned to settle in Japan, Niigata Prefecture and Heilongjiang Province established a sister-province exchange relationship.
8. See a series of memorial articles in *Niigata Nippo*, 16, 17, 19, 20, 21, 22, 26 and 27 June 2001.
9. Ichioka Masao, *Jichitai Gaiko: Niigata no Jissen-Yuko kara Kyoryoku e* [Local autonomous bodies' diplomacy: From practice-friendship to cooperation in Niigata], Tokyo: Nihon Keizaihyoronsha, 2000, pp. 43–51.
10. Katherine Burns, "International Cooperation at the Local Level: Primorye and Niigata in the Northeast Asian Context", available at ⟨http://srch.slav.hokudai.ac.jp/sympo/Proceed97/KatherineG.Burns.html⟩. See also Gilbert Rozman, "Backdoor Japan: The Search for a Way Out via Regionalism and Decentralization", *The Journal of Japanese Studies* 25 (1), Winter 1999, pp. 3–31.
11. See Shaun Breslin, "Decentralisation, Globalization and China's Partial Re-engagement in the Global Economy", *New Political Economy* 5 (2), July 2000, pp. 205–226.
12. Author interview with Mr Susumu Yoshida, Director, Economic Research Institute for Northeast Asia, Niigata, 18 September 2002.
13. Author interview with a Niigata Prefecture official, 10 December 2001.
14. Author interview with a Niigata Prefecture official, 15 January 2002.
15. The information was provided by Niigata Prefecture's Department of Industry and Labor.
16. Author interview with a Chinese wife, who came from Shanghai, living in Urasa, a rural village of less than 10,000 people.
17. Niigata-ken Kokusai Koryu Ka (International Affairs Section, Niigata Prefecture), *Kokusai Koryu Gaiyo* [Digest of international exchange activities], Niigata: Niigata-ken Kokusai Koryu Ka, 2000, p. 36.

18. Author interview in Niigata, 15 February 2002.
19. Ichioka, *Jichitai Gaiko*, pp. 106–107.
20. See Gilbert Rozman, "Japan's Images of China in the 1990s: Are They Ready for China's 'Smile Diplomacy' or Bush's 'Strong Diplomacy'?", *Japanese Journal of Political Science* 2 (1), 2001, pp. 97–125.
21. At the time of the survey, there was a dispute over the import of Chinese farm products to Japan. The quoted statement may express the view that if more Chinese came to know the realities of farm life in Japan, it might become easier for them to accept Japan's recently instituted curbs on Chinese agricultural imports.
22. *Asahi Shimbum*, 27 September 2002, p. 9.
23. The results of the survey are posted on the ministry's home page at http://www.mofa. go.jp/mofaj/area/china/yoron.html.
24. Office of the Prime Minister, "Opinion Survey Regarding Foreign Workers", Item Number 3, available at http://www8.cao.go.jp/survey/gaikoku/3.html.
25. Ibid., Item Number 13, available at http://www8.cao.go.jp/survey/gaikoku/3.html.
26. For example, each year the Heilongjiang government and the Niigata Prefecture and Niigata City administrations send one official to the other, and this obviates the need for China-specific expertise among the other officials in the international departments, where the exchange personnel are assigned. Job rotation between administrative units in Niigata also works against the accumulation of China-specific knowledge in the international departments.
27. This point was brought up by a Chinese researcher, interviewed on 10 March 2002, who had lived in Niigata for 10 years.

6

Koreans in Japan and Shimane

Mika Merviö

The Korean community among Japanese ethnic minorities

The Korean community is the largest ethnic minority in Japan, and its history there is closely linked with Japanese imperialism. Uneasy relations between Japan and the two Korean states have overshadowed the life of Koreans in Japan. On the one hand, the Japanese authorities, and even the Japanese public, have expected ethnic minorities to assimilate and become invisible. On the other hand, inflexible policies related to naturalization and also exclusion and discrimination against foreigners have hit the Korean minority hardest.

The biggest wave of migration from Korea to Japan took place in the 1930s and 1940s when, under Japanese colonial rule, hundreds of thousands of Koreans were brought to Japan. After World War II, a large number of Koreans had to live there without Japanese citizenship, and faced various forms of discrimination. Nowadays, the Korean community is made up of people of various types of Korean identity. However, Japanese authorities and statistics usually treat as Korean both people of South Korean citizenship, called "Korean permanent residents", and "special permanent residents", those Koreans who have North Korean citizenship (which is not recognized by Japan) and refuse to take South Korean citizenship. The implication is that many people in Japan assume that ethnicity can appropriately be described in terms of citizenship and that those Koreans who are allowed to naturalize are assimilated and should be seen and treated as Japanese.

This attitude means that most Japanese are unable to relate to Korean people in terms of being Japanese with varying degrees of Korean cultural background (compare them to Japanese Americans) and an asset to Japanese society. This is regrettable because under the pressures of globalization, Japan badly needs people with multicultural backgrounds and intercultural skills. The South Koreans and older generations of Koreans in Japan often have problems in facing the reality of de facto Japanization of Koreans in Japan. The Korean community has to juggle conflicting expectations, and many individuals have developed skills enabling them to adopt and switch roles and be part of several communities: Japanese, Japanese Korean and Korean. However, as this chapter shows, an absence of support for Korean culture and multiculturalism is contributing to the assimilation of Koreans in Japan and with it a loss of Korean identity.

Demography and statistics

Together, the two Korean groups made up 82.6 per cent of all foreigners, excluding tourists, legally in Japan in 1982. Although the absolute number of permanent Korean residents has been relatively stable over the decades, the number of other foreigners has grown steadily. In 1993, Koreans represented 51.7 per cent of registered foreigners in Japan; but by the end of 2003, they were only 32.1 per cent. Age structure and naturalization have together caused a slow but steady decrease in the number of all (categories of) "Korean residents". Their number dropped from 688,144 in 1992 to 613,791 in 2003 while the total number of foreigners in Japan grew from 1,281,644 in 1992 to 1,915,030 in 2003.[1]

However, as mixed marriages with Japanese have become the mainstream pattern and as there are relatively high levels of naturalization, the number of people with Korean ancestry (those whose ancestors came to Japan after the end of the nineteenth century) is steadily increasing and is already above two million people. It is quite interesting that most Japanese researchers on ethnic issues are usually not interested in the issue of mixed cultural identities, although this is already the reality, especially with Japanese citizens of Korean ancestry. Instead, most Japanese research on Koreans in Japan deals exclusively with those with foreign citizenship. The term most often used with reference to Koreans in Japan is *Zainichi kankoku chosenjin*, meaning "South Korean (Kankoku) or North Korean (Chosen) residents" in Japan, but it does not differentiate between recent Korean immigrants and third- or fourth-generation residents born in Japan. The focus is on their legal status as "resident in Japan" rather than on their actual identity or culture.

As most Korean residents are born in Japan and "repatriation" largely stopped in the 1970s, it is quite natural that there are no big differences in the gender distribution of any age group. There are, however, some differences between Koreans and Japanese in Japan. First, there are fewer children (0–10 years old) among resident Koreans than among the Japanese population of the same age cohort. Second, the proportion of people 65 and older, especially women over 75, is larger among Korean residents than among Japanese or among other groups of resident foreigners. Third, there are somewhat larger numbers of Koreans in the 25 to 49 age bracket, owing to the recent immigration of working-age people from South Korea.[2]

In terms of regional distribution, Korean residents in Japan are heavily concentrated in a few larger cities. The Kansai region and, to some degree, Fukuoka Prefecture are where Korean residents outnumber all other "foreigners" and where their sheer number makes the Korean community visible. In Tokyo, where Koreans have a strong presence, they have recently been outnumbered by Chinese (112,208 to 101,389). The regional distribution of Korean residents largely reflects the distribution of settlement in the colonial period (1910–1945) and the availability of job opportunities. Korean communities in most rural areas have remained very small.

Community divisions

Koreans in Japan are an increasingly heterogeneous body of people. The community is divided roughly in half on the basis of its members' relationship to or attitude towards the two main Korean organizations in Japan, Mindan and Chongryun, discussed farther below in this section. The political division of the Korean peninsula has made it difficult for these organizations to cooperate on issues of common interest to the Korean community because Mindan has close relations with the South Korean government and Chongryun has strong links with the North Korean government. As for ordinary people, this fundamental split is for the most part "inherited" by families, and it has little to do with the original place of origin of Korean ancestors (some 98 per cent of the Koreans who came to Japan during the colonial period were from the present-day South). Mindan is the more popular organization now, but initially many Japanese Koreans did not want to join it because of the unpopularity of South Korean military governments and their close ties to the United States. The overwhelming majority of Koreans chose to be repatriated to Korea soon after World War II, and those who remained in Japan had various personal reasons for staying. The other reason why many did not join Mindan was that the Koreans most active in social issues before and during World War II espoused communist and socialist ideologies, and after the war they were in a better situation to organize themselves and defend the interests of the Korean community.

A further factor adding to the community's heterogeneity is that during the colonial years, some individuals earned reputations as collaborators. In the 1950s, North Korean propaganda against wartime collaborators and *yangban* (aristocracy) found fertile ground among Koreans in Japan. Chongryun used the stigma of collaboration against its political opponents, as most of its supporters came from working people, who often associated higher social status with collaboration. Mindan could not afford to show too much understanding for people who, for their misfortune, were perceived as former collaborators; and as a result, accusations related to real or perceived collaboration poisoned community relations among Koreans in Japan and even their descendants.

The most important factor in winning hearts for Chongryun has been its consistent policy of running Korean schools (now numbering about 150, from primary level to a university). In contrast, Mindan has just four schools. The Japanese government, for its part, has done very little to help minority education in Japan. On the other hand, a few local governments, usually under leftist or independent leaders, have given some support to Korean schools. After the war, the Americans were slow to decide whether Koreans in Japan should be treated as Japanese. The Japanese government did not see the Koreans as Japanese nationals. It claimed that Koreans residing in Japan were subject to Japanese law, including its provisions on compulsory education and curricula. However, Koreans wanted to have their own schools and were quick to establish them. Most Japanese authorities were against them from the beginning, and in 1949 about 350 Korean schools were closed while just three were approved by the Japanese Ministry of Education. Only after 1955 was Chongryun able to re-establish Korean schools and get them accredited by the Ministry of Education as miscellaneous schools.[3] But in places, especially Osaka Prefecture, where the authorities have sympathized with Korean educational aspirations, there have been so-called ethnic classes (*minzokugakkyu*) for Korean children after regular school hours and on a voluntary basis.[4] Nowadays, about 90 per cent of Korean children in Japan go to regular Japanese schools, and in most cases they hide, more or less effectively, their Korean background from their classmates.[5]

It is incorrect to hold Chongryun responsible for all the acts of the North Korean government. Most members of Chongryun probably have no idea of the secret operations of the North Korean government. Each time there is news about North Korean spy activities or the North's missile/nuclear programme, hate crimes against Chongryun Koreans surge; and most attackers escape without being arrested.

Chongryun is an umbrella organization that directs permanent Korean residents' educational, social, political and financial affairs. For many, there is no other organization that could fill its practical role in these areas, although this has decreased owing to its bad business decisions and waning ideological appeal. (Ideologically, it has faced the difficult task of applying the established North Korean dogma flexibly in a Japanese setting.) In the end, Chongryun has to compete with Mindan for support among the Korean community and cannot afford to alienate its supporters. It is functioning in a society that is fundamentally different from North Korea, and the only way for it to stay influential has been to remain useful to its supporters, particularly in its most important function of providing Korean-language education on a large scale.[6] But Chongryun schools are facing an economic crisis: there is a decreasing number of students as a result of demography and assimilation as well as increasing political pressure on it. Korean schools rely heavily on tuition fees (in the absence of state support), and recent increases in fees are likely to deal a further blow to attendance.

Mindan has successfully used its relations with the South Korean government and been able to work for gradual improvements in the legal status of Koreans in Japan. The ideological rigidity of Chongryun education has also alienated some Koreans from Chongryun and made them approach Mindan.[7] For ordinary people, the ideological basis of the community's division often has remarkably little to do with their own ideological convictions. As indicated above, people are simply born to either Mindan or Chongryun, and it is up to individuals how active they become in one organization or the other.

Assimilation

From the 1950s to the early 1980s, Japanese laws, regulations and practices regarding foreign nationals were aimed predominantly at dealing with the Korean community. However, this situation has changed with the arrival of relatively large numbers of immigrants, mostly from other Asian countries, and the so-called *Nikkeijin* (ethnic Japanese) from Latin America. However, the new immigrant groups have proved to be very different from each other, and especially from the Koreans. At the same time, the vast majority of Korean residents have been born and raised in Japan and been assimilated to such a degree that many of the control measures were clearly useless or counterproductive if assimilation were seen to be the main goal. Japanese policies towards the Korean community have always had two contradictory objectives: to facilitate total assimilation and to maintain control, which would be more difficult if Koreans were protected by the rights that come with Japanese citizenship.

With regard to keeping Koreans under control, one of the most persistent stereotypes in Japan about them is that they are likely to have some kind of semi-criminal background; this is because many of them work in so-called ethnic businesses of ill repute or have links with the North Korean government. One of the most important reasons why many Koreans have started businesses in these fields and why many Koreans continue to seek employment in them is continued discrimination against Koreans in the labour market. It is true that between 60 and 70 per cent of the approximately 20,000 *pachinko* (game) parlours in Japan are run by Koreans and that, as they are a significant source of income, their economic impact on the Korean community has been enormous. The other moneymaker for the Korean community in Japan is Korean barbecue (*yakiniku*) restaurants. But the problem is that Japanese people often fail to see that ethnic businesses would not be profitable without Japanese customers.[8] It is also the case that many Koreans have links with the North Korean government through Chongryun. The abduction issue and North Korea's missile and nuclear policies have increasingly caused Japanese people to view anything related to North Korea as questionable or worse. Therefore, any link with either North Korea or Chongryun has increasingly been interpreted in the worst possible light.

There are a few high-profile "success stories" of Koreans who have become rich or famous or both on the basis of their own talent. Very often they are active in the arts, literature or sports, all fields where individual merit is what counts. However, most of them go by their Japanese names/aliases, and their Korean identity is a subject of gossip magazines. Among the exceptional business achievers, the most notable case is Son Masayoshi, the Bill Gates of Japan. In politics, a Korean background has thus far been a major handicap because Korean residents cannot vote, and only two men with a (known) Korean background (Pak Ch'un-gum and Arai Shokei/Pak Kyong-jae) have been members of the Diet.[9] Positive success stories are important, because they challenge stereotypes and provide role models for young people. In the long term, it may be far more important that in recent decades there have been quite a few lawyers and academics among the Korean community. They have openly fought against all odds and secured a good education and professional status, using Japanese laws against the very system that created them.

Social life and marriage

The other big issue that increasingly divides the Korean community is attitudes towards mixed marriages, with Japanese people. Since the mid-1970s, a majority of marriages involving Koreans in Japan have been with Japanese citizens (some of whom are of Korean background); and in the 1990s, this kind of marriage reached well over 80 per cent. But a mixed marriage does not necessarily signify total assimilation, and it is a clear problem that Japanese society does not support bi- or multiculturalism. Even some Japanese Koreans turn their backs on people who live in mixed marriages.

The issue of mixed marriage is closely tied to the citizenship issue, because for most people of mixed Korean and Japanese parentage, it is practical to renounce their Korean citizenship when they have to decide about this at the age of 22. Keeping Korean citizenship would suddenly make them subject to various forms of discrimination. Aspects of identity such as status of citizenship, a Korean/Japanese surname and the use of aliases divide the Korean community. In addition, the Korean community experiences all the social divisions resulting from occupation, education, wealth and gender. Especially for the older generations, the cultural divisions between different provinces of what is South Korea have also been preserved. In all, these divisions make the social lives of Japanese Koreans very complicated.

Approximately 90 per cent of Japanese Koreans normally use their unofficial "Japanese names" or Japanese pronunciations of their names. When most Japanese Koreans learn early on to hide their true identity, it becomes difficult for them (especially outside the Chongryun community) to widen their social contacts with other Koreans. Therefore, most young Japanese Koreans hide their Korean identity in their daily lives and end up socializing mostly with Japanese people. In some areas of the Kansai region, there are so many people of Korean background that there is no point in hiding it. The concealment of one's "true" identity and the use of aliases are typical patterns of behaviour within the Korean community in Japan. Effectiveness in passing as Japanese in daily life has a particularly large impact on marriage prospects, as it is often difficult for Koreans to find eligible Korean partners. Revealing one's Korean identity also tests severely the depth of love in Japanese–Korean romances. However, the large number of mixed marriages testifies to the possibility of accepting Koreans as individuals in Japan and to the growing number of Japanese who are not readily deterred by discrimination and feudalistic conventions.[10]

As for marriages, statistics also reveal that from the early 1970s, marriages between Japanese men and Korean women have been far more commonplace than those between Japanese women and Korean men. The difference was the widest in 1990, but has since narrowed. In 1990 and 1995, mixed marriages involving Japanese and Korean citizens were 83.7 per cent and 82.2 per cent respectively of all mixed marriages in Japan. They consisted of marriages between Korean men and Japanese women (19.5 per cent and 31.7 per cent respectively) and Korean women and Japanese men (64.2 per cent and 50.5 per cent respectively). Immigration data show that the number of Koreans entering Japan as "the spouse of a Japanese national" in those two years was 578 and 916 people respectively. The overwhelming majority of these marriages are between Japanese men and Korean women.[11] This gender difference has many explanations, as both categories (Korean/Japanese citizens) are quite heterogeneous. For instance, some of the Japanese grooms and brides have Korean roots. Gender roles in both countries place different expectations on men and women, and there are gender-specific differences in the construction of ethnic identity, national stereotypes and nationalism. The result is that in mixed marriages in both countries, men and women prefer different nationalities when they select their spouses. Both traditional and modern introductory services and practices involving Korean residents in Japan are more effective in finding husbands for women. In some cases, the higher income levels in Japan have helped to make Japanese men more marketable. Available statistics reveal that Korean men who are permanent residents have significant problems in getting married, and this can be explained at least partly by the fact that the eldest son faces the strongest pressure not to marry outside the family's ethnic group.[12]

New migration

For many years, new migration from both Koreas to Japan was tightly controlled by all three governments. However, there was a new wave of migration from Korea to Japan after the South Korean government liberalized travel restrictions in 1988. The rise of the South Korean economy has been reflected by the number of Korean professionals living in Japan. On the other hand, South Koreans have been among the leading ethnic groups on the official list of "illegal immigrants" in Japan. For many South Koreans, Japan is a large and wealthy neighbour in which to work and study or to try their luck for a time. Most newcomers go to large cities with good employment and educational opportunities. Their situation is radically different from that of the vast majority of the ethnic Koreans who have been born and raised in Japan and have never had a realistic option of "going back" to Korea. In particular, the difference in the degree of assimilation into Japanese life affects relations between newcomers and Japan-born resident Koreans. In other words, these groups have little in common except exposure to Japanese discrimination. However, because of job discrimination, the Korean community in Japan has, as noted earlier, relied heavily for a long time on so-called ethnic businesses for employment; and these businesses have also provided employment for some newly arriving Koreans.

Students play a special role among new Korean migrants to Japan. As of the end of 2002, there were 110,415 foreigners with a student visa in Japan, and Koreans (15.5 per cent) were the second largest group of foreign students after the Chinese (66.8 per cent). The number of Korean students in Japan rose moderately, from 12,381 in 1998 to 17,091 in 2002, while the number of Chinese students more than doubled, from 32,370 to 73,795.[13] After completing their studies, South Korean students have more realistic prospects of finding work in Japan or South Korea and are therefore in a completely different situation from most long-term Korean residents in Japan.

In 2002, there were 1,472,096 registered new entrants to Japan of individuals with South Korean citizenship/place of birth. The total number of non-Japanese who newly entered the country was 5,771,975. This means that South Korea was number one on the list of citizenship/place of birth of people entering Japan, followed by Taiwan (with 909,654) and the United States (with 755,196). The number of tourists from Korea was 577,946 people. This number is relatively small in view of the short distance between the two countries, and is even smaller than that of Taiwanese tourists (735,526). However, in the short-term business visa category, South Koreans are in their own group, with 341,781 new visas, followed by US citizens (233,001). In the categories of short-term cultural/academic activities (18,683 visas) and short-term family visits (70,208 visas), South Koreans are also at the top of the list.[14]

There is also a relatively strong South Korean official and business presence in Japan. In the categories of education, engineering, entertainment and mixed marriages, South Koreans are well represented. All the same, immigration from South Korea to Japan is still tightly controlled, and new immigrants from South Korea are closely screened.[15]

The issue of nationality

Hostile relations between Japan and North Korea have created additional obstacles to improving the legal status of Koreans in Japan. The Japanese authorities have wanted to maintain strict control over all Koreans because of the perceived security risks instead of trying to see to the human, social and cultural rights of this large minority community. As citizenship is used as a tool of control, some authors describe Japanese citizenship practices, both formal rules and informal requirements such as changing the surname, as institutional or systemic discrimination.[16]

In 1965, Japan recognized South Korea diplomatically and concluded a peace treaty with it. Since then, those Japanese Koreans who have wanted to take South Korean citizenship have been treated as permanent residents, provided that they have lived in Japan since 1945 or have been born there. As the Japanese government does not recognize North Korea, it treats Chongryun Koreans as resident aliens, not as North Korean nationals. However, in recent decades it has gradually liberalized the granting of permanent residence on an "exceptional basis" to those Koreans who are not South Korean citizens. Japan's ratification of the International Covenant on Human Rights in 1979 was helpful in improving the situation of resident-alien Koreans. After these measures had settled the legal status of Koreans in Japan, there were by 1990 over 323,000 South Koreans who had been granted a permanent residence permit and 268,000 who had permanent residence on an exceptional basis.

In 1991, the foreign ministers of Japan and South Korea signed a memorandum aimed at reforming the Japanese Alien Registration Law and the Immigration Control and Refugee Recognition Act and changing those practices seen as discriminatory against Koreans in Japan and a source of friction in Japanese–Korean relations. The memorandum covered practical issues relating to immigration control, alien registration, education, the appointment of teachers in state schools and the appointment of permanent residents to public office.[17] It was followed by relatively rapid changes in legislation and even in the attitudes of Japanese civil servants.[18]

The impact of the 1991 memorandum extended to all Korean residents when, in 1992, all Korean permanent residents were made "special permanent residents". Moreover, fingerprinting, which is still used to register other foreigners, was abolished and re-entry permits for special permanent residents were made multiple and valid for a maximum time of five years. Despite these changes, a lack of understanding of Koreans' status still frequently causes discrimination, and a non-Japanese nationality is still widely used as an excuse for excluding Koreans from employment, education and business life.

Since the establishment of diplomatic relations with South Korea in 1965, Japan has had to take into consideration the wishes of the South Korean government on matters that affect the lives of Koreans in Japan with South Korean nationality. Early on, the military governments of South Korea were not in a good position to preach human rights to Japan. With the democratization of South Korean society, however, Japan increasingly had to worry about its public image in South Korea. Also, in Japan many people raised their voice against the more unreasonable practices that Koreans were subjected to.

Naturalization is a tempting option for some as a way to avoid various forms of discrimination. Since the 1990s, about 10,000 Koreans have changed their citizenship each year, and there are signs that the rate of naturalization will remain high for the foreseeable future. Japanese naturalization practices (not law) have emphasized the importance of selecting a Japanese name; and with a Japanese name and their outward appearance, most Japanese Koreans pass as Japanese.[19] The Japanese government's insistence upon maintaining the household registration (*koseki*) system adds weight to the rigid interpretation of nationality in Japan. *Koseki* excerpts are routinely used in Japan to check the background of people and to keep their privacy to a minimum. Because only Japanese nationals can have *koseki* registration, an inability to produce one has become the favourite method of employers and businesses to exclude foreigners from work.[20] In addition, the *koseki* excerpt includes information that has helped to maintain discrimination against other groups, such as *burakumin*.[21]

The possibility of extending voting rights to permanent residents as well as opening public jobs to them has been discussed widely in Japan. Many "progressive" prefectures have gradually opened more and more job categories to foreign job seekers. This largely means Korean permanent residents, because most of these jobs require native-speaker fluency in Japanese and a Japanese educational background. However, the central government has fought against this by interpreting the "exercise of public authority" in a narrow way. The most influential politicians within the Liberal Democratic Party have opposed the granting of voting rights to foreigners in any elections on the basis that foreigners should first become Japanese citizens if they want to vote. This argument has increased the pressure to make the naturalization process less complicated.[22]

Case study: Koreans in Shimane Prefecture

At the end of 2002, there were 1,071 registered Koreans living in Shimane Prefecture. They were the second-largest group of non-Japanese people there, after the Chinese (1,790), and were ahead of people with a Philippines passport (1,022).[23] The total population of Shimane in 2000 was 761,503; and with its relatively small number of Koreans and other foreigners, it may typify a predominantly rural prefecture in which the Korean community is not very visible.

The great majority of Shimane Koreans (720) live in the four largest cities (see table 6.1), and the only cities where Koreans are the largest ethnic minority are Masuda and Yasugi. There is no single place in the prefecture with a conspicuous Korean presence. Indeed, for many "ordi-

Table 6.1 The largest concentrations of Koreans in Shimane, 2001

Area name	Number of Koreans	Total number of residents (2000)
Matsue	276	153,616
Izumo	200	87,330
Hamada	134	47,187
Masuda	110	50,128
Yasugi	64	30,520
Gotsu	56	25,773
Oda	47	33,609
Mito	25	2,691
Yoshida	20	2,434

Source: Shimane Prefecture.

Table 6.2 Korean residents in Shimane, 1913–1990

Year	Number	Year	Number
1913	51	1947	6,138
1920	717	1950	5,828
1930	2,733	1960	4,007
1940	8,075	1970	1,555
1942	9,803	1980	1,270
End of war	c. 40,000	1990	1,326

Source: *Mo Hitotsu no Kokusaika. Zainichi Kankoku-Chosenjin no Mondai o Gozonjidesuka* [Another internationalization: Do you know about the issue of Korean residents?], Matsue: Shimaneken Somubu Kokusaika, Shimane Prefecture, 1997, pp. 1–3.

nary" Japanese the presence of Koreans goes largely unnoticed. There are quite a few towns and villages without one Korean resident. In this respect, Koreans are in a different situation from all other, larger groups of foreigners. First of all, they are the only group of foreign citizens whose number has steadily decreased in the post-war era, in contrast, for instance, to the Brazilians, who are true newcomers and stand out by concentrating in just two locations and working for a small number of relatively large enterprises in Shimane.

After World War II, most Koreans left Shimane, as is shown in table 6.2. The number of those who remained continued to decline until the early 1970s, when it began to stabilize. (In the post-war period, the Japanese population of Shimane has also been in steady decline, and many young Japanese have sought jobs and education outside the prefecture.) As the Kansai region is relatively close by, it is only natural that some Shimane Koreans have moved there. Koreans in Shimane have moved for jobs to cities (in the prefecture and elsewhere) where employment is

Table 6.3 Shimane Korean respondents to 1996 survey

Age	20s	30s	40s	50s	60s	70s	Total
Registered Koreans	164	202	240	153	110	129	998
Returned replies	41	44	48	45	43	40	261
Percentage	25.0	21.8	20.0	29.4	39.1	31.0	26.2

Source: *Mo Hitotsu no Kokusaika. Zainichi Kankoku-Chosenjin no Mondai o Gozonjidesuka*, p. 5.

provided by Korean ethnic businesses such as restaurants, *pachinko* parlours, construction and used goods.[24] In short, Koreans in Shimane have major problems in finding employment outside the ethnic community; and if they do find it, they are likely to move outside the prefecture.

As for the ancestral origins of the Koreans in Shimane, the list in 1996 of Shimane Korean families by Korean province was as follows: Kyongsangnam-do: 586 people, 45.7 per cent; Kyongsangbuk-do: 402 people, 31.4 per cent; Chollanam-do: 93 people, 7.2 per cent; Pusan City: 46 people, 3.6 per cent; and others: 155 people, 12.1 per cent.[25]

The two south-eastern provinces of South Korea, with the city of Pusan next to them, are the origin of some 80 per cent of the Koreans in Shimane. This geographical origin, together with a shared interest in the Tokdo–Takeshima territorial dispute between Japan and Korea, has been one of the main reasons why Shimane has selected Kyongsangbuk-do as its sister prefecture/province. On the Korean side, Tokdo belongs to the County of Ullungdo Island, which is part of Kyongsangbuk-do; on the Japanese side, the same islands are under the jurisdiction of the Oki Islands, which are part of Shimane Prefecture. This political relationship is the most significant and active direct foreign official relationship that Shimane Prefecture has.[26]

The International Section of Shimane Prefecture's General Affairs Office has conducted, in cooperation with local organizations representing both sides (Mindan and Chongryun) of the Korean community, a survey to find out the basic distinctive life patterns of the Korean community in Shimane. Questionnaires were distributed by mail to all Korean residents (above the age of 20) twice, in February 1991 and February 1996. (On the respondents to the latter survey, see table 6.3.)

In addition, the same office conducted in 2000 a general survey of all foreigners in Shimane, sending a questionnaire to 4,728 foreigners. The return rate was 1,244 (26.3 per cent), of whom 234 were Korean residents, representing 18.8 per cent of all respondents.[27]

The Korean community is relatively small, and respondents would have had good reason to refrain from answering if they felt that it would be difficult to protect their anonymity. The reasons why so many did not return their questionnaire are not clear. The main difference between the 1991 and 1996 surveys and the 2000 survey was that the latter was mostly concerned about whether respondents had problems with the Japanese language or with using various public services. By contrast, the survey of Koreans asked questions that were more substantive and were sensitive for Shimane Koreans. Shimane Prefecture issued a publication in 2002 that tells the history of Koreans in Japan and Shimane and shows the results of the survey of 1991 and 1996. It adds examples of situations involving Shimane Koreans.[28]

Migration

Of the 998 respondents, 58 per cent were born outside Shimane, 84 of them in other parts of Japan and 67 in Korea. Among the post-war generation (people below 40), there was a large gender difference: 60 per cent of the women were born outside Shimane and 35 per cent in Korea; of the men, only 23 per cent were born outside Shimane and just one was born in Korea. As we know that the Korean population in Japan decreased rapidly from the 1950s to the 1970s, it seems that at the same time as many Koreans were leaving Shimane, other ethnic Koreans were coming in; and women were a majority of the newcomers. Most new migrants who came to Shimane from Korea were also women.

Marriage

Table 6.4 shows a very strong tendency among Shimane Koreans to choose their marriage partners from within their own ethnic community. This finding contrasts with the overwhelming tendency among younger

Table 6.4 Marital status of Koreans in Shimane (%)

	1991 survey*	1996 survey
Married to other Koreans	88.7	82.4
Married to Koreans with Japanese citizenship	0.4	1.9
Married to ethnic Japanese	9.9	13.9
Other	–	0.5
Not known	1.1	1.4
Total married	84.0	82.7
Total unmarried	14.1	16.9
Total not known	1.8	0.4

Source: Mo Hitotsu no Kokusaika. Zainichi Kankoku-Chosenjin no Mondai o Gozonjidesuka, p. 6.
* The figures in this column have been rounded to the closest decimal.

Japanese Koreans to marry Japanese citizens, a decades-long tendency among resident Koreans in the rest of the country. However, the difference between the 1991 and the 1996 surveys indicates that Shimane is rapidly moving in the same direction as the rest of the country. Among the youngest age group (people in their 20s), mixed marriages had reached 57 per cent; and among those in their 30s, 36 per cent had a non-Korean spouse. In interpreting these results, we have to keep in mind that Korean organizations were consulted when the survey was planned; and it is possible that among the 26.2 per cent of the Koreans in Shimane in 1996 who replied, those active in Korean organizations and having a strong Korean identity were over-represented.

Education

In the 1996 survey, the respondents were asked what schools they had attended or were attending (see table 6.5).

There is a strong tendency towards a rising degree of education among the ethnic Koreans in Shimane. This reflects a general trend among Koreans in Japan, to the extent that the general educational level of the survey respondents is very close to the national averages in all three stages of education.[29] As for so-called ethnic education, the respondents included a relatively large number of people who had attended Korean

Table 6.5 Educational background of Koreans in Shimane, 1996

Educational level	Number
Secondary school (%)	27.4
Korean ethnic school	3
Japanese schools	43
School in Korea	12
High school (%)	50.0
Korean ethnic school	21
Japanese schools	72
School in Korea	13
University (%)	22.2
Korean ethnic school	14
Japanese schools	31
School in Korea	3
Total	212
Korean ethnic school	38
Japanese schools	146
School in Korea	28

Source: Mo Hitotsu no Kokusaika. Zainichi Kankoku-Chosenjin no Mondai o Gozonjidesuka, p. 7.

Table 6.6 Respondents' facility in Korean language (%)

	1991 survey	1996 survey
Know well	27.6	28.7
Know somewhat	21.2	15.3
Know basic vocabulary	26.1	29.1
Do not know	22.4	26.8

Source: Mo Hitotsu no Kokusaika. Zainichi Kankoku-Chosenjin no Mondai o Gozonjidesuka, p. 8.

ethnic schools and even Korea University graduates. On the other hand, educational opportunities in the prefecture have been limited; and even among the Japanese population, there has been a strong pattern of moving out of the prefecture for higher education or for better employment. As for the educational "elite" among Shimane Koreans, there are very few people who have come from Korea with university degrees. This is understandable, as there have been and are limited employment opportunities in Shimane for first-generation Koreans with a professional background. Also, the relatively large number of Korea University graduates is explained by the existence of a Korean school in Matsue.

Language

In the two surveys, the respondents were asked as well about their use of and facility in the Korean language (see table 6.6).

The proportion of respondents who said that they spoke Korean often at home was 18 per cent. Those who spoke Japanese often amounted to 60 per cent and those who spoke only Japanese at home came to 22 per cent. Over 80 per cent stated that they communicated mostly in Japanese. Knowledge of Korean among Shimane Koreans seemed to be fairly good compared to trends among Koreans throughout Japan. However, the use of Korean seems to correlate strongly with attendance of ethnic schools. Few parents seem to teach Korean systematically to their children, who attend Japanese schools, or otherwise make an effort to help them to become bilingual. If the current trend continues, it is likely that the number of Koreans who do not know even the basics of their "mother language" will increase rapidly. As for the terms bokokugo (mother tongue) and kokugo (national language, i.e. Japanese) and wagakuni (our country), which are used widely in Japan, numerous Koreans have pointed out that in many schools, Korean students have been corrected/failed if they have replaced these nationalistic terms by more neutral ones, such as nihongo (Japanese) or nihon (Japan).

Table 6.7 Respondents' practice of Korean customs at home (%)

	1991 survey	1996 survey
Cuisine	92.3	91.6
Ethnic clothing	88.7	82.8
Festival/rituals	77.6	69.7
Wedding rituals	67.2	58.2
Books, records	58.9	49.0
Nothing	6.1	1.1

Source: Mo Hitotsu no Kokusaika. Zainichi Kankoku-Chosenjin no Mondai o Gozonjidesuka, p. 8.

Table 6.8 Awareness of respondents' Korean ethnic background among co-workers and neighbours (%), 1996

	Co-workers	Neighbours
All know	63.6	71.6
Some know	20.3	22.6
No one knows	1.1	1.1
Do not know	3.1	4.2
Unclear	11.9	0.4

Source: Mo Hitotsu no Kokusaika. Zainichi Kankoku-Chosenjin no Mondai o Gozonjidesuka, p. 10.

Korean customs at home

Table 6.7 shows the extent of the practice of Korean customs at home. The great majority of Koreans in Shimane keep at least some Korean customs alive. However, even in the short period between 1991 and 1996, there was a clear pattern of declining observance, although at the same time those who claimed that they did not observe any Korean customs had virtually disappeared. Since the 1990s, there has indeed been a greater popular acceptance of some aspects of Korean culture in Japan, such as food and popular culture.

Relations with Japanese

The 1996 survey asked the respondents if their co-workers and neighbours knew about their Korean ethnic background (see table 6.8). It also asked about their use of a Japanese alias (see table 6.9).

These figures reveal a strong tendency among Shimane Koreans to have a Japanese alias. They recognize that most acquaintances know that they are Korean but they still use their unofficial Japanese name widely.

Table 6.9 Shimane Koreans' use of Japanese aliases (%)

	1991 survey	1996 survey
People who have a Japanese alias	84.7	82.0
Using only official (Korean) name	2.2	5.1
Using official (Korean) name often	9.8	9.3
Using both about the same	18.8	15.4
Using Japanese alias often	35.1	22.9
Using mostly Japanese alias	26.1	40.2
Unclear	8.0	7.0
People who do not have a Japanese alias	10.1	10.3
People who previously had a Japanese alias	4.6	6.9
Unclear	0.6	0.8

Source: Mo Hitotsu no Kokusaika. Zainichi Kankoku-Chosenjin no Mondai o Gozonjidesuka, p. 10.

As for the reasons for this practice, the most popular answer was "no reason at all".

In recent years, there has been a campaign among the Japanese Korean community to get rid of Japanese aliases and start using Korean names; and especially for younger Koreans, the decision to start using their real name signifies "coming out" and letting others know about their Korean background. Some naturalized Koreans have been able to restore their original Korean name after a long legal battle. However, in rural Shimane, there is less point in trying to hide one's Korean identity. The inability of respondents to give clear reasons for their use of aliases may indicate that there is less bitterness there about this practice than among Koreans in some other areas of the country. The use of Japanese names among Koreans goes back to the days of Japanese colonial rule when Koreans were forced to use Japanese names. Koreans as individuals can avoid discrimination if they use Japanese names. Also, some Japanese employers still require their Korean personnel to use Japanese aliases, because they do not want their customers to know that they have employed Koreans. Moreover, the use of aliases often goes in families; and once a family starts to use a Japanese name, it is difficult to discontinue its use.

Japanese friends

As for socializing with Japanese, 24.1 per cent of respondents to the 1996 survey said that they had many Japanese friends, 55.2 per cent indicated that they had some Japanese friends and 20.3 per cent said that they had no Japanese friends. The most important factor in explaining these findings is attendance at ethnic Korean schools. Forty per cent of those who had attended ethnic schools said that they had no Japanese friends. This pattern has also been documented in many other studies conducted elsewhere in Japan.[30] Those students who attend ethnic Korean schools tend to have few close contacts with Japanese people. In addition, all Korea University students live on campus, and the most realistic employment opportunity for many of them is to become a teacher at an ethnic Korean school.

Experiences of discrimination

Discrimination is experienced in public administration (according to 25.7 per cent of the respondents), working life (18.8 per cent), neighbourhoods (16.1 per cent), school education (26.4 per cent), marriage (8.0 per cent) and "other" (8.8 per cent). It is remarkable that so few people complained about public sector discrimination, because many state policies are highly discriminatory against Koreans. However, many respondents probably interpreted the question to mean whether they personally had been harassed in a particularly cruel manner. The highest rate of discrimination was recorded in education, and this apparently reflects the Japanese school system's inability to tolerate differences and control rampant bullying among pupils.

The future

The 1991 and 1996 surveys both asked about respondents' future plans (see table 6.10).

The choices presented in table 6.10 are based on the present situation concerning citizenship status laws and the political, economic and social situation in Japan, South Korea and North Korea. However, it is clear that most Shimane Koreans are so deeply assimilated that they would have few prospects in any future Korea. The limited job opportunities in Shimane make it unlikely that there will be a significant new influx of

Table 6.10 Shimane Koreans' plans (%)

	1991 survey	1996 survey
Want to return to mother country	5.5	7.3
Continue to have resident Korean status	66.3	57.5
Naturalization	17.2	23.0
Other	7.7	6.9
Unclear	3.4	5.4

Source: Mo Hitotsu no Kokusaika. Zainichi Kankoku-Chosenjin no Mondai o Gozonjidesuka, pp. 8 and 14.

people of Korean background. On the contrary, it is likely that many younger Koreans will leave Shimane to find better job and educational opportunities.

Conclusions

Naturalization and assimilation will undoubtedly be the destiny of many Korean people in Japan, and the Korean community will become even less visible while other minority groups grow in size. Most permanent Korean residents can be seen as "culturally Japanese", and their needs are modest – quite different from those of most other (more recent) groups of immigrants in Japan.

The most urgent task is to eradicate all forms of discrimination and pave the way for a culturally more diverse and tolerant Japanese society. If Japan does not find ways to deal with a minority group that is largely monolingual in Japanese and physically indistinguishable from Japanese, then there is little hope for its successful globalization. There is a need to rethink how the legal status of permanent resident Koreans could better reflect the special and changing circumstances of their life in Japan and how the Japanese government and the international community could protect their rights, including cultural rights.

The establishment of dual citizenship would be a good start, and this would require close coordination between the Japanese and South Korean governments. The most important issue concerning Korean cultural rights is the future of Korean schools in Japan. By denying support to Korean cultural rights and to education in the Korean language, the Japanese authorities have divided the Korean community between those who try to minimize discrimination and gradually (and often grudgingly) assimilate and the Chongryun-led camp, which has actively resisted Japanese cultural influence. The Japanese authorities should realize that bad treatment of Koreans in Japan is the main reason why even among third- and fourth-generation Japan-born Koreans there is much support for North Korea. They should recognize too that it would be in the interest of Japanese society to make the Korean community feel that the Japanese government takes into account their interests and concerns as well.

New immigration from Korea is limited, and only a major political change could open the borders for significantly larger numbers of Koreans to settle in Japan. Real political leadership and vision is required to push through a free trade agreement (FTA) between Japan and South Korea, which would provide also for the free movement of people. An FTA would serve well the political and economic interests of both countries, and could demonstrate the virtues of multiculturalism in each society and the broader region of Northeast Asia. However, successful implementation of this scheme would require changes in both states' legislation and administrative practices, especially in the fields of immigration and the protection of human rights.

Notes

1. See Tani Tomio, "Zainichi Kankoku-Chosenjin Shakai no Genzai" ["The current situation of Koreans in Japan"], in Tanaka Hiroshi, ed., *Teijukasuru Gaikokujin* [Foreign permanent residents], Tokyo: Asahi Shoten, 1995, p. 137 and the Japanese Ministry of Justice statistics for the 1990s (under the heading "Heisei 15-nen Matsu Genzai ni okeru Gaikokujin Torokusha Tokei ni tsuite" ["On statistics of alien registration as of end of 2003"]), available at ⟨http://www.moj.go.jp/PRESS/040611-1/040611-1.html⟩ (accessed 7 July 2004).
2. See the Japanese Ministry of Justice, "Heisei 13-nen Matsu Genzai ni okeru Gaikokujin Torokusha Tokei ni tsuite, shiryo 2-1" ["On statistics of alien registration as of end of 2001, data 2–1"], available at ⟨http://www.moj.go.jp/PRESS/020611-1/020611-1-10.html⟩ (accessed 7 July 2004).
3. Inokuchi Hiromitsu, "Korean Ethnic Schools in Occupied Japan", in Sonia Ryang, ed., *Koreans in Japan: Critical Voices from the Margin*, London and New York: Routledge, 2000, pp. 140–156.
4. See, for example, Jeffry T. Hester, "Kids between Nations: Ethnic Classes in the Construction of Korean Identities in Japanese Public Schools" in ibid., pp. 175–196.
5. See Aoki Eriko, "Textbooks and Educational Practices", in ibid., pp. 157–160.
6. Ri Worusun, "Zainichi Chosenjin no Minzoku Kyoiku" ["Ethnic education of Korean residents in Japan"], in Paku Chonmyon, ed., *Zainichi Chosenjin* [Korean residents in Japan], 2nd rev. edn, Tokyo: Akashi Shoten, 1999, pp. 135–173.
7. For more on Chongryun education, see "History and Current State of Ethnic Education By Korean People in Japan", available at ⟨http://210.145.168.243/pk/⟩ (accessed 20 July 2004). The site is part of the Japanese-, English- and Korean-language North Korea–Chongryun homepage based in Tokyo, available at ⟨http://www.korea-np.co.jp/main/main.aspx⟩ (accessed 20 July 2004). See also Sonia Ryang, *North Koreans in Japan: Language, Ideology, and Identity*, Boulder and Oxford: Westview Press, 1997, pp. 23–67.
8. Kim Choru'un, "Zainichi Chosenjin no Keizai Mondai" ["The economic problems of Korean residents in Japan"], in Chonmyon, ed., *Zainichi Chosenjin*, pp. 101–134. For information on *pachinko* parlours, see pp. 123–125.
9. George Hicks, *Japan's Hidden Apartheid: The Korean Minority and the Japanese*, Aldershot: Ashgate, 1997, pp. 102–104 and "Editorial: Arai's Death Must Not Hinder Reform: 6", *Daily Yomiuri*, 21 February 1998.
10. For more on the issue of marriage, see Nakao Hiroshi, *Zainichi Kankoku Chosenjin Mondai no Kisochishiki* [Korean residents in Japan: Basic knowledge about the issue of Koreans] Tokyo: Akashi Shoten, 1997, pp. 49–56; Kim Chan-jung (Kimu Chanjon), *Zainichi to iu Kando* [Ostracism called zainichi], Tokyo: Sangokan, 1994, pp. 114–132; Hicks, *Japan's Hidden Apartheid*, pp. 107–110; Fukuoka Yasunori, *Zainichi Kankoku Chosenjin: Wakai Sedai no Aidentiti* [Korean residents in Japan: Identity of young generations of Koreans], Tokyo: Chuokoronsha, 1993; Fukuoka Yasunori, *Lives of Young Koreans in Japan*, Melbourne: Trans Pacific Press, 2000; and Kanai Yasuo, *Zainichi Korian Nisei-Sansei no Genzai – 13 Yureru Omoi* [The current situation of second- and third-generation Korean residents in Japan: 13 cases of anxieties], Tokyo: Bakushusha, 1997.

11. Fukuoka Yasunori, *Lives of Young Koreans in Japan*, pp. 35–37.
12. Ibid., pp. 37–38.
13. Japanese Ministry of Justice, "Heisei 13-nen Matsu Genzai ni okeru Gaikokujin Toroku-sha Tokei ni tsuite" ["On statistics of alien registration as of end of 2001"], available at ⟨http://www.moj.go.jp/PRESS/020611-1/020611-1-6.html⟩ (accessed 7 July 2004).
14. All statistics are as of the end of 2001. See Japanese Ministry of Justice, "Dai 5-hyo" ["Table 5"] available at ⟨http://www.moj.go.jp/PRESS/020322-2/table05.html, http://www.moj.go.jp/PRESS/020322-2/table05-01.html, http://www.moj.go.jp/PRESS/020322-2/table05-02.html and http://www.moj.go.jp/PRESS/020322-2/table05-03.html⟩ (accessed 7 July 2004).
15. Idem.
16. See, for example, Sorano Yoshihiro and Ko Chan-yu, *Zainichi Chosenjin no Seikatsu to Jinken* [The life and rights of Korean residents in Japan], Tokyo: Akashi Shoten, 1995, pp. 71–105.
17. Hicks, *Japan's Hidden Apartheid*, pp. 59–61.
18. Ryang, ed., *North Koreans in Japan*, p. 126.
19. For naturalization, see Chikako Kashiwazaki, "The Politics of Legal Status", in Ryang, ed., *Koreans in Japan*, pp. 26–29.
20. For examples of widespread company practices of making hiring and even golf club membership subject to *koseki* excerpts, see Hicks, *Japan's Hidden Apartheid*, pp. 120–126.
21. Editors' note: during the Tokugawa period (from the seventeenth century to the mid-nineteenth century), *burakumin* were associated with defiling occupations, such as burying the dead and tanning animal hides, considered offensive in Shinto and Buddhist belief systems.
22. On the issue of extending voting rights to Koreans, see Paku Kanhon, "Zainichi Chosenjin no Sanseiken Mondai" ["The issue of the right of Korean residents in Japan to participate in politics"], in Chonmyon, ed., *Zainichi Chosenjin*, pp. 213–243; Nakao, *Zainichi Kankoku*, pp. 65–68; and Hicks, *Japan's Hidden Apartheid*, pp. 98–104.
23. Unless otherwise noted, the statistics in this section are from unpublished Shimane Prefecture statistics.
24. *Mo Hitotsu no Kokusaika. Zainichi Kankoku-Chosenjin no Mondai o Gozonjidesuka* [Another internationalization: Do you know about the issue of Korean residents?], Matsue: Shimaneken Somubu Kokusaika, Shimane Prefecture, 1997, p. 3.
25. The list includes all Korean provinces (both contemporary South and North). *Mo Hitotsu no Kokusaika*, p. 4.
26. For details, see *Shimaneken no Kokusaika no Genjo* [The present situation of Shimane Prefecture's internationalization], Matsue: Shimaneken Somubu Kokusaika, Shimane Prefecture, 2002, pp. 5–21.
27. *Shimaneken Zaijugaikokujin Jittai Chosa* [Survey of the situation of foreign residents in Shimane Prefecture], Matsue: Shimaneken Somubu Kokusaika, Shimane Prefecture, 2001, pp. 6–7.
28. *Tabunka Kyoseishakai no Tame ni: Zainichi Kankoku-Chosenjin Anketo Chosa kara* [For multicultural coexistence: From a questionnaire survey of Korean residents in Japan], Matsue: Shimaneken Somubu Kokusaika, Shimane Prefecture, 2002. Pages 1–7 include a general introduction; the survey results are explained on pages 7–35.
29. For the rates of advancement in the Japanese school system from elementary school to university level, see Japanese Ministry of Education, Culture, Sports, Science and Technology, "Expanding School Education", available at ⟨http://www.mext.go.jp/english/statist/xls/012/xls⟩ (Excel file, accessed 20 July 2004).
30. See Ryang, *North Koreans in Japan*; Fukuoka, *Zainichi Kankoku Chosenjin*; and Fukuoka, *Lives of Young Koreans in Japan*.

Part IV

Migration issues in the Korean peninsula and Mongolia

7

North Koreans in China: Sorting fact from fiction

Hazel Smith

The presence of North Korean migrants in China has become a source of international political controversy even though very little knowledge is available as to the number involved, the migrants' reasons for migrating, their conditions and patterns of living in China and the outcomes for individuals and their families of their choice to migrate.[1] Instead, largely unfounded speculation has substituted for factual analysis and sober research, with the serious consequence that the policies of major countries, including the United States, are being based on hearsay, exaggeration and heavily skewed ideological agendas.

The purpose of this chapter is to set out what is known about the illegal migration of citizens of the Democratic People's Republic of Korea (DPRK) to China, to identify research lacunae, to suggest ways in which knowledge of this issue can be improved and to offer some policy options for states which are responsible for responding to the needs of those North Koreans living precarious and poverty-stricken existences in China. I do not deal specifically with the interests, agendas and activities of foreign governmental and non-governmental actors involved with North Korean migration to China except insofar as it is necessary to analyse or to illustrate the primary subject of this research. Such research and analysis is crucial in order to provide a full understanding of the internal and external dynamics of North Korean migration to China, but would warrant a lengthy investigation.

In the chapter, I first clarify the term "migrants" and identify the demographic and geographical context in which illegal North Korean migration to China takes place. Then I discuss five research problems and their attendant policy dilemmas. These are the pattern of migration and the number of migrants; the legal status of North Koreans in China; the different geographical origins of North Korean migrants; the conditions in which North Koreans live in China; and the nature of current assistance to North Koreans in China.

Of the five research problems, some have been fairly well covered in reputable literature, including the better journalistic accounts. Much of the available data and analysis on North Koreans in China, however, has been selectively filtered and disseminated in such a way as to support pre-existing ideological and policy biases, of whatever political hue. Not all this selection or filtering of facts has come about because of attempts to wilfully distort evidence. Sometimes, distortion occurs because those doing the analysis and reporting have relatively little understanding or experience of what it means to undertake (social) scientific research. Small interviewing samples undertaken by advocacy groups, for instance, are regularly used to make huge generalizations about North Koreans in China that simply cannot be sustained by the size of the sample or the interview methods. On the other hand, some groups do deliberately distort evidence, knowing that an oversimplified story makes for better press than an account that might reflect complexity and be more difficult to convey in sound bites to those abroad who are not familiar with North Korea or China.

Much more systematic research needs to take place before we can obtain a clear map of what is happening to North Korean migrants in China. This chapter is therefore deliberately written as a "research report": it attempts to chart what is reliable knowledge and what is not in respect of North Koreans in China. On the other hand, it also offers policy recommendations. We know enough already to be able to provide a basis for appropriate and realistic policy recommendations to those governments whose job it is to make and implement policy towards North Koreans in China. My own personal preference is in favour of policies that rapidly respond in a humane way to relieve the severe human insecurity experienced by many North Koreans in China today.

Terminology and politics

Terminology is never neutral; and in respect of North Koreans in China it is part of what is contested, because it reflects competing claims about migrants' legal status and the responsibilities of international organizations and governments. For the purposes of this chapter, I use the term "migrants" to categorize all citizens of the DPRK who have settled in

China. The use of this term is not an implicit judgement of the legal status of North Koreans living in China.

Koreans in China

Illegal migrants from the DPRK are not the only Koreans living in China.[2] There are around 2.2 million ethnic Koreans of Chinese nationality, of which some 854,000 live in the Korean Autonomous Region of Yanbian (referred to below as Yanbian), situated in Jilin Province in the far north-east of China.[3] Koreans in China are a tiny fraction of the total Chinese population, and the South Korean National Office of Statistics expects the number of Koreans in China to become even smaller as they disperse throughout China, intermarry with ethnic Chinese and migrate, some to South Korea.[4] Some citizens of the DPRK and the Republic of Korea (ROK) are also legally resident in China, in Beijing and other areas, particularly north-eastern China, for a number of reasons. Legal DPRK residents include diplomats, students and traders.[5] The largest concentration of Koreans is in Yanji City, the capital of Yanbian, whose total population is around 350,000; and approximately 210,000 are ethnic Koreans.[6]

Yanbian

Yanbian borders Russia and two of North Korea's provinces, North Hamgyong and Ryanggang. It is part of the Changbai mountain area, a major tourist attraction for Chinese and South Koreans. The region's main industries are agriculture, forestry, coal mining and power, and it is a hub for transportation to Russia and Japan. The local airport, in Yanji City, has frequent flights to Seoul as well as domestic connections. Yanbian residents are highly educated, with the rate of college education twice as high as for the whole of China.[7] The area's dynamism is fueled by South Korean investment, to the extent that Yanbian has sometimes been called "the South's Guangdong".[8] The shops are full of South Korean goods, and South Koreans invest in hotels, food processing and skills-training and run a university, the Yanbian University of Science and Technology.[9]

The pattern of migration and the number of migrants

China and the DPRK are divided by a long and porous border demarcated by the Yalu and Tumen rivers. The two most important official border crossing points are at Sinuiju in the west, in the North Korean province of North Pyongan, which faces Dandong in the Chinese province of

Liaoning and at Onsong County in the east, in the DPRK province of North Hamgyong, which faces Tumen in the prefecture of Yanbian. Hyesan, in the North Korean province of Ryanggang and midway between Sinuiju and Onsong County, provides another regular exit point into China. (See fig. 7.1 for DPRK provincial borders.)

The length of the border, about 1,000 miles, and its topography and demography make it easy to cross without official authorization. The border region is mountainous, forested and sparsely populated. It is relatively straightforward for North Koreans to cross at narrow sections of the river, especially in the winter when the temperature is as low as minus 40 degrees centigrade, the river freezes and it is possible to walk across.[10] Both sides of the border are non-militarized. There is a noticeable dearth of armed guards, barbed wire, sentry posts and lookout points.[11]

The pattern of migration

The most credible research on North Korean migrants in China, the results of which were published in the internationally respected medical

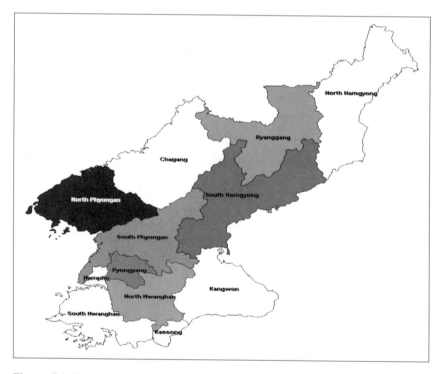

Figure 7.1 Map of DPRK provincial boundaries (*Sources*: UNOCHA, Pyong-yang, 1998.)

research journal *The Lancet*, reports that "Migrations into China can be characterized typically as short-term movements by a single member of a household whose other members remained in North Korea."[12] This conclusion resulted from a systematic survey of North Koreans in China carried out by the authors of the *Lancet* article between March and September 1998, towards the end of the worst of the food crisis in the DPRK. The findings of this survey, that most North Koreans spent only a few days in China before returning home, were reinforced by researchers from Yongnam University in the ROK, who also conducted fieldwork along the border in 1998.[13] These survey results confirm the pattern of North Korean migration into China as that of individuals crossing the Chinese border along the Yalu and Tumen rivers at different times of the year and for differing lengths of time. Some received authorization to leave and re-enter the DPRK and others crossed the border without papers.

The numbers game

There are great difficulties in quantifying the number of those who have made illegal cross-border journeys or how many times they have made these journeys. Because the pattern of migration is based on short-term stays and because individuals may come and go several times, particularly if they live in a North Korean border county and have relatives in China, it is almost impossible to calculate the number of North Korean migrants living in China at a particular time. It is also difficult to assess how this figure has changed over time. Neither the DPRK and China nor any organization publishes figures of cross-border journeys, the number of individuals involved or the number of North Koreans illegally resident in China. More importantly, neither China nor the DPRK has the means of collecting these figures, as, by definition, these migrants travel and live clandestinely and avoid contact with state authorities. Chinese and North Korean authorities would have figures for those North Koreans who are sent back to the DPRK, but they are not published.[14] Journalists and scholars have not systematically quantified the number of illegal North Korean migrants in China.

Estimates of the number of North Koreans living illegally in China, including those disseminated by journalists and scholars, come almost entirely from organizations that provide humanitarian aid to North Koreans or act as advocates for them or from religious and political groups. Those working directly with North Koreans in China tend to be the most muted in their public statements, as their aim is to be able to continue with humanitarian or faith-based organizational work on the ground. Their experience is that international media attention causes constraints to be placed on their work and a tightening by Chinese and DPRK authorities such as to make life more difficult for North Koreans in China. These organizations are less likely to provide frequent statements to the media than are foreign-based groups such as the human rights groups based in the United States and South Korea. They, by definition, are much more detached from the local environment than locally based organizations that work on a daily basis with North Korean migrants. The organizations based outside China are thus a main source of figures for the number of North Korean migrants in China that are circulated in the international media.

A March 2001 *Newsweek International* report cites "an estimated 300,000 [North Korean] refugees scattered across northeast China".[15] An April 2002 news report mentions unspecified "aid agencies" giving figures of "between 100,000 and 300,000 North Koreans hiding in China's northeastern borders".[16] Another, unsourced, report published in 2002 states that the number could be between 100,000 and 200,000.[17]

In August 2001, the Committee on International Relations of the US House of Representatives passed a resolution that included a reference to estimates of 100,000 to 300,000 North Koreans resident in China "without the permission of the government of China".[18] These figures were given "official" international status as reasonable estimates through their promulgation by a US government agency, although staffers and researchers for Congress had no research available to them on which these figures could have been based.

Congressional committees relied on highly partisan and politicized organizations, some with strong anti-communist and Christian fundamentalist agendas, as sources of information and figures that eventually were published as part of various Congressional resolutions.[19] At a May 2002 Congressional hearing, for instance, two of the four persons invited to give testimony were sponsored by an American foundation called the Hudson Institute and one represented Médecins sans Frontières, an organization that had last had personnel in the DPRK in 1998. Only one, John Powell of the World Food Program, represented an organization that had worked throughout the DPRK for a considerable length of time and had accrued systematic knowledge of the country. This knowledge was based on, among other things, around 500 visits a month to beneficiaries and institutions throughout the country, satellite photography and literally thousands of reports and analyses from international and DPRK-based experts.[20]

Only the two individuals from the WFP and the MSF were in any way representative of publicly accountable organizations. The Hudson Institute-sponsored pair – Norbert Vollertsen, a German doctor who had lived in Pyongyang for just over a year until his visa ran out in December 2000 and who called himself a "public relations manager of Jesus

Christ", and a US citizen resident in South Korea who called Vollertsen a "Christ-like figure" – were offered to Congress as representative figures of the humanitarian agencies in the DPRK.[21]

None of the hundreds of NGOs or any of the other UN agencies working in the DPRK to alleviate suffering were called on to give evidence.[22] No views were heard in Congress from more mainstream and more representative faith-based organizations such as the international Catholic relief organization CARITAS, the Canadian Foodgrains Bank, the network of Canadian protestant churches, the Mennonites or the Quakers in the United States, all of which have been active in the DPRK for many years.[23] Nor were broad-based Korean American organizations such as the Korean-American Sharing Movement (KASM), which has also provided substantial relief assistance to the DPRK, invited by Congress to give information and evidence.[24]

Applying rationality

If there were 300,000 North Koreans in Yanbian, this would amount to almost the entire population of Yanji City, and it would be 100,000 people more than the ethnic Korean population of that city. In other words, 300,000 North Koreans, or even 100,000, would be highly visible. Yanji City has the largest ethnic Korean population of any city in China; and if the purported 100,000 to 300,000 North Koreans are not settled in Yanji, it is most unlikely that they are being absorbed in any large number into non-Korean-speaking cities elsewhere. Yanji City is small and is surrounded by mountains. The mountain areas are sparsely populated, with small villages and tiny human settlements based around farms. There are few paved roads and the distances between settlements are large, making transportation necessary to obtain basic goods, including food. Destitute North Koreans would be highly visible if they were walking around in their hundreds of thousands. In the extreme temperatures of winter and summer, it would be especially difficult for large numbers of poor, hungry North Koreans to survive without support or to wander around the countryside without being noticed and picked up by the police.

There is, however, some less ideologically skewed information available about the number of North Korean migrants in China. The US Committee for Refugees estimated that by the end of 2000, there were about 50,000 North Korean refugees living in China.[25] It also cited a Johns Hopkins School of Public Health figure of 50,000.[26] This last figure is from one of the better sources of professional analysis about North Koreans in Yanbian, one working on the ground since 1997. In September 2002, workers for a Chinese Korean humanitarian agency in Yanbian gave a figure of around 10,000 to 20,000 North Koreans illegally resident in the area.[27] This source stated that the total had decreased sharply from the previous year, when it was around 50,000. The clearest reason for the decline in number was increased surveillance by the Chinese authorities in Yanbian in 2002 of vehicles moving in and out of Yanji City, with local police and the state security forces regularly stopping vehicles to check papers.[28]

It is difficult for poor North Koreans who do not speak Chinese to establish themselves in non-Korean-speaking areas of China, so most of those who manage to evade discovery and stay in China probably remain in Yanbian. The number of North Koreans illegally resident in Yanbian will not be equivalent to the total of all North Koreans resident in China, but probably it represents a large majority of the illegal North Korean migrants living there.

The research problem

There remains the research problem of mapping the pattern of migration, quantifying the number of North Korean migrants in China and determining how both have changed over time. It is difficult to assess whether there has been a change in the pattern of migration such that those intending long-term relocation in China or elsewhere now form the majority of migrants, as opposed to the pattern evidenced in 1998, when those who entered China for food and income and meant to return home formed the majority of North Korean migrants. The total number of migrants is likely to be less than the figures published by US government sources. A reasonable hypothesis is that there are smaller numbers staying longer and living in more difficult conditions than ever before, but such a hypothesis would have to be examined by careful empirical research.

The legal status of North Korean migrants

North Korean migrants to China have been termed refugees, asylum seekers, economic migrants, defectors and escapees. The first three of these labels are important, as they indicate legal status and consequent duties of states and international organizations in relation to migrants. The last two labels are entirely normative and have no legal connotation. They indicate a conception of the DPRK that assumes that it is an evil regime and lacking in legitimacy and therefore that migrants from the country must be considered morally legitimate, even if their individual or immediate motivation for leaving the DPRK is not self-defined as political.

Refugees, asylum seekers and economic migrants

According to the 1951 UN Convention relating to the Status of Refugees, a refugee is a person who "owing to a well-founded fear of being persecuted for reasons of race, religion, nationality, membership of a particular social group, or political opinion, is outside the country of his nationality, and is unable to or, owing to such fear, is unwilling to avail himself of the protection of that country".[29] An asylum seeker is someone applying to be treated as a refugee under international law.[30] For the UNHCR (United Nations High Commissioner for Refugees), the difference between a refugee and an economic migrant is that "An economic migrant normally leaves a country voluntarily to seek a better life. Should he or she elect to return home, they would continue to receive the protection of their government. Refugees flee because of the threat of persecution and cannot return safely to their homes in the prevailing circumstances."[31]

It is not the responsibility of the UNHCR to decide who is an economic migrant or a refugee. It is governments which establish procedures to decide who constitutes a refugee and who does not.[32] Governments can and often do interpret the 1951 Convention in a restrictive manner. There is no international machinery that can, legally, override the decisions of individual states as to how they apply the Convention.

The view of the Chinese government is that North Koreans illegally resident in China are economic migrants. The US Congress has argued that they should be treated as refugees. The UNHCR has on the whole been careful not to allege that the Chinese government has contravened international law. It has, however, made clear that it would prefer China not to send illegal North Korean migrants back to the DPRK because they are likely to face penalties and punishment.[33] Its view is that to return North Koreans to the DPRK is "inhumane" treatment, even if they are not "strictly speaking ... eligible [for refugee status] under [international] conventions".[34]

What does the research indicate?

The 1998 survey in *The Lancet* of North Koreans in China showed that the majority migrated to China for food and to earn money.[35] Interviews with North Koreans since 1998 indicate that such motivations remain important and probably still predominate.[36]

Most North Koreans leave home as economic migrants, but the evidence is sufficient to indicate that there is genuine fear of persecution if or when they return to the DPRK.[37] The most severe penalties face those who have aligned themselves with fundamentalist Christian organizations which have an explicit anti-communist, anti-DPRK, and often anti-China, agenda and whose avowed aim is to see the fall of Kim Jong Il. There have been uncorroborated reports of extreme penalties imposed on women who return to North Korea pregnant by a Chinese man, including forced abortion and baby killing.[38] It is impossible to verify these reports. However, given the DPRK government's refusal to allow regular social contact between DPRK citizens and foreigners and the intense social stigma of illegitimacy, it is not difficult to assume that single women as parents face very difficult times indeed if they return to the DPRK after a stay in China. The least punitive penalties face those who have crossed the border for a short time and are returning to families and communities after obtaining food and maybe some cash.[39]

There are few asylum seekers because few North Koreans illegally settled in China directly approach the Chinese authorities to request refugee status. There are a tiny number who have attempted to claim asylum by breaking into foreign embassies and consulates in China, but these activities are organized first and foremost as full-blown media "events" by non-Korean organizations based in Tokyo, Seoul, Los Angeles and Washington, DC.[40] For these events, press statements written in English are made available to the international media based in Beijing, who are always contacted personally before every attempt by North Koreans to gain access to foreign embassies. These events are always professionally organized: they are filmed and the tape is copied and sent to major news organizations.[41] Media access is straightforward, as some of the South Korean media assist the activists.[42] North Koreans who make it over the fence into the embassies end up with a ticket to Seoul. The Chinese police arrest those who do not make it.

Many North Koreans, because they arrive in China as economic migrants and because they do not seek asylum, would not satisfy the initial criteria for refugee status under the terms of the 1951 Convention. The North Koreans with a justifiable claim to refugee status are those who have worked closely with South Korean or Christian organizations, particularly ones with anti-communist credentials. It is unlikely, however, that all contact with all faith-based organizations is viewed as suspect by the DPRK authorities in view of the large number and variety of Christian humanitarian organizations working with the DPRK government, including some radical Christian groups such as the Christian Friends of Korea based in the United States.[43]

The policy problem

Some North Korean migrants are likely to qualify for refugee status, and the vast majority are in China because they are desperate to obtain food and a basic income for themselves and their families.

Policy recommendation (i)

The Chinese government should develop a package of policies towards North Korean migrants to China that identifies those who are refugees and takes appropriate action. It should also find ways to assist those who need food, basic goods and help with simple survival.

Which parts of the DPRK do migrants come from and why?

The 1998 survey published in *The Lancet* reported that most migrants come from the province of North Hamgyong, on the eastern end of the China–DPRK border, across from Yanbian.[44] Interviews with migrants since 1998 continue to report the province of origin as mainly North Hamgyong.[45] There is no evidence that there is widespread migration from the rest of the DPRK to China or, as might be expected, from the other three North Korean provinces that border China: Chagang, North Pyongan and Ryanggang.

North Hamgyong, the main source of DPRK migration

North Hamgyong is a mountainous province, with extreme temperatures in winter and summer, insufficient arable land to feed its population, a large urban population and a large number of unemployed industrial workers. It accounts for 10 per cent of the population of the DPRK (see fig. 7.2). In 2000, it had the third-lowest grain production of the 12 provinces of the DPRK (excluding Pyongyang), at 69 kg per capita.[46] This compares to a Food and Agriculture Organization-recommended min-

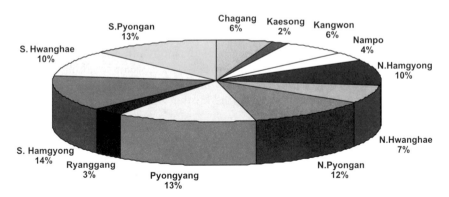

Figure 7.2 Population of North Korea by province and percentage, 2000 (*Source*: extrapolated from figures given by Flood Damage Rehabilitation Commission to UN WFP, 2001).

imum per capita grain ration for basic survival of 167 kg per year.[47] By 2001, there was an increase in food availability, to 126 kg per capita. However, there was still insufficient food for physical survival for most of those who live in the cities of North Hamgyong, whose estimated population was 2.2 million in 2001.[48]

Chagang, North Pyongan and Ryanggang – why so few migrants?

The mountainous border province of Chagang was almost as food-deficient as North Hamgyong in 2001: the per capita availability of grain was 122 kg for its 1.2 million population.[49] This province is one of the least accessible to humanitarian agencies, as only seven of its 18 counties are open for international assistance and monitoring.[50] Chagang is also where several military institutions are based, as well as munitions industries. Given the State's "army-first" policy, it is very likely that a disproportionate amount of the country's harvest goes to this province. This may reduce the push of "food migrants" to China. It may also be that the military sensitivity of this province ensures that border controls are tighter here than at other parts of the border.

North Pyongan, whose capital Sinuiju is the most important border crossing to China, is also reported to be a minor source of migration to China. Its 2.5 million population live in a mixed agricultural and industrial area, and grain production in 2001 was 299 kg per capita.[51] In addition, much of the DPRK–China land-based trade from the relatively major economic centres of Nampo port and Pyongyang passes through North Pyongan, giving some of its inhabitants the opportunity to earn an income from trade-related activity.

Ryanggang lies to the west of North Hamgyong, and its population is spread through a mountainous and forested area. Its winters are notoriously harsh; but because of its upland flatlands and its investment in potato production, the 223 kg per capita of grain production by 2001 was more than enough to meet the needs of the population.[52] Unlike North Pyongan and Chagang, Ryanggang borders the Korean-speaking area of China. The province's borders with China are relatively open, and the capital, Hyesan, is located right on the border with China.

Why North Hamgyong?

Chagang, North Pyongan and Ryanggang are not, as pointed out above, major sources of North Korean migrants to China. This suggests that there are specific characteristics of North Hamgyong that cause North Koreans to make the perilous journey to China and attempt to live in Yanbian for lengthy periods. All DPRK residents live under the same political regime and therefore face identical imperatives to migrate. If moving to China were mainly for political reasons, it would be unlikely that migration would be so heavily skewed towards North Hamgyong Province. If another reason were that people from the provinces bordering Yanbian could more easily assimilate in this Chinese region, one might expect to see more migrants from Ryanggang in China. It seems much more likely that the prime causes of migration are the extreme food deprivation and poverty facing the population of North Hamgyong as well as easy access to Yanbian. (fig. 7.1 and the map of Northeast Asia on p. ii illustrate the geographical contiguity of North Hamgyong to China and Russia.)

Not all North Korean migrants are the poorest

An absence of systematic research into the socio-economic background of migrants prevents identification of the various proportions of poor and better-off migrants or changes in the social background of migrants in the 1990s and early 2000s. There is, however, sufficient evidence from interviews of migrants to indicate social variation. Many interviews have been conducted with unemployed workers and poor farmers from North Hamgyong. There are fewer accounts from former party officials and the relatively well off.[53] This may indicate that there are fewer migrants from the relatively well-off groups in the DPRK or it may simply mean that these migrants have resources and need to maintain only minimal contact with humanitarian organizations, churches and those who are somehow engaged in providing services to North Koreans resident in north-eastern China. The DPRK migrants who have savings or assets to sell sometimes buy fake Chinese ID papers or pay Chinese and Chinese Korean middlemen to smuggle them into other parts of China or to third countries.[54]

Some of those who successfully breached security at diplomatic compounds in Beijing and Shenyang in 2001 and 2002 were carrying fake Chinese ID papers, which may indicate that they were better off than most of those hiding in north-eastern China. A useful addition to knowledge about the social origins of North Korean migrants in China would be the results of the debriefing of the North Koreans who defected to Seoul by invading embassies and consulates in 2001 and 2002. This information is available to the South Korean security services and other agencies of the ROK government that routinely engage in systematic debriefing of North Koreans who defect to Seoul.[55]

The research problem: The geographical and social origins of DPRK migrants

More research and more systematic research on DPRK migrants' background is necessary, and surveys similar to the 1998 *Lancet* survey that identified and analysed their geographical and social origins would be a useful next step. There is already sufficient information from NGOs, UN organizations, interviews and South Korean government sources to provide a basis for further research. Such data, if systematized, along with a new survey of migrants by independent researchers, could provide very credible knowledge about where in the DPRK North Koreans come from and why they migrate to China.

Policy problems

Impoverished, food-deficit counties in North Hamgyong are major sources of illegal North Korean migrants to China. For instance, Musan and Onsong counties on the border with Yanbian are extremely poor mining areas.[56] Undok is a ghost county, as heavy industry closed down after the economic collapse of the 1990s, leaving the population without food, income or coping solutions short of migration.

Finding solutions

It should be possible for governments, such as the South Korean government, and other interested parties to channel economic investment into the poor border counties of North Hamgyong. By 2002, engagement between North Korea and South Korea had developed to such an extent that joint economic cooperation projects existed and were expected to expand in the future. China remains on good diplomatic terms with both the ROK and the DPRK. In view of this propitious diplomatic environment and given that North Hamgyong is "open" to the international community, it would not be too difficult for the various parties to devise a plan for economic development in its neediest counties. This development should be project-based, transparent and subject to accountable auditing procedures. This type of investment would provide economic benefits for the neediest but, by encouraging transparency and accountability, it could help to introduce an element of political openness in DPRK policies and methods of operation.

Policy recommendation (ii)

A plan for project-based, transparent and accountable investment should be drawn up by a task force of North Korean, Chinese and South Korean technical experts. This investment should be managed multilaterally according to protocols overseen by an intergovernmental governing body of North Korean, Chinese and South Korean technical experts. A body specifically designated to coordinate this investment should be established for a finite time, and it should have finite goals. This should be a low-key enterprise designed to implement a defined programme of activity. It should not be a political entity.

The plight of migrants

The North Korean men, women and children who are illegally resident in China live in appalling conditions and are vulnerable to physical, emotional and sexual exploitation. Most are immobile, trapped in isolated settlements, whether these are in hidden rooms in apartments in Yanji City or in the surrounding mountains. Women and children are even more deprived and are subject to additional forms of exploitation. (North Korean children include orphans, children with families and children born in China. There are no reliable figures about the scale of the North Korean child population in China.)

North Korean migrants try to find food from individuals, humanitarian organizations and churches; and if they plan to stay long, they try to find work. The small population of Yanbian and the relatively high educational qualifications of its residents, along with the work opportunities available from South Korean investment there, mean that there is little local Chinese or Chinese Korean labour for menial jobs in the agricultural and forestry sectors. The demographics and economics of Yanbian thus provide opportunities for North Koreans and as such are a "pull" factor for North Korean migration to China. North Koreans can speak the language (Korean) and are prepared to work for literally next to nothing, to live in very poor conditions and to have no legal and few social rights and protections. They are unlikely ever to complain about low pay or poor treatment.[57]

In Yanbian, North Korean men, and some women, find work in the remote mountain areas.[58] They work for local farmers who are likely to be Korean Chinese and to have connections with local church or humanitarian organizations that help DPRK migrants. They are dependent on their employers for food, shelter and safety as well as work and are paid on a piecework basis. It is virtually impossible to save money or to find alternative employment. The condition in which these North Koreans live is akin to indentured servitude, irrespective of the motives of those who assist them.

North Koreans live in makeshift wooden structures lacking sanitation, running water or any facility apart from the *kang*, the raised platform heated by underfloor pipes upon which the Korean household sleeps, eats and spends any leisure time. In these remote areas, the household consists of groups of mainly men, sometimes related to each other, with a tiny minority of women who perform domestic work such as cooking and cleaning. North Koreans not only live in physically very poor conditions but are also without hope of improvement of these conditions. One North Korean, in a letter to the United Nations that does not exaggerate, stated, "We North Korean refugees in China ... live worse than dogs in a mountain hut."[59]

Women, young adolescents and children cannot risk being asked for papers to prove their legal residence and so, as noted above, live confined to "safe houses" in apartment blocks in Yanji City. They, as all Koreans, are subject to checks to see if they have legal residence, and these checks can take place in the street and in the home. Surveillance and checking for illegal North Koreans in China intensified after the beginning of the occupations of embassies and consulates in 2001. This increased surveillance was highly visible, and there was effective communication about it between Yanbian and northern DPRK counties by word of mouth among Chinese Koreans who regularly travel to the DPRK. This was probably a powerful deterrent to those considering migrating to China from the DPRK's northern counties.

Women are particularly subject to exploitation. There have been a number of reports indicating that women have paid money to traffickers/ smugglers in return for arranged marriages with Chinese men and, worse, that they have been sold into sexual servitude. These reports also indicate that such arrangements had become less common as of late 2002 because North Korean women have become aware of potential abuse and are no longer choosing to enter China as part of an arranged marriage or a liaison.[60] Sexual exploitation, however, remains an ever-present hazard for single North Korean women, especially for those living in isolated mountain areas, as they live communally, with large groups of men, and do not have the benefit of protection from their families or a local community.[61] As in the DPRK, these women are expected to perform a highly gendered role of cleaning, cooking and carrying out physically demanding household chores.[62] These gendered roles are not intrinsically or necessarily sexually exploitative but, in the event of abuse, these women have no legal protection or any way in which they can seek redress.

Homeless children and adolescents were regularly seen on the streets of Yanji City between 1994 and 1999. Since 1999, however, the Chinese and DPRK governments have both sought to prevent their migration and to return them to the DPRK if they are found in China. The combination of a slight growth in the DPRK economy since 2000 and the reasonably effective communication network with the northern counties of the DPRK probably ensured that the county authorities could provide some minimal resources for these children and that the children themselves were deterred from re-entering China. The North Korean children currently living in Yanbian reside in shelters provided by humanitarian organizations, and some receive basic schooling. A relatively new group of vulnerable children are those born in China since the start of the food crisis in the 1990s. Children with one Chinese parent who has not entered into a legal marriage with a North Korean partner and children born of North Korean parents who are illegally resident are without legal status. They are not eligible for health, education or welfare support.

Policy problems: The most vulnerable

The North Koreans in Yanbian include some very vulnerable groups: those living a life of indentured servitude in the forests and mountains of Yanbian, single women, children and adolescents, and the stateless infants and young children born in China during the past decade. They are relatively small in number, and policies could be designed to improve their conditions in the context of a larger package of measures to regulate migration between the DPRK and China.

Policy recommendation (iii)

The Chinese government could consider granting semi-resident status through a special visa to those North Korean individuals who can demonstrate that they have work and shelter. For those who are employed to carry out seasonal agricultural work but can demonstrate that the employer is prepared to house and feed them the year round, there could be an annual visa. These visas could be an extension of current arrangements whereby residents in China and residents of the northern counties of the DPRK have relatively easier access to the others' territory provided that they remain in those specific border counties.

Policy recommendation (iv)

The Chinese government should consider a one-off amnesty for the relatively low number of North Korean migrants in China. It should also consider granting citizenship to those infants and young children currently without any legal status who have been born in China during the past decade.

Policy recommendation (v)

In the medium and long term, the Republic of Korea, Japan and China should develop a plan of investment in the manufacturing and mining sectors of North Hamgyong, from where many of the refugees originate. Project-based investment that would allow for a partnership between foreign lenders and DPRK industry and for the scrutiny, transparency and accountability of those projects would achieve a twofold objective. It would create employment and income for the residents of North Hamgyong, who currently have few options other than at best badly paid and insecure employment in Yanji City. It would also help to reinforce the transition to a market economy that is taking place in the DPRK. Given that North Hamgyong was the centre of advanced industrial development in the country until the late 1980s, it has a comparative advantage in the pool of technically qualified (if in obsolescent technology) but currently unemployed personnel.

Current assistance

When North Korean migrants enter China, they look for help from legally resident Chinese Korean or Korean relatives or from individuals whose name or telephone number they have been given by friends or contacts in the DPRK, or they look for a church because they have heard back in the DPRK that churches provide assistance to North Koreans.[63] There are reports that the local Korean Chinese population has been sympathetic to North Koreans looking for food and sustenance, but there is no systematic research on the attitude of local people to North Korean migrants.

Identification and analysis of the work of the dozens of humanitarian and advocacy organizations is difficult. None of them publicize their work in any detail, as all are technically breaking Chinese law. They can be subject to penalties if discovered, but in practice the Chinese authorities tolerate those that engage solely in humanitarian assistance while they prosecute those who smuggle North Koreans out of China to South Korea. These organizations therefore lack transparency; and information as to their funding, structure, sponsors, links with foreign organizations, objectives, methods and achievements is scarce and almost wholly reliant on whatever data the organization itself wants to present. No systematic research has been undertaken on who is operating in the region and what they are doing. However, some organizations maintain websites, and it is thus possible to gain some, if inadequate and biased, information about their activities.

One experienced international humanitarian official states that there are three types of group operating in the Yanbian region to assist North Korean migrants: the humanitarian organizations, the advocates and the "lunatics".[64] This categorization, subjective as it may be, is useful in that it suggests the varied and differing priorities of these groups. It would be a mistake to assume that there is an automatic link between any of these three kinds of group and a particular faith. Not all Christian organizations, for instance, approve of activity by Christian fundamentalists who encourage migrants to re-enter the DPRK for the sole purpose of carrying out conversion or missionary work. These migrants have no organizational protection, least of all from the organizations that send them, and without doubt will face retribution against themselves and their families if they are caught.

The humanitarian organizations primarily offer food, shelter and humanitarian assistance sufficient to allow North Korean migrants to survive physically. Some of these groups also work in the northern counties of the DPRK, leaving "survival rucksacks" containing food, clothing and other basics at strategic locations.[65] The advocates visit Yanbian but are based in Tokyo, Washington, DC or Seoul. They raise issues of refugees' rights and try to encourage the Chinese government to recognize the claims of North Korean migrants to legal status in China. The lunatics, or extremists, can perhaps best be understood as those who are interested less in individual North Koreans per se living in Yanbian than in the general objective of replacing the governments in Pyongyang and Beijing.

Research problem

Research needs to be undertaken on the scale, scope and activities of the various organizations operating in and from Yanbian on behalf of North Korean migrants. Baseline information exists in the form of website data and journalists' accounts. There is also a realistic chance that independent researchers could persuade representatives and workers in these organizations to give interviews. It would be possible to establish a research protocol whereby organizations would not be identified when the research is disseminated.

Policy problem

The organizations working in Yanbian have differing priorities, motives and objectives. If governments are to be persuaded to respond effectively to the humanitarian needs of North Koreans in China, they must identify which of these organizations are credible and professional and which are not. Governments will need to work through reputable and locally based non-governmental organizations in order to address the poverty and deprivation facing North Korean migrants in China.

Policy recommendation (vi)

The Chinese government, in the context of the package of measures suggested here, should support those humanitarian organizations that provide for the basic needs of migrants from the DPRK.

Immediate and future needs

Short-term solutions are required by way of an immediate response to the extreme privations being suffered by women, children and men in Yanbian. Short-term solutions make sense, however, only if they are carried out in the context of dealing with the underlying conditions that make illegal migration to China a perceived necessity for so many North Koreans. They will be acceptable to the parties involved only if a diplomatic route can be found that minimizes risk and maximizes effectiveness.

One solution is for an "honest broker", trusted by all sides, to engage in some quiet diplomacy to try to produce a package of measures that responds to the needs, identified in this chapter, of North Korean migrants in China. But this mediator must avoid "megaphone diplomacy" and must produce a set of policy options that all parties can implement. The Swedish and Swiss governments are clear candidates for this role in view of their long-standing relations with the DPRK and China, their lengthy experience of working within these two countries and their global reputation for neutrality and even-handedness in foreign affairs.

Only a package of measures responding to the divergent sensitivities of the Chinese and DPRK governments would have any practical chance of being implemented. It could include the various policy recommendations made in this study. In addition, further research must be undertaken so as to fill in the knowledge gaps that have been identified here. Good policy needs to be based on accurate and reliable information – not speculative worst-case scenarios.

Policy recommendation (vii)

The Swiss and Swedish governments should consider whether they might have a role to play in facilitating the creation of a negotiating framework in which a comprehensive package of measures could be developed and implemented in order to respond to the urgent humanitarian needs of North Korean migrants in China.

Policy recommendation (viii)

The Chinese government, in the context of a general package of measures, should permit credible and independent researchers from any of the numerous good universities and research institutes in China, in partnership with researchers already engaged in this work from outside China, to assess the nature and scale of North Korean migration to China.

Conclusion

We have enough knowledge of North Korean migration to China to know that we should not wait until more substantive research is completed before policy solutions are found to meet the needs of the deprived, impoverished and hopeless North Koreans illegally resident in China. Instead, concerned parties should consider a package of policy measures that, with some goodwill, could realistically be implemented by governments and the more professional non-governmental organizations currently working to assist North Korean migrants.

There is a humanitarian crisis facing the North Koreans living in Yanbian and in China. Relative to the population of China, only a very small number of people are involved; but for each and every North Korean individual, especially the children, it is a crisis of extreme proportions. Given a little flexibility and imagination by all the parties concerned, it is also a crisis that is solvable.

Acknowledgement

The field research for this analysis was made possible by a very generous grant from the United States Institute of Peace, Washington DC. I am immensely grateful for their support and forbearance, and am all the more appreciative because I fully realize that some of my conclusions may not be shared by all at the Institute.

This chapter is based on written English-language sources, some of which refer to other language sources themselves and some of which do not. I have spoken with and formally interviewed hundreds of Chinese, North Korean and South Korean sources over the past 12 years, some with the aid of an interpreter and some not, and some on this particular subject and some on broader issues to do with the Korean peninsula. The chapter would undoubtedly have benefited from ready access to written Korean- and Chinese-language sources. But even if, as here, only currently available English-language resources can be drawn upon, it is still possible to improve the knowledge upon which to base policy, to identify exaggeration and disinformation and, most importantly, to develop and implement more appropriate policies for impoverished and insecure North Koreans living in China.

Notes

1. A useful but undated survey and analysis (1999?) is Young-hwa Lee, General-Secretary of RENK (Rescue the North Korean People: Urgent Action Network), "Situation and Protection of North Korean Refugees in China", available at ⟨http://www.nkhumanrights.or.kr/bbs/board2/files/55_young-hwalee.doc⟩. There have been a number of unscientific "surveys" of North Korean migrants in China. The major problem with them is that their methodology is rarely made explicit. Also, their creators seem to be unaware of basic research conventions such as the necessity both to guard against bias and to demonstrate, through making explicit their methodology, just how bias is being avoided in the "research". However well meaning the intention of the "surveys" is, the results developed from such naïve work do not provide credible data or the basis for generalization about the status of North Koreans in China. See, for example, The Commission to Help North Korean Refugees, "A Field Survey Report of the North Korean Refugees in China", undated (but conducted in 1999, as the text itself states), available at ⟨http://www.nk-refugees.or.kr/english/emain.html⟩. See also Good Friends: International Peace, Human Rights and Refugees Center, "The Food crisis of North Korea: Witnessed by 1694 Food Refugees", available at ⟨http://www.jungto.org/gf/eng/index.htm⟩.
2. A most informative piece of research on North Korean migrants in China is Jeanyoung Lee, "Ethnic Korean Migration in Northeast Asia", in Tsuneo Akaha, ed., *Proceedings, International Seminar: Human Flows across National Borders in Northeast Asia*, Monterey: The Center for East Asian Studies, Monterey Institute of International Studies, January 2002, pp. 118–140. The figure 2 million comes from this source. Ibid., p. 118.
3. "Tumen River Area, China", available at ⟨http://www.ecdc.net.cn/regions/english/tumen/tumenzone_e.htm⟩.
4. "Population of Ethnic Korean Community in China Expected to Be Halved by 2050", *The Korea Herald*, 13 September 2002, available at ⟨http://www.koreaherald.co.kr/SITE/data/html_dir/2002/09/13/200209130017.asp⟩.
5. North Korean business trainees, for instance, work in Yanji City at a Chinese hotel. See "Yanji region", ⟨http://www.korea-np.co.jp/pk/095th_issue/99051904.htm⟩.
6. Idem.
7. "Tumen River Area, China", available at ⟨http:/www.ecdc.net.cn/regions/English/tumen/tumenzone_e.htm⟩.
8. "The South's Guangdong", Asiaweek.com, 2001, available at ⟨http://www.asiaweek.com/asiaweek/97/0228/nat3.html⟩.
9. Idem.
10. For comments on how migrants simply walk across the river in winter, see Shim Jae Hoon, "North Korea: A Crack in the Wall", *Far Eastern Economic Review*, 29 April 1999. I travelled along the North Korean side of the border from North Hamgyong to Ryanggang in 2000 and on the Chinese side of the border up to Russia and back twice in 2002. It is mostly deserted and the river narrows at a number of points.
11. In Yanji City in September 2002, I spoke with a representative from the US consulate in Shenyang. He said that it had been a major surprise to observe that the Dandong–Sinuiju border crossing was not militarized.
12. W. Courtland Robinson, Myung Ken Lee, Kenneth Hill and Gilbert M. Burnham, "Mortality in North Korean Migrant Households: A Retrospective Study", *The Lancet*, 354 (9175), 24 July 1999, p. 293.
13. Shim Jae Hoon, "North Korea: A Crack in the Wall".
14. One researcher reports that 7,000 North Koreans were sent back to China in 1999 and that 5,000 were returned in March 2000. None of these claims are substantiated by

references to sources. Other parts of the paper are informative, for instance the discussion on international law. The point is that even this sober reflection on North Korean migrants in China is based on unsubstantiated claims and "common knowledge", which latter can be inaccurate and misleading. See James Seymour, "China and the International Asylum Regime: The Case of the North Korean Refugees in China", 28 July 2002, available at ⟨http://www.hrwf.net/newhrwf/html/north_korea_countries_polic. html⟩.

15. George Wehrfritz and Hideko Takayama, "Riding the Seoul Train", *Newsweek International*, 5 March 2001, available at ⟨http://www2.gol.com/users/coynerhm/riding_the_ seoul_train.htm⟩.

16. "China Police Storm Plane after Botched Hijack", available at ⟨http://latelinenews.com/ ll/1205714.shtml⟩.

17. James Seymour, "China and the International Asylum Regime".

18. "Text: Resolution Urges China to Halt North Korean Repatriations", available at ⟨http://usinfo.state.gov/regional/ea/uschina/nkrefuge.htm⟩.

19. See, for example, Chuck Downs, "Written Statement Submitted to the United States Commission on International Religious Freedom: Hearing on Religious Freedom for North Korea", 24 January 2002, available at ⟨http://www.familycare.org/network/p01_ chuckdowns.htm⟩.

20. John Powell, "Testimony Before the Sub-committee on East Asia and the Pacific, House International Relations Committee", 2 May 2002, available at ⟨http://www. house.gov/international_relations/powe0502.htm⟩.

21. These quotations come from a radio interview with Vollertsen and Peters on a Christian women's radio station – Concerned Women of America – in link to "interview", available at ⟨http://www.familycare.org/network/p01.htm⟩. The radio interview has Vollertsen and Peters professing that no one but themselves cares about the children of the DPRK, and Peters refers to Vollertsen as a "Christ-like figure" because of an incident in the DPRK when the latter cut off a part of his skin to donate to a burns victim. He does not say that Vollertsen did this in support of an entire workforce who had each cut off a tiny part of their skin to offer to their colleague. Would this make all these North Korean workers "Christ-like" figures too?

22. For a survey of humanitarian activity in the DPRK, see Hazel Smith, "Overcoming Humanitarian Dilemmas in the DPRK", Special Report No. 90, Washington, DC: United States Institute of Peace, July 2002.

23. Hazel Smith, *CARITAS, Evaluation of CARITAS activity in DPRK 1995–2001*, Hong Kong: CARITAS, 2001.

24. A widely circulated statement by KASM, which did not share the perspective of the unrepresentative groups advising the Congressional committees, was "KASM's Position on North Korean Refugee Issues", 22 May 2002, available at ⟨http://www.nautilus.org/ pub/ftp/napsnet/special%5Freports/kasm%5Fposition%5Fon%5Frefugee.txt⟩.

25. US Committee for Refugees, "Country Report: North Korea", available at ⟨http://www. refugees.org/world/countryrypt/easia_pacific/2001/north_korea.htm⟩.

26. Idem.

27. Interview of Chinese Korean humanitarian agency representative, Yanji City, September 2002. Anonymity is given in order to protect the source.

28. I witnessed this systematic stopping of vehicles to check for North Korean migrants on my visit to Yanji City and Yanbian in September 2002. Not all vehicles were stopped.

29. UNHCR, *Protecting Refugees: Questions and Answers*, Geneva: UNHCR, 2002, p. 4.

30. UNHCR, *Refugees by Numbers 2000 edition*, Geneva: UNHCR, 2001, p. 10.

31. UNHCR, *Protecting Refugees*, p. 10.

32. Ibid., p. 8.
33. UNHCR was itself involved in the drama of highly publicized occupations of international premises in June 2001 when seven North Koreans walked into the UNHCR office in Beijing, accompanied by a Japanese journalist, demanding to be repatriated to South Korea. UNHCR in Geneva went so far as to say that they believed the seven should be granted asylum. For discussion of the UNHCR occupation, see Elizabeth Rosenthal, "North Koreans in China Press UN on Asylum Issue", *New York Times*, 29 June 2001, available at ⟨http://www.snkr.org/stories/news/news.html⟩.
34. Kris Janowski, UNHCR spokesperson, quoted by Elizabeth Rosenthal, "North Koreans Widening Escape Route to China", *New York Times*, 5 August 2002, available at ⟨http://www.nkhumanrights.or.kr/newsletter_eng/news_view.html?no=282⟩.
35. Robinson, Myung, Hill and Burnham, "Mortality in North Korean Migrant Households", p. 293.
36. I interviewed two groups of North Korean migrants in Yanbian in September 2002. They had left the DPRK at various times over the previous two years. All informed me that the main reasons for leaving the DPRK were food shortages and lack of opportunities to work and provide for their family. See also Elizabeth Rosenthal's fine reportage from Yanbian as Beijing correspondent of the *New York Times*. See, for instance, Elizabeth Rosenthal, "North Koreans in China Now Live in Fear of Dragnet", *New York Times*, 18 July 2002, available at ⟨http://www.freeserbia.net/Articles/2002/Dragnet.html⟩.
37. Various reports on detention camps for those sent back to the DPRK from China include "Exclusive Detention Centers for NK Defectors Emerge, What is New about Defectors", October 2002, available at ⟨http://north-korea.narod.ru/defectors_new.htm⟩.
38. Patrick Goodenough, "Babies Killed in North Korean Prison Camps, Observers Say", CNSNews.com, 12 June 2002, available at ⟨http://www.cnsnews.com/ViewForeignBureaus.asp?Page=\ForeignBureaus\archive\200206\FOR20020612b.html⟩.
39. Elizabeth Rosenthal describes the lack of fear displayed by many North Korean migrants in China in respect of potential harsh penalties on their return to the DPRK. See Elizabeth Rosenthal, "North Koreans Widening Escape Route to China", *New York Times*, 5 August 2002, available at ⟨http://www.nkhumanrights.or.kr/newsletter_eng/news_view.html?no=282⟩.
40. For a discussion of Japanese involvement and balanced analysis of those organizing the embassy and consulate "invasions", see Philip Brasor, "Who's Got the Scoop on the Shenyang Five?", *The Japan Times Online*, 2 June 2002, available at ⟨http://www.japantimes.com/cgi-bin/getarticle.pl5?fd20020602pb.htm⟩. The Los Angeles-based organizer is Douglas Shin, who is quoted in Elizabeth Rosenthal, "N. Koreans Seek Asylum", *New York Times*, 4 September 2002, available at ⟨http://www.bayarea.com/mld/bayarea/news/world/3998743.htm⟩. Norbert Vollertsen moves between Seoul and Washington, DC. He is not a member of any organization and does not reveal who provides him with funds.
41. Interviews with foreign journalists, Beijing, September 2002.
42. One organization, appealing for help for four people imprisoned in Mongolia for smuggling North Koreans from China into Mongolia, noted that one of them was Oh Young-Phil, "a South Korean freelance video documentarist whose video features have often appeared on KBS TV". See "Appeal for Imprisoned South Korean and Chinese Activists and Ten North Korean Refugees", available at ⟨http://www.chosunjournal.com/announce.html#special1⟩.
43. The Christian Friends of Korea is an evangelical organization that draws on the experience of Christian missionaries who operated in Pyongyang before the 1940s. Some of

the children of these missionaries, who grew up in Korea, run the organization, which operates in the DPRK in partnership with the DPRK government as an openly faith-based Christian humanitarian programme. See various newsletters of the Christian Friends of Korea, PO Box 396, Montreal, NC 28757, USA.

44. Robinson, Myung, Hill and Burnham, "Mortality in North Korean Migrant House-holds", p. 294.

45. My interviewees in Yanbian in September 2002 were all from North Hamgyong, al-though they had entered China at different times and independently of each other.

46. World Food Program, *Review of Operations 2000*, Pyongyang: World Food Program, undated (but 2001), p. 12.

47. World Food Program, "Emergency Operation DPR Korea No. 5959: Emergency Food Assistance for Vulnerable Groups", in World Food Program, *WFP Operations in DPR Korea as of 14 July 1999*, Rome, WFP, undated (but 1999), p. 1.

48. World Food Program, *Review of Operations 2001*, Pyongyang: World Food Program, undated (but 2002), p. 17.

49. Idem.

50. Idem.

51. Ibid., p. 16.

52. Idem.

53. For reference to recent migration, including by teachers, doctors and other members of the middle and upper classes, see Robert Marquand, "A Refugee's Perilous Odyssey from N. Korea", *The Christian Science Monitor*, 16 August 2002, available at ⟨http://www.csmonitor.com/2002/0816/p01s02-wosc.html⟩.

54. One example is a North Korean physician who defected from the DPRK to the ROK in 1996. His daughter and granddaughter left for China in 1997. They were arrested at Harbin airport in 2002 because the daughter used a forged Chinese passport. See "De-fector Goes Back to China for Daughter, Child, Is Caught", *JoongAng Ilbo*, 2 February 2002, available at ⟨http://english.joins.com/nk/article.asp?aid=20020205101316&sid= E00⟩. The rate for a fake passport in 2002 was US$10,000, more than most North Kore-ans would expect to see in a lifetime. For the price of a passport, see Robert Marquand, "A Refugee's Perilous Odyssey from N. Korea", *The Christian Science Monitor*, 16 Au-gust 2002, available at ⟨http://www.csmonitor.com/2002/0816/p01s02-wosc.html⟩.

55. A February 2002 report from the ROK secret services, for instance, indicated that 20 North Koreans who had arrived that month through third countries were unemployed workers, farmers and labourers. Only one was in a white-collar job, a teacher. See "20 North Korean Defectors Arrive in South", *JoongAng Ilbo*, 25 February 2002, available at ⟨http://english.joins.com/nk/article.asp?aid=20020225102606&sid=E00⟩.

56. I have travelled extensively in the DPRK, and Musan, which I went through twice in October 2000, is the poorest place I have seen in the country.

57. A *Time Asia* article declares that North Korean refugees are subject to "unscrupulous farmers and factory owners who give them jobs but pay a pittance". See Donald Macin-tyre, "Nowhere to Run, Nowhere to Hide", *Time Asia*, 25 June 2001, available at ⟨http://www.time.com/time/asia/news/magazine/0,9754,131024,00.html⟩.

58. The description in this paragraph is taken from my own observations in the mountains outside Yanji City in September 2002.

59. Quoted in George Wehrfritz and Hideko Takayama, "Riding the Seoul Train", *News-week International*, 5 March 2001, available at ⟨http://www2.gol.com/users/coynerhm/ riding_the_seoul_train.htm⟩, p. 14.

60. Interview with a Chinese Korean humanitarian agency representative, Yanji City, Sep-tember 2002. Anonymity is given in order to protect the source.

61. Author's observations, Yanbian Prefecture, September 2002.

62. For an analysis of the gendered dimensions of women's life in the DPRK, see Hazel Smith, World Food Program, *WFP DPRK Programs and Activities: a Gender Perspective*, Pyongyang: WFP, 1999.
63. Interview with a Chinese Korean humanitarian agency representative, Yanji City, September 2002. Anonymity is given in order to protect the source.
64. I am loath to maintain the anonymity of the source, who is a senior humanitarian official; but the person continues to work in the field, and I protect their identity because I was asked to do so.
65. Interview with a Chinese Korean humanitarian agency representative, Yanji City, September 2002. Anonymity given to protect the source.

8

The realities of South Korea's migration policies

Shin-wha Lee

Introduction

Migration issues in the Republic of Korea (Korea or South Korea below) can be grouped into two categories. The first relates to Korean emigration, namely issues of overseas Koreans. The second concerns foreign immigration to Korea, both legal and illegal. This chapter will discuss both sets of issues.

Koreans living overseas number over 6 million today. Given this huge number, the South Korean government has come under increasing pressure to take a decisive role in promoting the status of overseas Koreans in both their countries of residence and their ancestral land, Korea itself. Although many overseas Koreans have successfully settled into their new environments with integrity and diligence, others have been unable to adjust to foreign political and social conditions. One significant case is that of the Korean Russians, who left for Yonhaeju (the maritime provinces of the Russian Far East) in 1863 because of a crop failure at home; they are viewed as the first Korean emigrants. In 1937, their descendants suffered Stalin's policy of forced migration and were deported to Central Asia. After the break-up of the Soviet Union and as a result of intensifying ethnic conflicts and civil war in Central Asia, many "Soviet Koreans" there moved to Yonhaeju.

With regard to foreign immigration to Korea, the most prominent and pressing issue today is how the government should deal with the influx of foreign workers, including rising numbers of illegal workers. Since foreign labourers first started to come to Korea a decade ago, their number has increased greatly; it is currently estimated to be over 300,000. Both legal and illegal immigrant workers have experienced discrimination, human rights abuses and social mistreatment in the country. There is also the problem of legal and institutional inadequacies, which has led to an increase in the pool of illegal immigrant workers in South Korea. Several religious organizations and research institutions have been established to protect foreign workers from exploitation, but the Korean government itself has remained passive in addressing their needs. It is encouraging that in 2003, the Korean National Assembly passed a bill related to the employment of foreign workers that provides a benchmark for the protection of foreign workers in accordance with international standards. However, it is still uncertain whether the new law can be effective because of its numerous restrictions, which are discussed below. In addition, the sexual exploitation of female illegal immigrants in Korea is a growing concern. They usually come to Korea to realize the "Korean dream", but many of them are forced or lured into the sex industry, at times selling themselves for almost nothing in return. Such practices must be eradicated at all levels of society, with the government taking an active role.

This chapter will first examine the present situation of Koreans living overseas and the evolution of the South Korean government's policies towards them. Next, it will discuss the national debate and the future tasks related to Korean emigration policies. Then it will look at the current situation of foreign immigrants in Korea, with particular reference to legal and illegal immigrant workers. The chapter will conclude with a brief discussion of some recommendations for government action.

Korean emigration: Past and present

The history of overseas Koreans

Koreans first began to go abroad approximately 140 years ago. The history of Korean emigration can be divided into four waves of mass emigration to the following countries or regions: Manchuria (Yonhaeju), Japan and the United States.

The first wave of Korean emigration, to Manchuria, started in the late nineteenth century: emigrants fled domestic political unrest in Josun, Korea's last dynasty, and sought land. Later on, after the "March 1st movement" (the Samil Independence Movement in 1910), emigration increased, as Manchuria became the base for the anti-Japanese resistance movement fighting for Korean independence. Subsequently, Korean schools were established, and stirred up anti-Japanese sentiments and Korean patriotism.

Immigrants in Manchuria suffered greatly under Japanese oppression. There were the Gando massacres in 1920 and the 1925 Mitsuya Agreement, concluded between Director Mitsuya Miyamasu from the Government-General of colonized Josun and Jang Jeorin, the head of the northeastern provinces of China. This aimed to eliminate the Korean national independence struggle in Manchuria. The invasion of Manchuria by the Japanese army in the early 1930s further weakened the activities of Korean armed resistance in the region.

Immigrants in Yonhaeju participated in the resistance movement after 1905 by establishing nationalist groups to oppose the 1905 Protectorate Treaty, recruiting loyal troops and setting up schools. They also contributed to the creation of the government of the Liberation Army in Vladivostok in 1914 and to the organization of the national rally during the "March 1st Movement" in 1919. These immigrants and their children would fall victim to Stalin's policy of the forced migration of Koreans to Central Asia in 1937.

The history of Korean immigration to Japan began in the late nineteenth century when a handful of Korean intelligentsia went to Japan for study. After Japan's colonization of Josun in 1910, Korean immigrants to Japan were primarily farmers looking for work in Japanese industries. Countless women, who came to be known as "comfort women", were subject to forced migration in order to provide sexual services to Japanese soldiers. After the devastating earthquake in the Kanto region of Japan in 1923, some 6,000 Korean immigrants were massacred for supposedly causing social unrest.

Korean immigration to the United States started in the early twentieth century when immigrants, mostly male farmers, went to work in the sugar cane plantations of Hawaii and the railway construction projects and vegetable farms on the west coast. Korean immigrants there also contributed to the anti-Japanese resistance movement by organizing patriotic groups, establishing newspaper and magazine companies, and forming a Korean army in the United States during World War II. In addition, some Koreans went to Mexico and Cuba. They were exploited as cheap labour and toiled under conditions almost indistinguishable from slavery.

Another important aspect of the history of Korean emigration is the adoption of children from Korea. Between 1958 and 2002, a total of 150,499 Korean children were adopted by citizens of the United States and European countries.

In brief, Korean emigration started as a means of surviving difficult living conditions in Josun or contributing to independence movements against the Japanese. It has changed in character in more recent decades, spurred on by a yearning for a better quality of life and education.

Current trends in Korean emigration

The number of overseas Koreans increased from 700,000 in 1971 to 2,320,000 in 1990 and 4,830,000 in 1991. The main cause of the sharp increase between 1990 and 1991 was the fact that after the end of the Cold War, ethnic Koreans living in China and the countries of the Commonwealth of Independent States (CIS) were included for the first time in statistics about overseas Koreans. The number of overseas Koreans has increased continuously: there are an estimated 6,080,000 as of July 2003 (see table 8.1). About 88 per cent of them are located in Asia (mostly in China and Japan) and North America (mostly in the United States). Of the 2,140,000 living in China, approximately 90 per cent have Chinese citizenship (see table 8.2). In all, Korean immigrants are currently found in 151 countries, with more than 2,000 Koreans living in 24 countries (see table 8.3). Over 2 million Korean immigrants live in the United States and in China; 640,000 live in Japan and 560,000 live in the countries of the CIS.

Although Korean immigrants living in Canada numbered only 170,000 in 2003, they had increased by 20.74 per cent from the previous year, and

Table 8.1 Overseas Koreans, 2003

Region	Overseas Koreans	Percentage of overseas Koreans by region	Percentage of increase compared to preceding year
Asia	2,979,736	49.03	11.73
Japan	638,546	10.51	−0.26
China	2,144,789 (1,923,800)*	35.29	12.03
Others	196,401	3.23	40.47
Americas	2,327,619	40.04	2.43
USA	2,157,498	35.50	1.62
Canada	170,121	2.80	20.74
Central and Latin America	105,643	1.74	−5.22
Europe	652,131	10.73	9.59
CIS	557,732	9.18	6.91
EU	94,399	1.55	28.65
Middle East	6,559	0.11	−9.41
Africa	5,095	0.08	−3.28
Total	6,076,783	100	7.56

Source: Korean Ministry of Foreign Affairs and Trade, *The Current Status of Overseas Koreans*, Seoul, July 2003.
* Ethnic Koreans who have obtained Chinese citizenship.

Table 8.2 The increase in overseas Koreans, 1971–2003

Year	Total
1971	702,928
1975	920,358
1980	1,470,916
1985	1,905,181
1990	2,320,099
1991	4,832,414
1995	5,228,573
1997	5,544,229
1999	5,644,558
2001	5,653,809
2003	6,076,683

Source: Korean Ministry of Foreign Affairs and Trade, *The Current Status of Overseas Koreans*, Seoul, July 2003.
Note: ethnic Koreans living in China and the CIS have been included since 1991.

their number is expected to continue to grow in the future. This trend seems to reflect the economic downturn and high level of unemployment in Korea. The increased difficulty in obtaining immigration permits or student visas to the United States after the September 11, 2001 terrorist attacks have contributed to a strengthening interest in emigrating to Canada and other English-speaking countries with relatively lenient immigration rules.

Koreans go abroad for various reasons (see table 8.4). Since the government's introduction in 1989 of a policy that allows the freedom to travel abroad, there has been a sharp rise in overseas travel, with the exception of a decline during the financial crisis of the late 1990s. In 2001, the main purposes of foreign travel among Koreans were tourism (43.5 per cent), commercial business (25.6 per cent), personal visits (10.3 per cent) and language studies (4.4 per cent). The percentages vary from year to year, but the priority of purposes has remained more or less the same. But now, more Koreans want to go abroad for longer periods of time, usually for study or a better life. One of the main reasons for emigration in recent years is the pressure Korean parents feel to give their children the best education possible, which in turn causes many young Koreans to settle abroad permanently.

The present trend in Korean emigration is a natural consequence of the wave of globalization. The presence abroad of Koreans must thus be viewed as an asset in making Korea an influential country in the globalizing world. To the extent that emigration is due mainly to dissatisfaction with the Korean educational system or Korean society, the government must develop a plan to counter it.

Table 8.3 Countries with more than 2,000 overseas Koreans, 2003

Country	Overseas Koreans
United States	2,157,498
China	2,144,789
Japan	638,546
Commonwealth of Independent States	557,732
Canada	170,121
Australia	59,940
Brazil	47,227
Philippines	37,100
United Kingdom	35,000
New Zealand	33,000
Germany	29,814
Indonesia	23,485
Mexico	17,200
Argentina	15,500
Thailand	15,100
France	10,900
Guatemala	7,943
Paraguay	7,097
Viet Nam	6,821
Singapore	5,820
Italy	5,432
Malaysia	3,983
Spain	3,568
Taiwan	3,076
Countries with less than 2,000 ethnic Koreans	37,068
Total (151 countries)	6,076,783

Source: Korean Ministry of Foreign Affairs and Trade, *The Current Status of Overseas Koreans*, Seoul, July 2003.

Table 8.4 Koreans "temporarily" going abroad, by purpose, 1985–2001

Year	Total	Tourism	Commercial business	Visit, study	Government business, conferences	Other
1985	484,000	2,000	134,000	46,000	17,000	286,000
1990	1,561,000	590,000	401,000	203,000	30,000	337,000
1995	3,819,000	1,771,000	900,000	436,000	63,000	649,000
2000	4,342,000	1,387,000	1,239,000	655,000	69,000	990,000
2001	6,084,000	2,647,000	1,557,000	626,000	99,000	1,156,000

Source: Korea National Tourism Corporation, available at http://www.knto.or.kr/eng/07 statistics/07 01.htm, accessed 28 September 2003.

Table 8.5 Overseas Korean associations, 1997 and 2000

Region	1997		2000		Increase/ decrease
	Number of associations	Countries	Number of associations	Countries	
Japan	291	1	286	1	−5
Other Asian countries	188	24	280	22	92
North America	1,089	2	997	2	−92
Central and South America	182	19	164	14	−18
Europe	475	30	503	24	28
Middle East	50	16	32	13	−1
Africa	28	17	27	9	−1
Total	2,303	109	2,289	85	−14

Source: Korean Ministry of Foreign Affairs and Trade, The Current Status of Overseas Koreans, Seoul, July 2003.

The status of overseas Koreans' associations

A unique characteristic of overseas Koreans compared to migrants from other countries is their concentration, as noted, in a few countries and regions of the world: Japan, China, the United States and the CIS countries. As shown in table 8.5, the United States is home to the largest number of overseas Koreans associations. This reflects the fact that these associations have the ability and the connections to exercise influence on the US government. However, the South Korean government, in the midst of tense relations with North Korea, has shown its preference and support for Mindan (a pro-South Korean association) in order to gain advantage over Chongryun (a pro-North Korean association) in the competition between these organizations in Japan. This has taken priority over focusing on lobbying in the US Congress for a North Korean policy that would be more favourable to South Korea. This emphasis by the South Korean government has caused discontent among Koreans living in other countries, particularly the United States.

Currently, the Overseas Koreans Foundation (OKF), a non-profit public corporation affiliated with the South Korean Ministry of Foreign Affairs and Trade (MOFAT), acts as a cornerstone of support for the more than 6 million overseas Koreans. The OKF was established by legislation in 1997. It aims to promote a sense of community among ethnic Koreans and works to expand a cyber community among them, Korean. net. In October 2002, the OKF launched the Hansang Network, consisting of a network of commercial and industrial experts, information technology specialists and science and technology-related organizations. Its purpose is to promote business opportunities for Koreans around the world.

Overseas Koreans policy: Progress and tasks

Development of Korean emigrant policy

There was practically no standard policy towards Korean emigrants during the first and second republics, when government leaders were preoccupied with the problem of post-colonial social instability and the post–Korean War reconstruction effort. The Third Republic, under President Park Chung Hee, encouraged Korean emigration by enacting the Emigration Law in 1962, but this legislation failed to achieve its goal, largely owing to inadequate government management. Meanwhile, mounting complaints about the legal status of Korean residents in Japan prompted proposals for investigations into the situation of Koreans there. In June 1971, the then presidential candidate Kim Dae Jung pledged to establish a department for overseas Koreans. However, fierce diplomatic competition between South Korea and North Korea during the 1960s and 1970s, in which it focused on preventing South Koreans' defection to the North, prevented the South Korean government from developing a national policy towards overseas Koreans.

The new constitution of the Fifth Republic under President Chun Doo-Whan, promulgated in 1980, stimulated the country's interest in overseas Koreans. Clause 2 of Article 2 prescribed the government's duty to protect overseas Koreans. The expanding number and role of overseas Koreans, along with the strengthened political and economic position of Korea in the world as demonstrated during the 1988 Seoul Olympic Games, helped South Koreans to realize the importance of Koreans overseas.

There was also a positive change in the attitudes of overseas Koreans towards South Korea as Korean political leaders, including presidential candidates, began to emphasize the importance of policies that would enhance the status of overseas Koreans. For instance, during the campaign in 1987 for the thirteenth presidential election, the three candidates, Roh Tae Woo, Kim Young Sam and Kim Dae Jung, all pledged to promote the rights of Korean emigrants and to ensure the efficient implementation of emigration policies. The post–Cold War environment, in which ideological conflict was no longer a major obstacle, increased the goodwill and support of policy-makers and the South Korean public towards overseas Koreans. For instance, with President Roh's Nordpolitik, which aimed to pursue wide-ranging relations with socialist countries and to promote contacts and dialogue with North Korea, the government and people of

South Korea showed greater interest in ethnic Koreans living in China and Russia and the other CIS countries.

In the early 1990s, the Kim Young Sam administration presented the New Policy for Overseas Koreans, which followed from its globalization policy. In December 1995, it announced a plan to strengthen ties between Koreans and ethnic Korean communities and to promote the participation of overseas Koreans in developing Korea's globalization policies and strategies. The plan was based on a recognition of the significant roles and status of overseas Koreans, and its outcome was the enactment of the Overseas Koreans Foundation Bill and the establishment of the Overseas Koreans Foundation in 1997. This bill was the first official measure to provide a systematic approach to promoting the rights and interests of Koreans living abroad. In September 1999, the Kim Dae Jung administration established the basis for the promotion of the rights and interests of Korean emigrants in the form of the Special Act on the Legal Status of Overseas Koreans (called the Overseas Koreans Law below).

Limitations of policies towards Korean emigrants

The South Korean government's policy towards Korean emigrants has been developed with a view to "helping overseas Koreans fully adapt and settle in foreign countries without losing their national identity". According to an official of the South Korean Ministry of Foreign Affairs and Trade, the assumption underlying this policy is that the integration of ethnic Koreans into foreign societies will help in promoting the rights and interests of overseas Koreans. However, non-governmental organizations (NGOs) and the academic community have criticized this policy, asserting that it promotes assimilation rather than integration.[1] Some also assert that MOFAT should not be in charge of government policies towards overseas Koreans. They say that the Ministry has concentrated on minimizing diplomatic conflict with other countries rather than on dealing with issues regarding ethnic Koreans. Its only efforts on behalf of overseas Koreans have been limited to the cultural dimension and matters such as language education; it has stayed away from more important but controversial political, economic, judicial and human rights issues. For example, the government has shown little concern for new emigrants seeking employment or for computer and other technical training for second- and third-generation ethnic Koreans living in the CIS countries and China. The Korea Education Institute has also been criticized for concentrating narrowly on projects related to language and cultural education.

Proposals for the establishment of a Department of Overseas Koreans have been opposed by the Ministry of Foreign Affairs and Trade. In fact, it even opposed creation of the OKF. The Ministry was also against the passage of the Overseas Koreans Law in 1999. From the start, the party in power and the Ministry of Justice have defined an overseas Korean as a person of ethnic Korean origin who had obtained citizenship of a country other than South Korea. But owing to opposition from MOFAT, the government has adopted the more restrictive definition of an overseas Korean as "a person who either had Korean citizenship in the past or was a direct relative of a foreign national who had been designated by the president". This definition has resulted in the exclusion of 2.6 million ethnic Koreans who are descendants of the migrants who moved to Russia, China and Japan in the nineteenth century. The government's definition also runs counter to that of the Overseas Koreans Foundation Bill, which defines an overseas Korean as "a person of ethnic Korean origin, regardless of his/her nationality, who is currently living in a foreign country". The OKF and NGOs have called for a revision of the current definition.

In November 2001, the Constitutional Court ruled that the definition of ethnic Koreans with foreign citizenship under the Overseas Koreans Law violated the principle of equality and called for its amendment by 31 December 2003. As a result, public and political debate over how and where to set the boundary of the definition of "overseas Koreans" intensified, as did the government's efforts to develop a policy plan to accommodate the needs and interests of overseas Koreans. As we shall see below, however, the issue remains unresolved.

It is regrettable that there is no single government organization representing the interests of people who make up 11 per cent of the entire Korean population in the world. A stronger commitment by the Korean government is necessary in order to promote the welfare of overseas Koreans and also to take advantage of the resources they represent. Education is a case in point. For the 6 million ethnic Koreans living in 151 countries, there are only 25 Korean schools in 15 countries, most of them in Asia; and for the 2.4 million Koreans (more than one-third of all overseas Koreans) who live in North America, there is only one Korean school. In contrast, the majority of Korean-language schools overseas are in North America (1,085 of the 1,923 schools in 96 countries). It is evident that overseas Koreans are very interested in teaching their children the Korean language while relying on American educational institutions for standard education. A similar situation is found in Europe and the CIS, where there is only one Korean school but 593 Korean-language schools (see table 8.6). As of July 2001, the government had dispatched only 12 officials to support and monitor Korean educational institutions abroad. In order to enhance the diplomatic position of South Korea and the national identity of overseas Koreans through educational programmes, the

Table 8.6 Educational institutions abroad for overseas Koreans

Region	Korean schools			Korean educational institutes			Korean-language schools			Public offices related to education	
	Number of schools	Number of teachers (dispatch)*	Number of students	Number of institutes	Number of teachers	Number of ethnic Koreans	Number of schools	Number of teachers (dispatch)*	Number of students	Number of offices	Public officials (dispatch)+
Japan	4	167 (22)	1,672	14	22	640,234	46	123	1,552	3	5
Asia	12	439 (25)	3,448	1	1	2,030,489	111	1,111	10,243	1	1
North America	1	17 (–)	164	7	8	2,264,063	1,085	8,758	64,363	2	2
Central and Latin America	3	81 (4)	568	3	3	111,462	54	410	3,561	–	–
Europe and CIS	1	17 (1)	62	10	12	595,073	593	1,467	30,590	4	4
Middle East and Africa	4	42 (4)	108	–	–	12,488	34	215	994	–	–
Total	15 countries 25 schools	763 (56)	6,017	14 countries 35 schools	46	5,653,809	96 countries 1,923 schools	12,084	111,303	6 countries 10 schools	12

Source: Korean Ministry of Foreign Affairs and Trade, *The Current Status of Overseas Koreans*, Seoul, July 2003.

Notes

"Korean schools" refer to the educational institutions that teach the standard educational curricula in the Korean language.

"Korea educational institutes" refer to the institutions that aim to promote education in Korea's history, culture, society, economy etc.

"Korean-language schools" refer to institutions whose main purpose is to teach the Korean language.

The number of Korean educational institutions was counted in July 2001.

* Number of teachers directly dispatched from South Korea.

+ Number of public officers directly dispatched from South Korea.

government should expand its support for Korean schools and Korean-language programmes abroad.

Future tasks for Korean emigrant policies

Proposed revision of the Overseas Koreans Law

In November 2001, an amendment to the Overseas Koreans Law was proposed for the inclusion of ethnic Koreans living in China and Russia in the definition of "overseas Koreans". Unfortunately, there has been little agreement on how to achieve this objective. The law was amended in February 2004, but the so-called definition clause remained unchanged. As a result, Korean Chinese, that is Chinese citizens of Korean ethnicity, and also Korean Russians, are not regarded as overseas Koreans. Meanwhile, the amended law contravenes the Supreme Court's decision.

Although the revision of the law is supported by the moral and legal justifications provided by the Constitutional Court, it is not a simple task. This is because the revision itself presents several problems. One of the most serious obstacles is that the offering of special privileges to overseas Koreans in the form of a special law, such as the Overseas Koreans Law, goes against the spirit of international law, notably the International Covenant on Civil and Political Rights. International law prohibits discrimination against people on the basis of ethnic, religious or racial background and advocates the principle of equality of people both at home and abroad. More concretely, the proposed inclusion of ethnic Koreans living in China in the definition of overseas Koreans could bring Korea into diplomatic conflict with China. It could also negatively affect the domestic labour market, in which Chinese citizens of Korean ethnicity are an increasingly important element.

Despite these problems, if the Korean people demand, and social circumstances require, a revision, it will be appropriate to overcome the obstacles to amending the law. The first problem can be eased by adopting a system or law that best suits the interests and needs of overseas Korean residents in the short run but still conforms to international norms and standards in the long run. The second problem is more difficult to tackle: diplomatic tensions with China could possibly cause serious damage to Korea's national interests, as the two countries are highly interdependent in the political, diplomatic, security and economic spheres. But it would be wise for the Korean government to make its Chinese counterpart aware that in this age of increasing interdependence, China depends on Korea nearly as much as Korea depends on China. The Korean government should constantly remind the Chinese government that the *Josun-jok* (Chinese of Korean descent) who come to South Korea play an important role in increasing foreign earnings for China and in enhancing the productivity of China's work force. Moreover, the strengthening of the *Josunjok* community would have a positive effect on improving relations between South Korea and North Korea; and improved North–South relations would contribute to peace and stability in Northeast Asia, which is also in China's interest. Korea must also convince China that dual nationality is becoming a general international trend and that the Overseas Koreans Law is not a system that is against China's minorities policy.

It is also imperative to establish an institution that has executive power to handle the affairs of overseas Korean residents. This institution would need to have access to experts who have the professional knowledge, willingness and commitment to help overseas Korean residents and the ability to execute policies in a consistent and effective manner. For this to happen, the Policy Commission of Overseas Koreans, which has been dormant since the late 1990s,[2] should be revived and the overlapping tasks of MOFAT and the Ministry of Justice should be rearranged. Concrete solutions to this problem would include the establishment of a secretariat in the Policy Commission as a permanent entity. This would allow it to provide the basic guidelines and foundations for a policy towards overseas Koreans that would eventually lead to the creation of a body independent of MOFAT and ensure stronger executive measures. This agency would need to be integrated into the Bureau of Overseas Koreans Affairs under the auspices of the Prime Minister or become an independent body under the Policy Commission of Overseas Koreans.

Better policies towards overseas Koreans

Until now, the government's policy towards Korean residents overseas has been criticized for being self-serving because the government has placed large demands on overseas Korean communities while doing little or nothing for them in return. In addition, it has been criticized for being passive and concentrating only on cultural exchange projects, as noted above, and for ignoring human rights violations against Koreans abroad so as to avoid worsening diplomatic relations with host countries. Since its beginning in 2003, the Roh Moo Hyun administration has emphasized that Korea should become a "core nation in Northeast Asia": it would take the initiative in leading the region to an era of peace and prosperity as well as develop Korea into an economic hub of Northeast Asia. In order to realize this goal, the government must recognize that overseas residents are "assets to their homeland". Both South Korea and North

Korea should collaborate in establishing cooperative policies towards overseas Korean residents. Additionally, overseas residents must be recognized for their role as mediators between the two Koreas who facilitate exchange and cooperation and help to ease mutual mistrust and hostility. Furthermore, it is essential that the principle of equality be maintained at all times, thus preventing social, political and economic discrimination among groups of overseas Korean residents.

Another major issue facing the Roh Moo Hyun administration concerns the restoration of the right to participate in South Korean political life to Korean nationals residing overseas. Korean nationals abroad should be able to vote in Korean elections, much as US soldiers and civilians stationed at the Yongsan garrison in Korea are able to vote in US presidential elections. All modern countries grant their nationals living abroad the right to participate in the political process at home. Korea allowed this in the past, but the "Yushin" (revitalizing reform) constitution, which gave President Park Chung Hee the possibility of remaining President indefinitely, took this right away. Its restoration should be the first priority on the foreign policy agenda of the current administration, and Korean nationals overseas should propose this change to the government. This restoration can be more easily justified than creating an overseas resident foundation or enacting a special overseas residents law. All South Korean citizens, be they students, businessmen or permanent residents overseas, should be able to participate in elections in South Korea. Moreover, voting by absentee ballot has become much easier with the spread of the Internet. Although it might be difficult to grant these rights to overseas Koreans for local elections, their voting right for presidential elections should be honoured.

The proposed legislative change can be facilitated by promoting a sense of national identity and pride among overseas Koreans. This would be achieved by enhancing Korea's international standing, actively protecting overseas residents from discrimination and human rights abuses and promoting government-supported cultural performances abroad. Of course, these measures must be taken while respecting the interests and rights of other ethnic groups and nationalities. The ideals of "open nationalism" and "open Korean community" will play a pivotal role in establishing a Korean community that is in step with the information age of the twenty-first century and that emphasizes freedom, individuality, equality and sharing.

Foreign migrants in Korea

During the past decade, Korea, one of the few ethnically homogeneous nation-states in the world, was indifferent to the interests and concerns of foreign migrants in the country. In 1992, the number of foreigners entering the country was only in the thousands. This was a result of the Korean government's strict immigration control, which reflected a fear that foreign workers could depress the working conditions of Korean workers and eventually displace marginal workers. However, Korea slowly changed its perspective and started to accept foreign workers in the early 1990s, when factory operations faced serious labour shortages. Even though the Korean economy experienced a severe blow in the wake of the 1997 Asian financial crisis, the demand for foreigner workers continued to grow. The need to attract foreign businesses and investment to South Korea increased further when China, South Korea's neighbouring competitor, joined the World Trade Organization in 2000.

In an attempt to attract foreigners to Korea, the South Korean government, in partnership with many large corporations, has conducted an industrial training programme since 1993, which provides more incentives to foreign workers. In addition, the number of foreigners coming to South Korea has increased for various reasons, including employment, business and investment, education and tourism. The 2002 soccer World Cup attracted international attention to South Korea and brought a large number of foreigners and substantial amounts of foreign currency to the country. Although the number of international migrants declined by two per cent that year, it was still more than a 100 per cent increase from the levels of the 1990s. As of 31 December 2002, the number of foreign residents in South Korea was estimated at 629,006, comprising 339,767 legal aliens and 289,239 illegal aliens. The total number was an increase of 11 per cent over 2001 (see table 8.7).

Foreigners in South Korea can be divided into three categories: legal and illegal workers, migrants and asylum seekers, and tourists and other foreigners. The following sections will discuss briefly the issues of asylum seekers and North Korean defectors but will focus more on the situation of foreign workers, who account for the majority of the foreign presence in Korea.

Table 8.7 Foreign residents in South Korea, 31 December 2002

Legal foreigners	Percentage increase (compared to 2001)	Illegal foreigners	Percentage increase (compared to 2001)	Total	Percentage increase (compared to 2001)
339,767	9	289,239	13.3	629,006	11

Source: Korean Ministry of Justice, Press Release (in Korean), 9 January 2003.

The state of foreign workers in Korea

Foreign workers officially began to enter Korea when the country launched the industrial training system in 1993. In an effort to offset the shortage of labour, they were permitted to work in sectors such as manufacturing, clothing, footwear, textiles, rubber and plastics, synthetic metal, automotive equipment and coastal fisheries. Coming from China, the Philippines, Vietnam, Indonesia, Bangladesh, Myanmar (Burma), Sri Lanka, Nepal and Pakistan, the foreign workers were originally permitted to stay in the country for up to one year. They earned hourly wages in the rage of 2,000–3,000 won (approximately US$2); illegal workers earned approximately 3,580 won per hour. As the number of foreigners in the country continued to grow, the limit on their length of stay was extended to two years. To qualify for the training programme in South Korea, foreign workers had to be between 18 and 35 years of age, to have no criminal record and to be from one of 14 countries designated by the government.

Foreign workers have experienced various forms of policy discrimination and social prejudice. For example, more than 70 per cent of all foreign trainees work overtime (50–60 hours a week), in comparison with the average of 40–44 working hours for Koreans in the manufacturing industry. Also, owing to poor working conditions and malnutrition, several foreign trainees have suffered health problems such as tuberculosis and pneumonia. The working conditions faced by foreign trainees result from the presence of a huge number of illegal foreign workers, who are officially labelled as "unregistered foreign laborers". Illegal workers often enter Korea on a tourist or visitor visa and find employment, or they replace foreign trainees in small and medium-sized firms who have deserted their posts because of highly unsatisfactory working conditions.

Becoming an illegal worker is not a wise decision. Most illegal workers are employed or re-employed by very small, poorly equipped firms near metropolitan areas. Violations of human rights and labour laws are common in these firms. A protest initiated by the Citizens' Coalition for Economic Justice in 1994 provided the impetus for the passage of a bill requiring employers to provide a minimal level of financial compensation to illegal workers who are injured on the job. However, illegal workers rarely get their compensation. They are afraid of being forcibly deported from the country if their employers report their illegal status to the government. In many cases, illegal workers either give up receiving compensation or receive only a small proportion of what they are entitled to.

Another problem arises when an illegal foreign worker wishes to marry a Korean citizen. In the case of foreign women, they are able legally to marry Korean men and become naturalized citizens of Korea. But foreign men do not acquire Korean citizenship when they marry Korean women. The foreign husband would have to apply continually for a three-month visitor's visa and repeatedly enter and exit the country in order to stay with his spouse legally. Many foreign men live with their Korean spouses without registering their marriage. Their children are not able to acquire Korean citizenship because they are classified as illegal immigrants, like their fathers.

These problems notwithstanding, the number of illegal migrants in Korea has continued to increase, from 68,000 in 1992 to 115,000 in 1999 to more than 300,000 in 2004. This increase has been associated in part with the Korean government's policy towards foreign workers. In the face of serious labour shortages, the government has encouraged the inflow of foreign workers. The expansion of the job market stimulated by a growing economy has resulted in the employment of people from Southeast Asia and China in the so-called "3-D (dangerous, dirty and demeaning) jobs", which Koreans are reluctant to hold. Critics argue that the government has "used" foreign workers but failed to assume responsibility for the social consequences of its policy.

Labour strife has increased sharply in Korea in recent years as the demand for foreign workers has risen rapidly. In 1995, there were demonstrations in Seoul drawing public attention to the plight of foreign workers, including serious violations of their human rights. In response, the government has proposed measures to improve the working conditions of foreign trainees. In July 2003, the Ministry of Justice, with the approval of the National Assembly, introduced Laws Concerning the Employment of Foreign Workers, to grant legal status to 227,000 unregistered foreign labourers. If properly implemented, the law is expected to result in an increase in the number of foreign workers in the country, including officially recognized employees and trainees, to between 300,000 and 400,000 in 2004.

Policies towards foreign workers

In 1992, the Korean government began to offer amnesty to undocumented foreign workers. At that time, 61,126 foreign workers of about 68,000 were officially registered and allowed to stay in Korea until the end of 1992.[3] In September 1993, there was a shortage of 120,220 workers in the manufacturing sector. (In the entire economy, there was a 4 per cent shortage of production workers, about 250,000 workers.) The industrial training system introduced by the government in 1993 (see above) allowed 20,000 foreign trainees into Korea that year. In

1994, some 30,000 industrial trainees entered Korea, and the number increased to 50,000 in 1995, 70,000 in 1996, 80,000 in 1997 and 85,000 in 2002. The foreign trainees have been processed by the Korea International Training Cooperation Corps, which was established in 1992 under the aegis of the Korea Federation of Small Businesses.[4]

The government's position on the import of foreign labour has been mixed. The Ministry of Labor called for the introduction of a work permit system for foreign workers in 1994 but the Ministry of Trade, Industry and Resources claimed that the foreign trainee system should be maintained in order to prevent the cost increases of authorized foreign labour that the proposed work permit system would cause.[5]

In 2002, the Korean government provided a two-month registration period for the estimated 265,848 unauthorized foreigners; the majority of them had entered Korea legally but had overstayed or violated the terms of their visas. During this period, 255,978 foreigners registered (151,313 Chinese, including 91,726 ethnic Korean Chinese, followed by 17,087 Bangladeshis and smaller numbers of Filipinos, Mongolians and Vietnamese). They were permitted to stay in the country until March 2003. Most of these registered workers (77 per cent, or 220,000) were in Seoul and its suburbs, and 89,174 of them worked in manufacturing, 55,907 in construction, 34,573 in restaurants and private houses and 2,400 in farming.[6]

Since its establishment, the International Labor Organization (ILO) has been an advocate of the rights of foreign workers as "migrant workers", not "foreign labor". It has called for the protection of those who are currently working or searching for employment abroad owing to economic or other reasons. According to the ILO, human rights policies for foreign workers should be based on the principle of equality: equal treatment for foreign and domestic workers. The Korean government should embrace this principle and the international standards for the protection of foreign workers by ensuring, for example, the protection of industrial trainees under Korean labour law.

The aforementioned fact that 227,000 illegal foreign workers will gain legal status according to new legislation is a welcome development. However, it remains to be seen whether the implementation of this law will bring about the desired results. These workers must meet several conditions in order to obtain legal status. They must have lived in Korea for less than four years as of 31 March 2003 and must be currently employed in one of six specified areas: manufacturing, construction, service, agriculture, livestock farming or fishery. Otherwise, they must leave the country. And a total of 900,000 illegal workers, those who have lived in Korea for more than four years and those who have attained illegal status after March 2003, are not entitled to apply for legal status.

Asylum seekers, North Korean defectors and human trafficking victims in South Korea

Asylum seekers

According to the UN High Commissioner for Refugees (UNHCR), South Korea ranks among the lowest countries in the world in terms of the number of asylum seekers it admits.[7] In 1994, the Korean government amended its immigration law, permitting individuals to file asylum appeals with it. However, according to the UNHCR, the actual process of applying for asylum has been extremely difficult. Between 1994 and 1999, more than 50 people from at least 14 countries, including Algeria, Iran, Afghanistan and China, applied for asylum in South Korea, but the government denied all applications.[8]

The government finally granted an Eritrean man refugee status in February 2002. This was the first refugee it had recognized since it joined the UN Convention relating to the Status of Refugees of 1951 and the 1967 Protocol relating to the Status of Refugees. A Congolese asylum seeker was the second to be granted refugee status, in December 2002.[9] As of September 2003, a total of 181 foreign nationals had officially requested refugee status, and 14 of them had been granted it (see table 8.8). Of the other applications, 37 were voluntarily withdrawn and the rest were either denied or were pending. A review of the status of asylum seekers by region reveals that 74 asylum seekers were from 6 Asian states, 20 from 2 Middle Eastern countries and 87 from 14 African states.

In order to receive refugee status in Korea, a petitioner must go through a process of investigation by the Refugee Recognition Council, under the aegis of the Ministry of Justice. Although Korean law on refugees has received much international criticism for being excessively strict, it must be recognized that 12 of 14 petitions had been granted during the nine months to September 2003. This reflects the government's changing attitude towards refugees. It is particularly encouraging that on 19 September 2003, the Ministry of Justice granted refugee status to two Arab

Table 8.8 Acceptance of refugees by South Korea, 1994–2003

Year	1994	1995	1996	1997	1998	1999	2000	2001	2002	2003
Number of asylum seekers	5	2	4	12	26	4	48	32	33	15
Number of people accepted as refugees	0	0	0	0	0	0	0	1	1	12

Source: This information was acquired from the South Korean Ministry of Justice at the author's request.

men in their 30s who had converted to Christianity. Almost all the asylum cases that had been recognized by Korea and other countries were of people who had fled political persecution. As the granting of refugee status on religious grounds is rare, this decision is worth noting.

North Korean refugees

The sudden surge of North Korean refugees in recent years has resulted from the structural food crisis in North Korea since the mid-1990s. Despite international relief aid to North Korea, over 2 million people are estimated to have died from starvation, with hundreds of thousands leaving the country for China. The number of defectors too has increased. According to the Korean Ministry of Unification, North Korean defectors to South Korea numbered below 100 before 1998. Since then, the number has risen every year: 148 in 1999, 312 in 2000, 583 in 2001 and 1,141 in 2002, an annual increase of almost 100 per cent. In 2003, 1,281 defectors came to South Korea; and as of June 2004, 760 had arrived. In July 2004, 460 came to the South. At this rate, more than 2,000 were expected to come by the end of 2004.

In the past, North Korean defectors, mainly male political elites or soldiers, defected to the South for ideological and political reasons. South Koreans welcomed them as *Kwysoon Yongsa* ("brave soldiers", who surrendered themselves to the South). However, the nature and type of North Korean defector has been changing, particularly during the past decade. More and more North Korean defectors are coming to South Korea with their families for economic and social reasons. The proportion of women defectors arriving in the South has also been increasing. In 2001, it was 42.3 per cent, but it increased to 49.6 per cent in 2001, 53.2 per cent in 2002 and 59.2 per cent (354 people) in 2003.[10]

Direct defection to the South through the heavily land mined and tightly guarded Demilitarized Zone has been rare. The majority of defectors have illegally crossed the Yalu River or the north-eastern Chinese border to enter China and then have sought refuge in foreign embassies or have travelled to a third country in order to come to South Korea.

Estimates of the number of North Koreans fleeing to China vary widely, ranging from tens of thousands in official accounts (100,000 by the UN and other international organizations) to as many as 300,000–400,000 according to some NGOs. These defectors are now scattered mostly in the Korean autonomous district of Yanbian in Jilin Province, as well as in Heilongjiang and Liaoning provinces; some have found their way to larger cities such as Tianjin and Shanghai.

According to the 1951 UN Convention relating to the Status of Refugees and the 1967 Protocol, these North Korean escapees, who are mainly in search of food, are not "refugees". The Chinese government has without exception labelled all North Korean escapees in their country as "illegal aliens". Most escapees have been forcibly repatriated to North Korea, in accord with the 1962 Chinese–North Korean border treaty. Most North Korean refugees live under the constant fear of being arrested and forcibly repatriated to North Korea by the Chinese police, North Korean espionage operatives or the Chinese *Josunjok*, who have North Korean citizenship. Furthermore, these escapees in China are suffering human rights violations, such as being victims of human trafficking or labour exploitation; but despite this, they remain silent, for fear of being deported.

The South Korean government has been practising "soft diplomacy" on the issue of North Korean refugees in China by requesting that they be provided with "special treatment" based on humanitarian principles while it respects China's rights under international law. In recent years, many Korean escapees in China have voiced their desire to defect to South Korea, but the South Korean government has not been eager to help them, mainly owing to its concern about diplomatic relations with China.

The "sunshine policy" of the Kim Dae Jung administration and the succeeding "peace and prosperity policy" of the Roh Moo Hyun administration were initiated in the hope of slowly changing North Korea into a partner for dialogue and reconciliation. Still, diplomacy involves both the "carrot" and the "stick". Aid and the "sunshine policy" are the South's carrot for North Korea, but the South Korean government also needs to raise the "stick" when the safety of escapees is threatened. Some argue that aid to North Korea, especially monetary cash relief, and the "sunshine policy" have actually ended up giving the North Korean government all the profit and the opportunity to strengthen itself while leaving millions of North Korean citizens starving. Thus, in addition to the need for continued diplomatic talks, exchanges and cooperation, South Korea should insist on the North's adherence to universal principles of humanity, such as human rights and humanitarianism.

Without principles and strategies as anchors, without any advance analysis of the consequences of its policies, the South will only present a reactive response to Chinese and North Korean government policies on North Korean refugees. South Korea must try to convince China that China's involvement in resolving the escapees issue will not lead to the collapse of North Korea and instability in the region. But it must also make it clear that China's acquiescence to the North's demand that North Korean escapees in China be forcibly repatriated will only ensure the continuation of instability in the region, to the detriment of China's own interests. It is important to constantly remind the Chinese government that engaging actively in resolving the North Korean defection issue according to humanitarian terms will not only support China's image as "a responsible superpower" but also help it to develop into a world-leading country.

If the ultimate goal of South Korea's policy towards North Korea is to secure the rights and well-being of the North Korean people, then that policy must be extended to include the hundreds of thousands of North Korean refugees as well. Given the seriousness and urgency of the issue, it is imperative for the South Korean government to set clear principles, develop concrete and comprehensive plans and undertake measures to coordinate and lead international efforts to achieve that goal.

The trafficking of women

South Korea is one of the states serving as a source, transit and destination country for the trafficking of women for prostitution. Victims come mainly from the Philippines, Thailand, China, Russia, Uzbekistan and Kazakhstan. Women normally enter the country on "entertainer" visas and are forced to work as prostitutes in private clubs and bars. Meanwhile, South Korean women are kidnapped and sent to countries such as Japan and the United States. At present, the Korean government fully complies with all international laws and regulations on the prosecution and prevention of kidnapping (e.g. the Protocol to Prevent, Suppress and Punish Trafficking in Persons). The government prosecutes traffickers through a variety of criminal statutes. In 2002, for example, it detained and investigated 450 suspected traffickers, of whom 90 were indicted and 68 were convicted. Also, in cooperation with Interpol and foreign governments, South Korea has been one of the key players in identifying and arresting traffickers. NGOs advocating human rights and women's issues have also been actively engaged in the protection of victims of human trafficking and the prevention of smuggling of women. It is important for the government to provide comprehensive guidelines so as to effectively coordinate the efforts of the parties concerned.

Conclusion

The migration policies, past and present, of the South Korean government have been mostly passive, despite some changes in recent years. This is the case whether the policies deal with the emigration of Korean citizens to foreign countries or the immigration of foreigners to South Korea. Its policies have failed to reduce the vulnerability of overseas Koreans and of foreign immigrants in Korea to discrimination and violations of individual rights.

In the past, the government's passive approaches towards migration were justified by the logic of the Cold War, traditional diplomatic games and state security. But today, the growing interdependence of states, a manifestation of globalization, presents opportunities as well as threats to the State.

On the one hand, interdependence can be an opportunity in that the network of 6 million Koreans living around the world could contribute to the advancement of South Korea's political and diplomatic interests in the international arena. For this to be possible, however, the Korean government must change its attitude, from one of regarding overseas Koreans as "former Korean citizens" to one that views them as "permanent Korean nationals" whose needs and rights it should consider in its policies.

On the other hand, interdependence poses a serious challenge to South Korea because the country can no longer keep its doors closed to international immigrants who wish to come there. Strict immigration regulations could have the unintended consequence of increasing the number of "unauthorized" immigrants in the country. The fact that these immigrants are "illegal" implies that there are only a limited number of legal and institutional channels to help them make a living in the country. Through its restrictive immigration policy, the South Korean government not only subjects "unauthorized" individuals to a threat of personal insecurity but also potentially threatens the security of society and even the State itself if these individuals decide to resort to unlawful means of making a living. In view of the increasing number of illegal immigrants in the country in recent years, the South Korean government should find a way to incorporate unauthorized immigrants into the population of authorized migrants. This would also help it to respond more effectively to transnational crimes such as human and drug trafficking.

The above examination of the realities of South Korea's migration policies in the context of interdependence could be a guide for the country's future policies towards Koreans living abroad and immigrants in South Korea.

Acknowledgement

The author wishes to acknowledge Ms Hyun Myoung Jae of the Department of Political Science and International Relations, Korea University, for her valuable assistance in the conduct of this research.

Notes

1. As, for example, Lee Soo Hong, Director of the Institute of Overseas Koreans Study, points out, the current policy implies that the government is unwilling to implement a policy towards Korean emigrants, as it assumes that Koreans living abroad will

naturally assimilate into the societies in which they live. He argues that the government's policy neglects the needs and interests of the second- and third-generation ethnic Koreans who have fully assimilated into foreign societies. Annually 20,000 overseas Koreans give up their Korean nationality. *Maeil Business Newspaper*, 16 September 2003, available at ⟨http://www.msn.co.kr/webinclude/exredir.asp?startid=edi&adgroup= KRMIVG&URL=http per cent3A//news.mk.co.kr⟩ (accessed 19 February 2004).

2. It is a nominal organization that does not even have the physical presence of a secretariat. The Commission was last convened in December 1997.

3. Asia Pacific Migration Research Network, "Issue Paper from the Republic of Korea", 1999, available at ⟨http://unesco.org/most/apmrnw12.htm⟩ (accessed 28 August 2003).

4. Idem.

5. Idem.

6. Korea Registration, "Migration News", 2002, available at ⟨http://migration.udavis.edu/ mn/ARCHIVE_MN/july M2002-16mn.html⟩ (accessed 23 August 2003).

7. Worldwide Refugee Information, "Country Report: South Korea, 2001", available at ⟨http://www.refugees.org/org/world/countryrpt/easia_pacific.../south_korea.htm⟩ (accessed 28 August 2003).

8. Worldwide Refugee Information, "South Korea", 2003, available at ⟨http://www. refugees.org/org/world/countryrpt/easia_pacific.../south_korea.htm⟩ (accessed 28 August 2003).

9. UNHCR, "South Korea Grants Rare Refugee Status to African Asylum Seekers", 2003, available at ⟨http://www.unhcr.ch/cqi-bin/texis/vtx/home/⟩ (accessed 6 August 2003).

10. Korean Ministry of Reunification, available at ⟨http://www.unikorea.go.kr⟩ (accessed 13 September 2003).

9

Foreign migration issues in Mongolia

Tsedendamba Batbayar

Introduction

The strength of the Russian presence in Mongolia has diminished in recent years but it remains strong in newer cities such as Erdenet and Darkhan in the north, closer to the border with Russia. Their Russian civilian populations have remained after the departure of the military, and many are now involved in Mongolian–Russian business partnerships that support the local and national economy. Today, these still mostly industrial communities, which are engaged in mining and some manu-facturing, are a cause for anxiety concerning Mongolia's future, as some worry about the possible participation of Russian criminal groups in illegal activities, such as money-laundering, the narcotics trade etc.

Most important, however, to Mongolia, its national security policies and strategies is its ever-present and powerful neighbour China. Al-though Chinese–Mongolian relations have improved significantly since 1990, China's economic and social influence in the country has gradu-ally been increasing, a cause of worry for Mongolians. This is demon-strated in legislation adopted in June 2002, the Law on Land Owner-ship of Mongolian Citizens. It gives all Mongolian citizens the right to own land, except pastures, for personal and business purposes, but it prohibits them from selling, giving as a gift or transferring their land to a foreign citizen or a person without Mongolian citizenship. This pro-hibition was a response to the fear of Chinese acquisition of land through a local agent.

China has a huge population – some 1.3 billion to Mongolia's 2.5 million. The neighbouring Inner Mongolian Autonomous Region has a population of approximately 20 million. At any time, some 100 million people are on the move in China; they seek a better life, coming from rural to urban areas in search of employment, or they are looking for new opportunities abroad. China's population density is 127 times greater than Mongolia's, making Mongolia seem like a land of frontier opportunity to some Chinese. Mongolia has difficulty in defending itself against Chinese influence on a variety of fronts – from imported goods and foodstuffs to business and investment, intermarriage and illegal immigration or settlement. Both countries are opening their economies to freer trade, but at a price that threatens Mongolia's cultural identity and economic independence.[1]

The interplay of Chinese and Russian factors: A historical perspective

The process of settling Chinese nationals in Mongolian lands has a long history. This history began in 1725 when, by decree of the Qing emperors, the first Chinese farmers settled in the fertile lands of the Orkhon and Tuul river basins; in 1762, more settled in the Khobdo region. The basic duty of the Chinese settlers was to provide food for Chinese soldiers stationed in Mongolia, who were fighting the rebellious Jungar Khanate. Farming was scaled back with the onset of peace and the withdrawal of the Chinese soldiers.

During the more than 200 years of rule by the Manchu Qing dynasty, Mongolia was effectively sealed off from any foreign, especially Chinese, presence. Knowing that the nomadic Mongols did not like the Han Chinese and despised Chinese sedentary culture, the Manchu rulers of China were careful not to mix the two cultures. Indeed, they were interested in maintaining the Mongols as a strong ally, and they introduced and implemented several anti-Chinese laws that remained effective well into the beginning of the twentieth century. These laws forbade the Chinese from crossing the Mongolian border, from cultivating Mongolian pastoral lands and from marrying Mongolian women.

Trade was the main Chinese activity in Mongolia. Virtually every town had either a small branch of a Chinese trading company or a commercial agent who would collect raw animal materials from the Mongols in exchange for tea, tobacco, china, fabrics and the like. In order to limit the number of Chinese traders in Mongolia and prevent their permanent residence there, the Manchu court carefully devised a policy whereby a special licence to trade in Mongolia had to be sought in Peking. Beginning in 1720, Chinese merchants were required to get special permission to enter Mongolia, and in addition were required to return to China.

Chinese merchants were concentrated in major cities such as Khobdo, Uliastai, Ulaangom and Yihe Khuree. By some estimates, there were about 500 Chinese firms and 100,000 (or 50,000 by other estimates) Chinese settlers in northern Mongolia by the end of the nineteenth century. The Chinese commercial network dominated all of Mongolia: the volume of trade between northern Mongolia and China, estimated at 50,000,000 roubles in 1905, was six times as large as that between China and Russia.[2]

Until 1911, Russian commerce and the number of Russian citizens in Mongolia were relatively small compared to the Chinese presence. Their trade with Mongolia was worth about 8 to 10 million roubles per year, and there were probably only around 800 Russians in the entire country. Yihe Khuree, which the Russians called Urga and the Soviets later renamed Ulaanbaatar, had become the largest population centre in Mongolia and also the centre of trade and commerce. Naturally, the principal traders and merchants in Yihe Khuree were the Chinese and the Russians. By some estimates, Yihe Khuree had some 4,500 Chinese craftsmen, along with about 40 large Chinese firms, 25 Russian firms and around 100 small shops and stalls. By this time, small Japanese and Korean communities had appeared; their members engaged in small-scale trading, provided medical services and owned barber's shops.

The People's Revolution in Mongolia in 1921, supported by Soviet Russia, brought an entirely new dimension to the foreign presence in the country. According to the official report given to the Second Congress of the State Hural (the Mongolian parliament), which convened in 1925, there were 51,207 foreigners living in Mongolia, including 23,919 Chinese, 318 Tibetans and 161 Southern Mongols. Another report lists about 2,700 people of German, British, American, Danish, French, Polish, Hungarian and Italian origin residing in Mongolia by the mid-1920s. (Government reports do not specify the nationality of the other, more than 20,000, foreigners, but it is safe to assume that they were mostly Russian.) The tolerant policy of allowing foreigners to live in Mongolia and engage in various activities ended by 1929. All foreigners except Russians were required to leave the country; those who resisted were forcibly expelled. In 1929 alone, more than 4,000 foreigners, including German, Swedish and Danish industrial experts, were driven out of Mongolia.[3] This was in line with the Soviet Union's desire to isolate Mongolia completely from the outside world so as to pursue its economic interest of establishing a monopoly of trade with the Mongolian market.

The birth of communist China in 1949 was most significant, as it opened up broad opportunities for landlocked Mongolia. Until the mid-

1960s, Mongolia benefited from growing cooperation between the USSR and China. Chinese labourers arrived to build a number of projects in Mongolia, including the first apartment buildings in Ulaanbaatar. These workers and their families numbered between 17,000 and 18,000 in the years 1955–1964. The Chinese built their own school and hospital in Ulaanbaatar. The first large-scale departure of Chinese labourers occurred in May 1962, and most left Mongolia in 1963–1964.[4]

The Russian presence was greatest in the 1960s and 1970s, when Soviet economic assistance enabled the construction of several hundred industrial projects. The large industrial town of Darkhan, second in size only to Ulaanbaatar, was built in northern Mongolia by an international team mainly of Russians and east Europeans. Soviet construction activity in Mongolia began in 1964, and by the 1970s it focused on building mostly high-rise apartment buildings in Ulaanbaatar. The Soviets invested most in constructing a huge copper plant, called Erdenet, between 1973 and 1981. By 1989, about 19,000 Soviet citizens, including 9,700 construction workers, 1,700 technicians, 3,000 geologists and another 3,000 working in joint-venture entities, were registered in Mongolia as "Soviet civilian specialists".[5] Most of the Russians left Mongolia in 1990–1991 when bilateral relations ceased upon the collapse of the Soviet Union.

The current status of the foreign presence in Mongolia

Mongolia held its first free elections in 1990, and since then it has taken important steps towards building a pluralistic and democratic society. Political liberalization in the country has opened up unprecedented freedoms of religion and travel for its citizens. Additionally, Mongolia's openness has made it very attractive to foreigners, leading to a dramatic increase in the number of foreign residents in the country, both legal and illegal.

During the socialist period (before 1990), Mongolian citizens had very limited access to passports necessary for travelling abroad. At the same time, foreign nationals, except those from the USSR and east European countries, had to contend with visa issuance policies that made travel to Mongolia almost impossible. A foreign citizen's travel and residence in Mongolia were regulated by the Regulation on Entry to the Mongolian People's Republic and Exit from the MPR and the Law on Rights and Obligations of Foreign Citizens in the MPR.[6] During the period of Sino-Soviet confrontation, Moscow was Mongolia's only entry/exit point for both foreigners and Mongolians.

After 1990, every citizen of Mongolia was given an equal opportunity to obtain a passport and travel abroad. Businesses, both private and public, were provided with the same right to engage in international trade and commerce. By some estimates, about 30,000 Mongolian citizens travelled abroad in 1990, a dramatic reversal of the pre-1990 trend. This situation prompted the authorities to draft two important pieces of legislation, which were passed by the State Great Hural in 1993.

The first act, the Law on Foreign Travel of Mongolian Citizens for Private Business, was passed by the parliament on 24 December 1993. This law gives every citizen of Mongolia the right to travel abroad and also the right to emigrate, i.e. to reside permanently in a foreign country for private purposes. It regulates procedures for the approval and issuance of national passports and the rights and obligations of citizens travelling abroad. In accordance with this law, the Civil Registration State Center was established in Ulaanbaatar. The Center is responsible for the issuance of ordinary passports to Mongolian citizens travelling abroad and for the registration of foreigners residing in the country for longer than 30 days. It keeps a record of Mongolian passport holders as well as of foreign residents.

The second piece of legislation, the Law on the Legal Status of Foreign Citizens, was also passed by the State Great Hural on 24 December 1993. The purpose of this law is to define and regulate the rights and obligations of foreign citizens, aliens without Mongolian citizenship, with regard to citizenship, entry, exit, transit and residence. This law consists of five chapters: an introduction, the legal status of foreigners, visa issues (entry, exit and transit through Mongolia), travel and residence in Mongolia, and other issues. Foreigners entering Mongolia are divided into six categories: travellers; transit travellers; temporary residents; long-term residents both for official and private purposes; permanent residents; and immigrants. A traveller has the right to stay in the country for up to 30 days, a temporary resident for up to 90 days, a permanent resident for up to 5 years and an immigrant for more than five years.[7]

Foreigners in Mongolia: Status and number

The most debated issue in the State Great Hural was whether or not to limit the number of permanent residents and immigrants residing in Mongolia. The decision that finally prevailed called for a numerical limit or "ceiling" on the number of foreigners who plan to stay permanently in the country. The law states that the number of permanent foreign residents and immigrants should not exceed one per cent of the Mongolian population, i.e. Mongolian citizens, at any given time and that those from one country should not exceed per cent of the total number of permanent foreign residents and immigrants already in the country. This stipulation clearly reflects a deep-rooted concern about national security. The State Great Hural later went further and established numerical limits on the number of immigrants for 2000–2004. It specifies that each year, up to 100 immigrants, including 30 Chinese and 30 Russians, may be allowed into the country.

The law on the legal status of foreign citizens was amended by the State Great Hural in December 2000. The amendment requires all foreigners, except those invited in by the government, to register within seven days of their arrival in Mongolia. This strict regulation met bitter resistance and harsh criticism from foreign embassies and from foreign citizens residing in Mongolia. Some foreigners even complained that such a requirement was tantamount to a secret police surveillance network. This resistance forced the Mongolian government to request that the State Great Hural modify the regulation. It agreed to exclude travellers (those planning to remain in-country for up to 30 days) from the duty of registration.

The most important amendment made in December 2000 to the 1993 law was the creation of a new government service responsible for dealing with matters relating to foreign citizens and immigrants. Its purpose was to set up a unified professional immigration service that would handle all issues relating to the residence and citizenship of foreign citizens in Mongolia and to their immigration there. The Immigration Service, inaugurated in May 2001 under the jurisdiction of the Ministry of Justice and Home Affairs,[8] subsequently took over the corresponding functions of the Civil Registration State Center.

As of the end of 2003, according to the Immigration Service's director Ts. Buyanbadrakh, there were 15,036 foreign residents and immigrants registered in Mongolia. They included 146 long-term foreign residents for private purposes, 10,460 long-term residents for official purposes, 912 permanent residents and 2,258 immigrants from 13 countries. The number of long-term residents for private purposes had not exceeded 150 since 2000. Among the 146 foreigners from 21 countries, 12 came from China and 20 came from Russia. One hundred and thirty-three of them lived in Ulaanbaatar, and others resided in rural areas. Long-term residents for official purposes included those who worked in international and foreign NGOs or in business entities with foreign capital or who studied in Mongolian universities. Among the 10,460 foreigners registered as long-term residents, there were 3,760 Chinese citizens and 2,700 Russians.

The number of permanent residents, mostly foreigners married to Mongolians, has been growing year by year. Their number was 588 in 2001, 609 in 2002 and 912 in 2003. The 912 permanent residents included

227 Chinese and 413 Russians. The category of immigrants deserves special attention. Immigrants included 1,323 Chinese, 888 Russians and 47 others, who had come from 11 countries. Their number had not exceeded 3,000 since the year 2000. The number of immigrants admitted per annum is around 30 people. For example, 34 immigrants were admitted in 2001, 26 in 2002 and 22 in 2003.[9]

The majority of foreign nationals represented in the category of immigrants are Chinese and Russians. Mongolia's Law on Citizenship does not recognize dual citizenship. Therefore, all 1,323 Chinese permanent residents of Mongolia are Chinese citizens. Most of them live in Ulaanbaatar and are concentrated in the Sukhebaatar and Chingeltei districts. Traditionally, the Chinese in Mongolia have engaged in small-scale shopkeeping and vegetable growing. Since the 1990s, however, the right to travel freely has created opportunities for resident Chinese to set up joint-venture companies with partners in China proper, most commonly in the service, retail and wholesale trade sectors. Also, using their language skills and familiarity with the local market, Chinese permanent residents in Mongolia have begun to work as brokers for Chinese trading companies.

Most of the Russian permanent residents in Mongolia have Russian citizenship. Although having Russian citizenship was beneficial during the socialist period, Russian nationals have faced increasing difficulties since 1990. For example, Russians were excluded from privatization schemes and social security benefits. Gradually, however, the Mongolian government has agreed to extend social security insurance coverage to Russian nationals and to privatize their apartments, as was done for its own citizens. Although Russian citizens in Mongolia have established the Association of Russian Citizens in order to protect their rights, those who are termed "local Russians" continue to face high unemployment.

Issues and problems

As indicated earlier, the number of foreigners visiting Mongolia has increased dramatically since 1990. Most of them are short-term visitors or tourists, who usually come to enjoy Mongolia's virgin land during the summer. The number of foreigners working with international organizations, such as the United Nations Development Program, has also increased significantly. Contract workers, mostly from China, employed by foreign-invested companies comprise a large part of the foreign presence in Mongolia today. There are also a considerable number of missionaries,

Table 9.1 Number of arrivals and departures in Mongolia by country, 2000–2002

Year	Inbound			Outbound		
	2000	2001	2002	2000	2001	2002
Country/region						
USA	6,451	6,653	6,860	6,511	7,122	7,058
Australia	1,008	1,262	1,761	1,134	1,278	1,752
UK	2,800	3,122	3,537	3,032	3,021	3,306
South Korea	8,039	10,098	14,536	8,239	10,214	14,392
Germany	4,206	5,388	6,856	4,068	5,869	6,395
Denmark	602	617	863	639	627	721
Italy	743	961	987	801	914	958
Kazakhstan	1,677	1,569	1,976	1,510	1,536	1,740
Canada	611	825	1,062	663	782	1,058
Netherlands	1,391	1,352	1,739	1,302	1,595	1,665
Russian Fed.	49,456	66,415	71,368	48,712	62,037	66,985
Sweden	904	1,331	1,388	729	1,167	1,411
China	57,546	67,360	92,657	48,024	62,960	90,771
France	1,841	2,764	2,891	1,918	2,732	3,378
Switzerland	637	666	875	326	869	1,502
Japan	11,392	11,565	13,708	13,987	17,576	13,527
Other	8,901	10,109	12,201	8,168	9,826	13,727
Total	158,205	192,057	235,165	149,763	190,125	230,346

Source: *Mongolian Statistical Yearbook 2002*, Ulaanbaatar: National Statistical Office of Mongolia, 2003, p. 225.

especially from Korea, who are trying to establish Christian churches and are actively recruiting young believers.

The number of foreigners arriving in and departing from Mongolia reached a peak in 2002 (see table 9.1); it declined in 2003 because of concern about SARS (severe acute respiratory syndrome). The majority of foreign visitors came from China and Russia. In 2002 alone, 92,657 and 71,368 people visited from these countries respectively. Visitors from South Korea, Japan, the United States and Germany followed in terms of their number.

A common problem among foreigners in Mongolia, especially among the Chinese and Russians, occurs when they overstay their visas. If a foreigner stays for longer than 30 days, he/she must register with the Immigration Service or its offices in the provinces. In 2003 alone, 1,732 foreign citizens from 52 countries were fined for illegal visa extension or for violation of the registration policy. Among them, Chinese citizens numbered 1,224 (70.6 per cent), Russians 132 (7.6 per cent) and others 376 (21.8 per cent).[10] The most likely explanation for disregard of the registration requirement is that the low fine imposed on offenders has not sufficiently encouraged compliance. Some of the violators have been deported from the country for overstaying illegally or for violating the registration rules. For example, 350 foreigners were deported in 2001 and 580 in 2002.

Because of geographical proximity, Mongolia offers citizens of Russia and China ample opportunities for low-cost living and profitable trade, and it also serves as a transit point to more advanced countries. During the 1990s, the privatization of small-scale services and state-owned apartments generated much interest among the citizens of foreign countries, particularly Russia and China, who have had traditional connections with Mongolia. Foreign interest-backed groups and individuals made the bulk of the new acquisitions when much of the previously state-owned property and many companies were sold at auction. Chinese restaurants, German beer houses, Korean fast food shops and Korean dry-cleaners now predominate in the streets of Ulaanbaatar.

As of 31 August 2003, there were 8,090 foreign contract workers from 72 countries registered with the Ministry of Social Welfare and Labor. Among them, Chinese workers numbered 2,890 (35.7 per cent), Russians 1,744 (21.6 per cent) and Ukrainians 1,741 (21.5 per cent). These workers were employed mostly in construction (2,257 or 27.9 per cent), mining (2,673 or 33.0 per cent) and wholesale and retail trade (1,433 or 17.7 per cent).[11]

The cashmere industry in Mongolia is an interesting example of an expanding trade that increases the uneasiness characterizing Sino-Mongolian relations. Chinese buyers, who are able to pay the highest prices, are penetrating the domestic cashmere industry. The price of cashmere has come to be dictated by them, who in turn recruit local brokers to buy raw cashmere at the exchange markets in Ulaanbaatar. The export of raw cashmere (by Chinese buyers in Mongolia) to China for processing and manufacture has eliminated a raw export product that previously was a major source of domestic industry and employment. The goods making up Sino-Mongolian trade pass through one permanent and nine seasonal border crossings, and Mongolians point to the rapidly growing prosperity of these places of entry on the Chinese side as a sign of one-sided profit.

Russians residing in Mongolia on a contract basis work mainly in the major Mongolian–Russian joint venture companies that were set up during the socialist period. These include the Erdenet copper plant, the Mongol-Russian Mining Company (MonRosTsvetmet), which is engaged in gold and fluorspar extraction, and the Ulaanbaatar Railway Company. Currently, 250 Russian and Mongolian–Russian joint companies are registered in Mongolia, and they are engaged in such diverse industries as gold mining, transportation, construction and services. The border and proximate regions of Mongolia and the Russian Federation are beginning to develop direct ties. Frequent visitors to Mongolia include Governor

Aman Tuleev of Kemerovo, Governor B. Govorin of Irkutsk, President L. Potapov of Buriyatia and President Sh. Oorjak of Tuva. They visit almost every year or every two years.[12]

Although Mongolia's proximity makes it very attractive to citizens of neighbouring states as a transit point to more advanced countries, it has also created some problems. In May 2001, for example, a Chinese citizen was arrested at Buyant-Ukhaa airport for illegally trying to bring 104 Chinese passports into Mongolia. He allegedly claimed that the purpose of the passports was to procure Mongolian visas for Chinese workers on contract with a Mongolian company. The police suspected that the passports were to be sold to Chinese citizens *already* residing illegally in Mongolia.[13] In other cases, Chinese citizens have illegally bought forged Mongolian passports and subsequently used them in attempts to enter a third country.

Human trafficking in Mongolia

The Korean national Pak Song-ki was deported from Mongolia in January 2004 for attempting to sell over 400 Mongolian girls to Japan and South Korea. He came to Mongolia in 1996 in order to establish a private business. He received a licence from the Foreign Investment and Foreign Trade Agency to set up an auto service company, capitalized by his private investment of US$18,000. His illegal activity was revealed by law organizations during the December 2003 investigation of seven girls seeking visas for travel to Japan. According to the official report, Pak had registered over 400 girls since 2002. He registered and researched their weight, age, nationality, ability, health, religion and their parents' work and positions. He drew registrants into his scheme through a classified ad calling for women aged 20–25, tall and pretty, and interested in working abroad and marrying South Korean men. The announcement brought many women to the company's office, a rented space in the Od cinema. Pak sorted the applicants into two categories, girls bound for employment in Japanese nightclubs and adult bars and women selected to be offered for marriage to South Korean men. The investigation revealed that he demanded US$300 from each applicant. It was confirmed that 50 of the women had gone to Japan.[14]

The Center for Human Rights Development (CHRD), a Mongolian NGO, has carried out independent studies of human trafficking in the country. They have focused on topics such as social groups vulnerable to the threat of trafficking and the capability of the current legal system to deal with the crime. Victims of this kind of crime are primarily women, students or those working in bars and nightclubs. Those who are unmarried and without children are at highest risk, according to the report. When trafficking in Mongolia was first brought to light, the people in charge of operations were largely foreigners who were using translators to enrol or coerce clients. Now, according to a CHRD report, the trafficking network is well established there, and native residents have become more and more involved in private trafficking schemes, as they are able to speak with and associate directly with targeted women.[15]

Specialists consider a trafficking case in 2000 to mark the crime's first real inroad into Mongolia. A CHRD lawyer represented two female victims who were sold to a citizen of former Yugoslavia by two Russians. The offenders ran an ad in a local newspaper about their service: "mediating for high-paying jobs in European countries, particularly in Yugoslavia and Romania". The two Mongolian women responded to the ad and were falsely told that they would be given a monthly salary of US$3,000 for performing Latin American dances in bars and restaurants. The Russian offenders then flew the women to Yugoslavia via China and forced them into prostitution. After obtaining illegal passport extensions for the women, the perpetrators sold them to the citizen of former Yugoslavia. After the victims managed to call members of their family and inform them of their situation, arrangements were made through the Ministry of Foreign Affairs to bring the women back to Mongolia. The offenders were sentenced to prison for six years under the Mongolian Criminal Code.[16]

In a different kind of human trafficking, it was reported that a US-backed plan to use a former Soviet military base in eastern Mongolia as a temporary shelter for North Korean defectors remained uncertain owing to strong opposition from the DPRK.[17] According to the report, the plan to use the empty barracks and apartment buildings of Choibalsan, an old border post in Dornod province 480 km east of Ulaanbaatar, was proposed by the mayor of Choibalsan, South Korean missionaries and aides to US Congressmen. One South Korean Christian group, the Doorae Community Movement, had acquired land for the possibility of future refugee processing. The same report said that since the late 1990s, missionary groups had quietly brought hundreds of North Koreans to Mongolia for eventual settlement in South Korea. But after the Chinese border police intercepted 29 refugees in 2001, the missionaries stopped running their underground route.[18]

International expectations of a Mongolian role in the North Korean refugee situation are growing. According to a *New York Times* report, for example:

Bolstered by President Bush's re-election and a new American law that calls for spending $20 million a year to help North Korea's refugees, refugee advocates would like to see Mongolia, sandwiched between Russia and China, play roughly the same role as Portugal's during World War II; a neutral state where refugees could be processed for settlement in other countries, preferably by the United Nations High Commissioner for Refugees.[19]

Other types of criminal activity, including narcotics trafficking, are of increasing concern to Mongolian law enforcement agencies. In 2000, a controversy surrounding medicine production in the province of Bayankhongor was widely reported in the Mongolian mass media. According to some experts, a Chinese businessman had tried to obtain a contract from the governor of that province in order to gather a naturally occurring ingredient of opium. The experts claimed further that the businessman intended to engage in the production of a certain type of narcotic. Finally, Mongolian police detained about 50 foreign citizens, including 23 Chinese and 21 Russians, on charges of illegal narcotics distribution.

Mongolia's policy on the travel of Mongolian citizens

As stated above, the number of Mongolian citizens travelling abroad has increased dramatically since 1990. The right to travel abroad was one of the main freedoms instituted by democratic reform in Mongolia. Passports were liberally issued to all Mongolian citizens 18 years of age and older. Thirty thousand Mongolians travelled abroad in 1990; by 1997 and 1999, that number had increased by 20 and 30 times respectively. Because of their proximity, China and Russia were naturally the main destinations of Mongolians. China offered the additional attraction of being a large market of cheap consumer goods. Other common destinations included east European countries such as Poland, the Czech Republic and Hungary, as well as Germany. Many Mongolians had received their higher education in those countries during the socialist period and thus felt an affinity to them.

Initially, both China and Russia allowed Mongolian citizens to travel within their borders without a visa. During the early 1990s, many Mongolian private citizens benefited economically from this policy, especially in the so-called suitcase (shuttle) trade. Trade also flourished in the Mongolian–Chinese and Mongolian–Russian border regions. The exchange of consumer goods in these regions and the number of visitors increased rapidly during this time.

Mongolia might have become an important transit corridor between China and Russia, but Russia became concerned with the massive influx of Asians, especially Chinese. In the Irkutsk border region, for example, the "army of migrants" were viewed negatively by Russians because, in

their view, they were creating an unwanted permanent resident community. This community was increasing at an alarming rate through marriage, study, guest working, the establishment of businesses and the pur-
chase of property. In response, Russia ended its no-visa policy towards
the Chinese and Mongolians in 1994 and 1995 respectively. In order to
protect its domestic industry, Russia also tightened its taxation policy towards "itinerant traders", i.e. peddlers and retailers. In these ways the
Russian authorities tried to curb the wave of illegal settlers.

Mongolia shares a 3,485 km border with the Russian Federation and
a 4,677 km border with the People's Republic of China. The agreement
in place between the governments of Mongolia and Russia (the Inter-
government Treaty and the attached protocol between the MPR and
the USSR on the border regime, concluded on 26 November 1980) officially designates 29 points of entry, including four as international points
for passengers and goods, nine as bilateral points for passengers and
goods, nine as bilateral points on a seasonal basis and another seven as
transit points. At present, a total of 19 points are functioning, including
16 on a permanent basis and another three on a seasonal basis. Among
them, Sukhebaatar-Naushki plays a prominent role as an international
point because it is open to citizens of third countries. Three other international points operate only bilaterally, owing to a lack of adequate
facilities.

Between Mongolia and China, one international point of entry currently operates on a permanent basis and nine bilateral points of entry
operate on a seasonal basis. Most prominent among these is Zamiin-
Uud-Erlian, the international point. Nine others, including Bulgan in the
province of Khobdo, Gashuunsukhait in the province of South Gobi and
Shiveekhuren, also in South Gobi, are very crowded during the short season in which they operate. Passengers and vehicles are issued temporary
permits for seasonal entry and are then allowed to cross the border.
Table 9.2 shows the number of Mongolian citizens who travelled through
the various points of entry to Russia and China in 2002.

Beginning in the latter 1990s, South Korea became a popular destination for Mongolian citizens. Estimates suggest that at present, 15,000–
17,000 Mongolians are in South Korea, where they are engaged mostly
in low-wage factory labour. Most of these migrants have travelled there
on a 30-day tourist visa and then stay illegally in order to make money.
An increasing number of Mongolians are reportedly being sent back
from South Korean points of entry because of lack of financial support.
The Mongolian government has repeatedly asked the South Korean government to protect the interests of these Mongolians, most of whom are
illegally employed and thus face the hardships of little or no pay and in-
eligibility for medical care and insurance programmes.

Table 9.2 Outbound Mongolian passengers by point and purpose, 2002

Purpose Immigration point	Total	Official	Private	Tourism	Permanent residence	Other
Buyant-Ukhaa (airport)	45,217	8,118	25,323	1898	480	9,398
Sukhbaatar (to Russia)	22,067	360	19,847	240	278	1,342
Altanbulag	50,676	923	48,854	144	474	281
Tsagaan Nuur	13,286	1,615	11,671	–	–	–
Ulgii	432	5	359	28	–	40
Khankh	3,568	10	3,558	–	–	–
Arts suuri	6,420	73	6,331	1	1	16
Ulikhan	2,210	241	1,959	–	4	6
Ereentsav	1,945	130	1,810	–	–	5
Borshoo	12,714	241	12,433	5	13	49
Zamiin Uud (to China)	296,140	10,199	275,311	5,324	89	5,217
Gashuun-Sukhait	22,025	–	22,025	–	–	–
Bichigt	3,451	77	3,374	–	–	–
Bulgan	20,819	75	20,744	–	–	–
Dayan	794	4	790	–	–	–
Baitag	6,045	15	6,030	–	–	–
Burgastai	1,025	–	1,025	–	–	–
Shivee-Khuren	12,101	–	12,101	–	–	–
Khavirga	14,051	8	14,043	–	–	–
Total	536,306	22,156	488,819	7,693	1,338	16,354

Source: *Mongolian Statistical Yearbook 2002*, Ulaanbaatar: National Statistical Office of Mongolia, 2003, p. 226.

Survey of public attitudes in Mongolia towards foreigners

A survey of popular attitudes towards foreigners was conducted in February 2004 in the capital city Ulaanbaatar. Two hundred and twenty-eight people responded.[20] Men constituted 46.5 per cent of the respondents; 53.5 per cent were women. Of all the respondents, 39.5 per cent were under the age of 30; 49.1 per cent were between the ages of 30 and 45; and 11.4 per cent were 46 and older. In terms of educational level, 4.4 per cent were primary school graduates, 29.8 per cent were graduates of secondary schools and 29.8 per cent had finished vocational school. Holders of a bachelor's degree constituted 29.8 per cent, and the remainder (about 6 per cent) held a master's degree or a more advanced degree. As for their professions/occupations, 37.7 per cent of the respondents were engaged in intellectual work, 21.9 per cent in manual labour and 12.3 per cent in jobs combining intellectual work and manual labour. The other 28.1 per cent were unemployed. One-fourth of the respondents

Table 9.3 Mongolian attitudes towards Russians and Chinese (%)

	Accept as unwelcome strangers	Friendly	Flexible	Difficult to answer	Total
Russians	6.1	68.4	22.8	2.7	100
Chinese	49.1	7.9	27.2	15.8	100

Source: author's survey, Ulaanbaatar, Mongolia, February 2004.

Table 9.4 Mongolian attitudes towards Japanese and Koreans (%)

	Accept as unwelcome strangers	Friendly	Flexible	Difficult to answer	Total
Japanese	17.5	28.9	36.8	16.8	100
South Koreans	13.2	23.7	48.2	14.9	100

Source: author's survey, Ulaanbaatar, Mongolia, February 2004.

showed a friendly attitude towards foreigners, 8.8 per cent accepted them as unwelcome strangers or outsiders and three-fifths were flexible. The remaining respondents did not indicate their attitude.

Mongolia is one of the few countries in the world that shares common borders with only two countries. The historical and twentieth-century experiences of Mongolia largely determine the Mongolian people's attitudes towards their northern and southern neighbours.

It is surprising that the attitudes of Mongolians towards Russians and Chinese are quite different (see table 9.3). In recent years, Mongolian–Chinese relations have become very close at a high political level as well as at the local and cross-border regional levels. However, the people's negative attitudes towards Chinese probably originate from their memory of Qing imperial domination, the Cultural Revolution in China and the "cheating of each other" between individuals and businesses during the "suitcase" trading period of the early 1990s. By contrast, relations with Russians, stagnant in recent years, have revived although they have yet to reach the former "brotherly and friendly" level of Soviet times. The people's positive attitudes towards Russians result from many reasons, such nostalgia about the Soviet period, when the USSR provided a massive amount of aid to build factories, roads, hospitals, schools and housing, but also from inertia.

Mongolia has chosen democracy and a market economy, and its society has opened up and its foreign policy has diversified. Japan and South Korea have played a crucial role in this process. This fact is apparent in the favourable attitudes of the survey respondents as shown in table 9.4.

Japan provides a major portion of the foreign aid for Mongolia while South Korea is home to a great number of "illegal" Mongolian workers.

Mongolians have also developed very different attitudes towards North Koreans and South Koreans. The survey shows that 29.1 per cent of 103 respondents regarded North Koreans as unwelcome strangers or outsiders, 24.3 per cent had a friendly attitude, 34 per cent were flexible and 12.6 per cent did not indicate a view. On the one hand, Mongolia and North Korea have maintained good relations ever since their partnership in the former Soviet bloc. (The DPRK still values Mongolia's help by way of material assistance in the Korean War. Most importantly, Mongolia established a special orphanage for North Korean war orphans.) This is a positive factor informing respondents' views. On the other hand, North Korea is one of the few countries left in the world with a totalitarian regime; it has a nuclear programme and is a subject of international criticism. For these reasons, it receives disapproval from many of the survey respondents.

Although Mongolia is challenged by a number of transitional difficulties such as widespread poverty and unemployment, its political stability, adequate national income and friendly business environment attract foreigners. This fact is translated into the perception of the survey respondents that the number of foreigners in Mongolia has increased (see table 9.5). The table does not need elaboration, except to point out that virtually every respondent to the survey indicated that the number of Chinese in the country had increased and that a significant number of respondents thought that immigrants and people without citizenship had increased. If their perceptions are correct – and there is no reason to doubt that they are, then the registration of foreign citizens in the country needs to be improved and also to be made more transparent.

Table 9.6 shows the respondents' views on the countries and international organizations with which they think Mongolia should develop close partnerships. The most preferred foreign partner was Russia, followed by the United States, Japan, Germany and South Korea. Among the inter-

Table 9.5 Perceived changes in the number of foreigners in Mongolia (%)

	Increased	Decreased	Unchanged	Do not know	Total
Russians	5.3	73.7	17.5	3.5	100
Chinese	93.0	2.6	3.5	0.9	100
Koreans	67.5	5.3	21.9	5.3	100
Immigrants	42.1	11.4	36.8	9.7	100
People without citizenship	50.9	13.2	27.2	8.7	100

Source: author's survey, Ulaanbaatar, Mongolia, February 2004.

Table 9.6 Desirability of Mongolian partnerships with countries and international organizations (%)

Country		International organizations	
Russian Federation	89.5	UN	81.6
USA	78.1	WTO	72.8
Japan	67.5	IMF	36.8
Germany	50.0	EU	30.7
South Korea	44.7	Regional organizations	28.1
UK	43.0	APEC	20.2
China	23.7	ASEAN	19.3
France	20.2	Others	5.3
India	20.2		
Others	4.4		

Source: author's survey, Ulaanbaatar, Mongolia, February 2004.

Table 9.7 Mongolian preferences in dealing with foreigners (%)

	Favour	Dislike	Flexible	No answer	Total
Become a migrant	23.7	28.9	40.4	7.0	100
Become wife of foreigner	6.1	68.4	19.4	6.1	100
Become husband of foreigner	6.1	58.8	24.6	10.5	100
Work "illegally"	43.0	10.5	40.4	6.1	100
Obtain foreign citizenship	14.0	59.6	20.2	6.2	100

Source: author's survey, Ulaanbaatar, Mongolia, February 2004.

national organizations, the United Nations and the World Trade Organization were preferred as the most important partners.

The survey also asked for what purpose the respondents interacted with foreigners. Language study was the principal purpose according to 71.1 per cent. The next most important purpose was business (56.1 per cent), followed by education (41.2 per cent), employment (36.8 per cent) and making friends (30.7 per cent).

Table 9.7 shows the distribution of the respondents' preferences in developing or seeking opportunities to deal with foreigners. A significant proportion (43.0 per cent) supported the idea of working "illegally" in a foreign country. Those who wished to emigrate to another country constituted nearly one-quarter (23.7 per cent) of the respondents. In contrast, a majority of the respondents disliked the idea of marrying a foreigner: 58.8 per cent of the men and 68.4 per cent of the women. Acquiring foreign citizenship was not a very popular choice either, with only 14.0 per cent of the respondents supporting that idea.

Table 9.8 shows some differences in attitudes among the respondents towards the Russians and the Chinese. Somewhat more women showed

Table 9.8 Mongolian attitudes towards Russians and Chinese by age and gender (%)

	Russians			Chinese		
	Friendly	Accept as unwelcome strangers	Flexible	Friendly	Accept as unwelcome strangers	Flexible
Men	64.2	9.4	26.4	7.5	62.3	30.2
Women	72.1	3.3	24.6	8.2	37.7	51.4
Under 30	57.8	8.9	33.3	2.2	60.0	37.8
30–45	75.0	3.6	21.4	10.7	39.3	50.0
Above 45	76.9	7.7	15.4	15.4	53.8	30.8

Source: author's survey, Ulaanbaatar, Mongolia, February 2004.

friendly attitudes towards the Russians than did men, but both genders showed the same lack of friendliness towards the Chinese. The younger the respondents, the less likely they were to have friendly feelings towards either Russians or Chinese. Although not shown here, neither level of education nor profession was a differentiating factor in the respondents' attitudes towards the Russians and the Chinese.

Conclusion

After the democratic reforms of 1990, Mongolia became one of the most open countries in Asia on account of its liberal immigration policies. Its initial euphoria regarding foreigners reflected in those policies gave rise to interesting stories of adventure seekers and self-claimed millionaires who travelled to Mongolia from countries as far away as Australia and the Netherlands. The country's low cost of living and comparatively high degree of basic freedoms made it attractive to foreigners, especially those from neighbouring Russia and China, as a place to settle permanently. The economic slowdown and uncertainty in East Asia in 1997–1998 led to the discovery of Mongolia as a safe place to invest small fortunes, bringing in citizens from countries such as South Korea. More recently, land reform and the privatization of large-scale state enterprises have generated much interest from foreigners.

Mongolia has already established a good foundation for the human security agenda, initiating a follow-up on papers and recommendations from the May 2000 international conference on human security that it hosted.[21] The final report of the conference offered suggestions on economic policy and job creation, education, scientific technology and information, ecological protection and sustainability. The assessment of a human security agenda in Mongolia could incorporate a better under-standing of vulnerabilities arising from a range of potential political, eco-logical, economic, demographic and military "threats". These may in-clude challenges from neighbouring China as a growing regional and international power in terms of "uncertainties", among them illegal mi-gration, transnational crime and foreign investment. Other problems are real and growing environmental and socio-economic threats from climate change, privatization and economic transition, which may lead to more natural disasters, food insecurity and human suffering.

I conclude this chapter with four general recommendations, mainly di-rected to the government of Mongolia.

First, there is a need to improve Mongolia's general legal framework, so as to better address new immigration issues and concerns. The numer-ical limit on the number of immigrants – the number of foreigners should not exceed one per cent of the Mongolian population at any given time – and the ban on dual citizenship have been questioned more and more by foreigners and Mongolians alike. Mongolia's emphasis on regional integra-tion in Northeast Asia shows how necessary it is to balance sovereignty with mechanisms for allowing transnational movements of goods, people and services through special economic zones. Exceedingly low wages and incomes in Mongolia compared to developed countries make it difficult for many Mongolians to stay at home if they think that they can find a better life abroad. The youngest, the best and the brightest, those repre-senting Mongolia's future, are among the most susceptible to brain drain through emigration or not returning from study abroad. The introduction of dual citizenship can help to prevent brain drain and also to attract highly skilled workers from abroad.

Second, the government must put more effort and resources into edu-cating the public and changing their attitudes towards foreigners. Over-emphasis on the protection of ethnic identity, way of life, culture and language leaves the public ignorant and sometimes makes for rude treat-ment of foreigners. More Mongolian citizens are supplementing their in-comes with the help of foreigners: they are making contacts with foreign companies or agencies, renting apartments to foreigners and establishing small businesses with foreign capital. It is not surprising, however, that crime, prostitution and corruption have risen, creating false security for some and jeopardizing human security for both foreigners and Mongolians.

Third, the increased exposure of Mongolia and its citizens to the forces of globalization has brought new problems, such as human trafficking, il-legal migration and transnational crime. Mongolia should join the UN conventions addressing these matters and strengthen its coordination with regional and foreign organizations dealing with them. Newspapers report a growing number of cases of the trafficking of Mongolian women overseas. This is indicative of many other problems facing the country, e.g. poverty, unemployment and domestic violence. What drives many citizens of Mongolia to go abroad, even at the risk of personal safety or problems with the law? Low income, high unemployment and the desire to earn hard currency cause many of them to seek a better life abroad. Although expatriate Mongolians may send their family remittances from abroad, the exodus of workers may further impoverish the country's human resources.

Fourth, hundreds of North Koreans have come to Mongolia since the late 1990s, obviously for reasons of personal safety. Most of these "defectors" have been allowed to travel on to Seoul, their destination of choice. Although Mongolia has dropped its earlier policy of moving North Koreans to China, partly because of pressure from international human rights groups, it has yet to join the 1951 Convention relating to the Status of Refugees. It is urgent for Mongolia to join the Convention and actively participate in promoting the human security of international refugees, including those on its territory.

Notes

The opinions expressed in this chapter are the personal opinions of the author and do not necessarily represent those of the Mongolian government.

1. This observation is drawn from the broader overview of human security perspectives of Mongolia found in Wayne Nelles, "Reconciling Human and National Security in Mongolia: A Canadian Perspective", *Regional Security Issues and Mongolia*, Ulaanbaatar: Institute for Strategic Studies, 2001, pp. 67–68.
2. Ts. Batbayar, *Modern Mongolia: A Concise History*, Ulaanbaatar: Mongolian Center for Scientific and Technological Information, 2nd edn, 2002, p. 20.
3. B. Baabar, *History of Mongolia*, Ulaanbaatar: Monsudar Publishing, 2001, pp. 299–300.
4. L. Begzjav, *Mongolian-Chinese Relations, 1949–1999*, Ulaanbaatar: Admon Publishing, 1999 (in Mongolian), pp. 42–43.
5. D. Bayarkhuu, "Soviet-Chinese relationship and Soviet military and civil specialists in Mongolia", *Olon Uls Sudlal* [International Studies], Ulaanbaatar: Institute of International Studies, 2004, No. 2, pp. 114–115.
6. *Collection of National Laws on Immigration*, Ulaanbaatar, Civil Registration Center, 2000 (in Mongolian). MPR was the abbreviation of the country's former name, Mongolian People's Republic. The change of name took place in 1992.
7. Idem.
8. *Zuunii Medee* [Century News], 26 June 2001.
9. Author interview with Mr Ts. Buyanbadrakh, 26 February 2004.
10. Author interview with Mr Ts. Buyanbadrakh, 26 February 2004.
11. Reference material, Department of Employment, Ministry of Social Welfare and Labor, 8 September 2003.
12. The most recent visitor was Governor Tuleev of Kemerovo Oblast in June 2004.
13. *Zuunii Medee*, 25 May 2001.

14. *UB Post* (Mongolia's English weekly newspaper), 30 January 2004.
15. *UB Post*, 19 February 2004.
16. Idem.
17. *New York Times*, 28 September 2003, reported in *UB Post*, 2 October 2003.
18. *UB Post*, 2 October 2003.
19. *New York Times*, 21 November 2004.
20. The author would like to thank Kh. Gundsambuu, Professor of Sociology, National University of Mongolia, for designing and administering the opinion survey exclusively for the purpose of this study.
21. International Conference on "Human Security in a Globalized World", 8–10 May 2000, Ulaanbaatar, Mongolia. Papers from this conference were posted at http://www.un-mongolia.mn/undp.

10

Conclusion: Implications for regional international relations

Tsuneo Akaha and Anna Vassilieva

International migration is an increasingly important part of the economic and demographic changes in Northeast Asia. Russia, Japan and South Korea have become the three most important destinations of labour migration in the region. In 2000, Russia had the second-largest migrant stock in the world, with 13,259,000 migrants, after the United States with 34,988,000 migrants.[1] Russia's willingness to absorb surplus labour from China is a function of political and cultural tolerance rather than economic logic. In strictly economic terms, China's need to find employment for its citizens, particularly in its north-eastern provinces, and Russia's need to provide food and consumer goods and to maintain construction and agricultural production, especially in its Far Eastern regions, are quite complementary. Although Chinese migration to Russia is currently under control, growing unemployment in north-eastern China and continuing depopulation in the Russian Far East will continue to present serious policy challenges to the two countries.

Just as in Europe in the 1990s, pressure is growing in Japan for the introduction of temporary worker programmes for highly skilled professionals. Japan's net immigration gain increased from 37,000 in 1990 to 56,000 in 2000, nearly doubling its migrant stock from 877,000 to 1,620,000.[2] The further ageing of the Japanese population will no doubt prompt more labour migration from neighbouring countries.[3] Although public acceptance of foreign workers remains muted, Japan's need to respond to the shrinking labour market is beginning to change its labour import policy. In the face of an estimated 580,000 non-Japanese illegally working as unskilled labourers in the country, the Ministry of Justice is considering new immigration policy guidelines that open up opportunities for "non-specialists or engineers", i.e. unskilled workers, to seek employment in Japan. The guidelines also call attention to the concern that allowing more foreigners to enter the country might negatively affect security.[4] Balancing the need to import foreign labour with the need to maintain cultural homogeneity and social order is an important but difficult task for Japan and other labour importing countries. As the Commission on Human Security states, effective policies are necessary in order to overcome the gap between economic need and public perception.[5]

South Korea is a net migrant exporter, but growing labour migration to the country is reducing its net migration loss – from 23,000 in 1990 to 18,000 in 2000. As a result, its migrant stock increased from 572,000 to 597,000 during the 1990s.[6] In August 2004, the government launched an employment permit system designed to increase the legal import of foreign labour from selected countries, including Mongolia. Seoul was also reported to be holding talks with Beijing about concluding a memorandum of understanding on the supply of skilled workers from China.[7]

China has been and continues to be the largest exporter of migrants in Northeast Asia. In 1990, it sent 381,000 more migrants abroad than it received from other countries, and the same migrant export–import gap was seen in 2000.[8] Mongolia and North Korea are also net migrant exporters. Between 1990 and 2000, Mongolia's net migration loss doubled, from 8,000 to 16,000.[9] Although official statistics are not available on North Korea's migration situation, there is no doubt that the country is a net loser, and its economic emigration is likely to continue. In July 2004, there was a dramatic evacuation of several hundred North Koreans from Southeast Asia to South Korea, prompting an expected North Korean accusation of the South.[10] In September 2004, 29 people claiming to be North Koreans broke into a Japanese school in Beijing demanding safe passage to South Korea, and were placed under the protection of the Japanese embassy.[11] The human drama is certain to continue for the foreseeable future.

Although crossing borders by ordinary citizens in Northeast Asia is motivated mostly by economic reasons and clearly has economic impacts on the home and destination countries, the phenomenon has political, social, cultural and security implications as well. As Larin and Wishnick have shown in chapter 2 and chapter 3 respectively, the influx of Chinese traders and migrant workers into the Russian Far East is an important and necessary stimulant to the region's economy, but it is also a source of irritation to the local population, whose sense of vulnerability has been aroused by the economic stagnation and depopulation they have been experiencing in recent years. The case studies presented by Zha in chapter 5 and Lee in chapter 8 show that abuses of visa overstayers and illegal foreign workers by shrewd employers are a growing concern to immigration and law enforcement authorities in the host countries.[12] Also of concern are the deceptive practices of some labour export and import agents, as well as human trafficking organized by criminal groups which exploit the vulnerable status of people crossing borders in China, Russia, Mongolia, Korea and Japan.[13]

Crimes committed by foreigners are attracting growing attention from the general public and law enforcement agencies in all Northeast Asian countries. As Akaha and Vassilieva note in chapter 4, criminal developments are testing the tolerance of affected communities towards foreigners, whom they often cast in negative stereotypes. Lack of mutual understanding between foreign residents/visitors and the local population, as the two authors show in the case of the Russian presence in Japan, results from language and cultural barriers as well as perceived disparities in the distribution of benefits from their interaction. So far, the problem remains an issue largely at the individual level in Japan, but in the Russian Far East it has become politically charged. Discrimination against and loss of ethnic identity among younger generations of Koreans in Japan and elsewhere concern older members of the Korean communities in Japan, as discussed by Mervio in chapter 6, and those South Koreans who desire solidarity with overseas Korean communities, as described by Lee. As Batbayar notes in chapter 9, brain drain is of concern to Mongolia, as some of the most skilled and best educated citizens leave the country in search of opportunities abroad, although their remittances represent an important benefit for the home economy.

The migration issue potentially the most troubling in political and security terms is the status of North Koreans who have left their country and are living in China and elsewhere – the subject of Smith's analysis in chapter 7. Unfortunately, we do not know what impact, if any, the highly publicized "defection" of North Korean citizens to other countries is having on the regime in Pyongyang.

Currently, there is no institutional framework in Northeast Asia for the multilateral coordination of policies to address these issues. As Scalapino points out in the Foreword, the need for multilateral cooperation is evident. How likely is it that the Northeast Asian countries will move beyond their present unilateral (internal) responses and bilateral adjustments and engage in serious multilateral cooperation?

Generally, the movement of people across national borders has lagged behind transnational movements of information, capital, technology, goods and services. This is because the movement of people involves the difficult task of reconciling cultural and social differences and mediating and negotiating political loyalties between different ethnic and national groups. Most of the case studies in this volume present evidence of this. Growing contacts between people of different ethnicities and nationalities are generating various degrees of tension for the affected communities and diverse challenges for government authorities in all Northeast Asian countries.

So far, no summit meetings among the state leaders of the region have dealt with international migration issues. Nor has there been any serious effort to establish institutional mechanisms for multilateral coordination in this field. Virtually all policy changes in the migration sector have been, as noted above, through domestic (unilateral) or bilateral processes. The change in Russian migration policy in the winter of 1993–1994 in response to the consequences of the unmanaged influx of Chinese traders into the Russian Far East was unilateral. More recently, however, there has been some bilateral coordination between the Russian and Chinese governments regarding mutual migration flows. But there has been no multilateral discussion of the issue of North Korean migrants in China. If anything, these issues have strained relations between the countries concerned. None of the other migration issues discussed in this volume have yet given rise to any region-wide dialogue.

Is cross-border migration contributing to the development of a regional identity among the peoples of Northeast Asia? To the extent that individuals crossing borders help to create new social networks between communities in their home and host countries, they can potentially contribute to the sharing of cultural values and the development of a sense of a common future across national boundaries. However, the case studies presented in this book indicate that ethnic, cultural and national identities are still very powerful forces in Northeast Asia and that the influx of foreign migrants and visitors into local communities is reinforcing those identities.

What is the impact of international migration on the security concerns of the governments and peoples of Northeast Asia? The Commission on Human Security states, "Massive population movements affect the security of receiving states, often compelling them to close their borders and forcibly prevent people from reaching safety and protection. Armed elements among civilian refugee populations may spread conflict into neighbouring countries."[14] Northeast Asian countries have yet to face such a dire situation. However, they face some difficult issues of national and human security related to cross-border human flows. Although none of the cases that have been presented in this book involve immediate national security challenges to the countries of the region, instability on the Korean peninsula and possible North Korean refugee flows of massive proportions have the potential to disrupt peace and stability. Human security issues in Northeast Asia include the plight of North Koreans in

China and elsewhere in the region, countless cases of discrimination, exploitation, human rights abuses against migrant workers and others crossing borders, and the illegal status of growing numbers of migrant labourers. There is also evidence that some migrants in vulnerable legal positions and without basic social support resort to crime. Criminal elements in both sending and receiving countries also present serious challenges to national and local governments in the region.

Against the background of globalization, cross-border human flows cannot but grow in the future in this and other parts of the world. In Northeast Asia, economic interdependence is gradually deepening through market forces, particularly among Japan, China and South Korea. As market economies continue to grow in Russia and Mongolia, so the complementary linkages between the economies of the rest of the region will increase. Social integration proceeds through networks of individuals, enterprises and other groups and organizations whose activities transcend national borders. Cultural integration can also deepen through exchanges between individual citizens, business organizations and civil society groups. The region also needs integration through cooperation in non-traditional security fields, such as environmental protection, resource management, the control of illegal trafficking in drugs, weapons and humans, containment of the HIV/AIDS and SARS epidemics, counter-terror measures and the management of cross-border human flows.

We conclude this study with a survey of further issues to be considered, including possible solutions to some of the problems identified in the book.[15] Regarding Russians in Japan, Japan and Russia should expand opportunities for cultural and social interaction by organizing government-sponsored exchange programmes and supporting private initiatives for citizens' interaction. In chapter 4, Akaha and Vassilieva propose locally sponsored orientation programmes for Russian residents and visitors about Japanese culture and a partnership among public agencies, educational institutions and non-governmental groups in addressing the common cultural and social issues facing Russian residents and members of local communities.

The Japanese government should join and vigorously apply the terms of international conventions for the protection of the rights of migrant workers and their families and for the elimination of human trafficking.[16] Japan should energetically apply the principles and letter of international human rights conventions to which it is already a party[17] and protect Korean residents and other ethnic minorities from discrimination. In particular, the government should consider a legal reform with a view to introducing explicit and specific rules against crimes based on race, religion, ethnicity and gender. It should also consider establishing an ombudsman for aliens (primarily asylum seekers and recent immigrants) or an ombudsman for minorities. This ombudsman would collect information on the status of asylum seekers, recent immigrants and ethnic minorities, especially concerning various forms of discrimination against them.

As Merviö proposes in chapter 6, public education efforts are necessary in order to promote understanding of multiculturalism and cultural rights, especially in relation to the issues of education and the Korean language. For those Korean minorities who wish to maintain their ethnic and cultural identity and to use the Korean language, the opportunity to do so should be available. Without a cultural, particularly language, education, the Korean community will be assimilated rapidly and lose its potential role as a bridge between the Japanese mainstream and the Korean minority.

Japanese immigration policy should be reformed so as to reduce the illegal immigration and illegal labour that the current policy unintentionally encourages. Visa categories should be revised in order to root out exploitation of illegal and legal immigrants. One example is the "entertainment" visas, which serve as an incentive for human trafficking and the violation of the human rights of women. The Japanese government has recently decided to reduce substantially the number of "entertainment" visas to be issued. As Zha shows in chapter 5, Japanese employers use "trainee" visas to justify the import of unskilled workers as cheap labour, and many foreign nationals also abuse the "trainee" system in order to find employment in Japan.[18] Here too the Japanese government is beginning to respond to the problem. It is considering the possibility of allowing "non-specialized" personnel to work in the country. Visa overstayers as well are becoming a serious problem in Japan.[19] It will be able to reduce this problem by opening certain sectors of the domestic labour market to foreign workers.

The treatment of foreign citizens who have committed minor offences should be made more humane and be proportional to the impact of their unlawful act. For example, it does not make sense for visa overstayers who have been caught by the police to be placed in detention cells for three months before being afforded a hearing with immigration officials or for them to be "handcuffed and roped together like cattle" on deportation day.[20] Although Japanese authorities' requirement for law and order is understandable from the perspective of traditional Japanese culture's emphasis on conformity and social harmony, their open call for the public to report "suspicious illegal aliens" in their midst to law enforcement authorities smacks of racism and xenophobia.

The Japanese people generally support the United Nations and the universal ideals and aspirations it represents. UN diplomacy has been one of the main pillars of post-war Japanese foreign policy. The most recent example is Japan's high-profile contribution to the promotion of human security through the work of the UN Commission on Human Security. At an international symposium on the international movement of people and immigration policy in Tokyo in 2002, a high-ranking Japanese diplomat stated that human security was a "guiding principle" in dealing with the issue of the international movement of people.[21] The Japanese government should realize that the ill-treatment of Koreans and other minorities, as well as of foreign migrants, in Japan compromises its credibility as a promoter of human security.

As we have noted earlier, China has become the most important source of migration in Northeast Asia.[22] It should incorporate as many internationally recognized legal standards for dealing with illegal outward migration as possible. Its legal code has its own tradition, and often inflicts severe punishment on those Chinese who have migrated abroad illegally. But when the price of voluntary return to China is high for the migrants and their families, Chinese laws discourage Chinese migrant workers who would otherwise choose to return home. Beijing should work closely with Tokyo to crack down on criminal human trafficking networks in the two countries, which are responsible for much of the illegal labour migration. In late September 2003, the Chinese government finally agreed to establish a small law enforcement presence in Japan for assisting the Japanese police in identifying crimes committed by Chinese nationals in Japan. This is a step in the right direction, but the two countries should do much more to eliminate illegal migration to Japan. China and Japan may follow the model of Sino-American cooperation in which China has agreed to the establishment of an FBI office in Beijing in order to track down criminal elements, Chinese and/or American, operating in China.

The Chinese government should tighten the enforcement of its emigration regulations, to stem illegal labour migration to Japan and other countries. By design and by default, outward labour migration has been an accepted means of easing China's domestic employment pressures. Those pressures are bound to grow as the level of industrialization rises in the country and its education system remains ill-equipped to provide adequate retraining for its workforce.

The Chinese and Japanese governments should do away with the pretence of technology transfer under the "trainee" system and deal squarely with the needs of the labour market in both countries. Demographic changes in the two countries are such that Japan needs to import unskilled Chinese workers and China needs to export them. The "technology transfer" scheme was conceived of in the 1980s, when most of the Chinese going to Japan did so to acquire new skills. However, the situation has changed since then. China and Japan should call a spade a spade and acknowledge Japan's need to import and China's need to export unskilled labour. Doing so can be helpful in dealing with the often negative societal responses to disputes between Chinese employees and their Japanese employers.

As for Chinese migration to the Russian Far East, steady economic development on both sides of the border would help to alleviate the pressure of Chinese emigration and reduce Russians' sense of vulnerability.[23] This would require a commitment of substantial resources to the economic development of both the Russian Far East and adjacent eastern Siberia and the north-eastern provinces of China, namely Heilongjiang, Jilin and Liaoning. An improvement of the quality of educational institutions and human resources development facilities would also be important. In the foreseeable future, however, the push and pull factors on the two sides of the border are likely to continue to stimulate Chinese migration to Russia. This being the case, bilateral cooperation is essential to the management of the flow of traders and migrant workers. Sharing accurate information about the scale and nature of Chinese migration, eliminating official corruption and strictly enforcing the law and regulations on both sides of the border are essential for effectively managing bilateral migration flows.

As twice as many Russians travel to China as Chinese travel to Russia each year, clearly a stable and effectively managed border regime is in both sides' interest. Instead of focusing exclusively on restricting entry, which tends to encourage illegal migration and corruption, the Russian and Chinese governments should work together to facilitate legal travel in both directions. This would involve simplifying procedures for business travellers, expanding the number of cities where one can apply for a business visa, reducing fees and processing time, and keeping track of travellers from one country once they have entered the other. Even if the two sides undertake these initiatives, however, it is still highly likely that the depressed economy of the Russian Far East and the demographic and development trends on the Chinese side that cause unemployment will keep up migration pressure on the border for a long time to come.

Mongolia's restrictive immigration policy, particularly its severe numerical limit on immigration, has come under domestic and foreign criticism.[24] This also runs counter to its express interest in economic integration with other Northeast Asian countries. On the other hand, its liberal emigration policy and a lack of employment opportunities in the country are causing a brain drain. Batbayar suggests in chapter 9 that one of the solutions could be the introduction of dual citizenship, to retain the country's indigenous human resources and also to attract highly skilled workers from abroad. Public education is also required in order to improve Mongolian citizens' attitudes towards foreigners. It is in Mongolians' interest to supplement their income by working for foreign companies or agencies, renting apartments to foreigners or establishing small businesses with foreign capital. On the other hand, Mongolia needs to take effective measures to stem the growing tide of crime, prostitution and corruption involving foreigners.

Regarding North Koreans in China, Smith presents in chapter 7 a series of recommendations. Suffice it to reiterate here the importance of giving priority to the human security of North Korean migrants and the urgent need for the international community and the Chinese government to extend humanitarian assistance to them out of legitimate concern for their safety and well-being. Smith also emphasizes the importance of serious research into the scale, motivations, conditions and future plans of the migrants so as to provide reliable information on which to base national and international policies. Not isolation of North Korea but engagement with it is the only realistic way to improve the economic crisis in the North, which is the main factor pushing hundreds of thousands of North Koreans out of the country.

As part of South Korea's effort to accommodate more overseas Koreans and foreign workers in the country, the government should reorganize its legal framework so as to include Korean Chinese as one group of overseas Koreans.[25] According to Lee in chapter 8, the most important step would be to amend the Overseas Koreans Act of 1999 so that Korean Chinese would be accorded the same legal rights as other overseas Koreans. The exclusion of Korean Chinese from the definition of "overseas Koreans" in the Overseas Koreans Act has forced many of them to seek illegal entry into South Korea. Some are also overstaying their visas. The illegal status of Korean Chinese in South Korea encourages employers to exploit them and violate their rights. Such violations include overtime work without compensation, non-payment of salaries, physical beating and sexual harassment. Policy-makers in Seoul and Beijing should address the issue of Korean Chinese labour migration to South Korea. China-based brokers are charging Korean Chinese wishing to work in South Korea US$10,000–US$20,000 for finding real or prospective employers; this amounts to 10 years' salary for most Korean Chinese. Many of these brokers also illegally facilitate labour migration of Korean Chinese by forging passports and other documents and bribing consulate officials.

The labour migration of Korean Chinese to South Korea will be helpful to the economic development of north-eastern China, from where most of them come. However, the Chinese government opposes South Korea's possible inclusion of Korean Chinese in the category of overseas Koreans. Beijing argues that according a special legal status to Korean Chinese, who are Chinese citizens, would impinge on China's ethnic minority policy. If dual nationality is out of the question, as appears to be the case, South Korea should consider according a special status to overseas Koreans, including Korean Chinese, with their special rights limited to employment in the country. A precedent already exists in Northeast Asia, in the Japanese government's special treatment of foreign nationals of Japanese ancestry, particularly those from Latin American countries, who are given preferential access to the Japanese labour market.

South Korea and China should cooperate as well in facilitating the legal migration of Korean Chinese to South Korea. In 2003, a South Korean consulate-general opened in Shenyang in Liaoning Province. However, most Korean Chinese live in Yanbian Korean Autonomous Prefecture in Jilin Province and also in Heilongjiang Province. The establishment of a South Korean consular office in Yanbian would facilitate the issuing of visas for legal entry to South Korea.

Some administrative reforms are necessary in order to improve interagency coordination on immigration policy. Currently, various aspects of Korean Chinese activity in South Korea come under the jurisdiction of the Ministry of Legal Affairs, the Ministry of Foreign Affairs and Trade, the Ministry of Labor, the Ministry of Industry and Resources and the Ministry of Education. Even though a committee has been set up under the Prime Minister's Office to facilitate communication among them, their coordination has not gone much beyond clarifying each agency's position on Korean Chinese issues. The government should give the committee greater power or establish a higher-level body so as to ensure effective coordination among agencies.

Finally, all Northeast Asian countries need to cooperate with each other in strengthening and harmonizing human rights laws and practices in the region. As in the case of European integration, in which the European Council and the European Convention on Human Rights play a central role, so in Northeast Asia regional cooperation is necessary for improving human rights-related policies and practices as part of regional integration efforts. As the movement of people across national borders increases, new institutions should be established and agreements should be concluded for protecting the human rights of migrant and minority populations. More liberal migration policies and greater protection of human rights will help to reduce crime, alienation and other social risks involving migrants and minorities.

Notes

1. United Nations, Department of Economic and Social Affairs, *International Migration Report 2002*, United Nations, New York, 2002 (ST/ESA/SER.A/220), p. 3.
2. See ⟨http://www.un.org/esa/population/publications/ittmig2002/locations/392.htm⟩ (retrieved 27 April 2003).
3. In mid-2004, Japanese people above 65 made up 19 per cent of the total population of

the country, whereas those under 15 constituted 14 per cent. The comparable figures were 7 per cent and 22 per cent for China, 6 per cent and 27 per cent for North Korea, 8 per cent and 20 per cent for South Korea, 5 per cent and 36 per cent for Mongolia and 13 per cent and 16 per cent for Russia. *2004 World Population Data Sheet of the Population Reference Bureau*, Washington, DC, pp. 10 and 12.

4. *The Japan Times*, 4 March 2005, available at ⟨http://www.japantimes.co.jp/cgi-bin/getarticle.pl5?nn20050304a2.htm⟩ (accessed 6 March 2005).

5. Commission on Human Security, *Human Security Now*, New York: Commission on Human Security, 2003, p. 44, available at ⟨http://www.humansecurity-chs.org/finalreport/⟩ (accessed 21 August 2003).

6. The statistics are available at ⟨http://www.un.org/esa/population/publications/ittmig2002/locations/410.htm⟩ (retrieved 27 April 2003).

7. The programme was expected to bring in 25,000 workers from six countries in 2004 alone, with increasing numbers in subsequent years. *Asia Pulse Businesswire* via News-Edge Corporation, Seoul, 16 August 2004.

8. The statistics are available at ⟨http://www.un.org/esa/population/publications/ittmig2002/locations/156.htm⟩ (retrieved 27 April 2003).

9. The statistics are available at ⟨http://www.un.org/esa/population/publications/ittmig2002/locations/496.htm⟩ (retrieved 27 April 2003).

10. BBC News online, 27 July 2004, available at ⟨http://news.bbc.co.uk/2/hi/asia-pacific/3928523.stm⟩ (retrieved 30 July 2004).

11. Asahi Shimbun online, 5 September 2004, available at ⟨http://www.asahi.com/international/update/0905/009.html⟩ (accessed 5 September 2004).

12. In 2001, there were 255,000 overstayers in South Korea. *International Labor Conference, 92nd Session, Report VI, Toward a Fair Deal for Migrant Workers in the Global Economy*, International Labor Office, Geneva, 2004, p. 12.

13. Widespread labour recruitment malpractices, fraud and abuses in many Asian countries are noted in International Labor Office, *Summary of Conclusions*, Report of the Regional Tripartite Meeting on Challenges to Labor Migration Policy and Management in Asia, 30 June–2 July 2003, Bangkok, p. 1.

14. This is from the Commission on Human Security, p. 42.

15. The case study authors submitted the issues and possible solutions presented below to us. Most case authors benefited from the discussion at a project meeting held in Monterey, California, on 9–10 May 2004. The following individuals also attended this meeting, and we are grateful for their contribution to the discussion: Edward Newman of the United Nations University, Tokyo; Hiroshi Komai of Tsukuba University, Japan (now with Chukyo Women's University); Cristina Chuen, Daniel Pinkston and Jing-dong Yuan of the Monterey Institute of International Studies, California; Mitsuhiro Mimura of the Economic Research Institute for Northeast Asia, Niigata, Japan; Robert Scalapino of the University of California-Berkeley; and Joanne van Selm of the Migration Policy Institute, Washington, DC. We also extend our thanks to the United States Institute of Peace (USIP), Washington, DC, particularly Taylor Seybolt, and to the Migration Policy Institute, especially Demetri Papademetriou and Joanne van Selm, for co-hosting the meeting at the USIP on 24 June 2004, where the findings and recommendations from the project were presented. The authors alone are responsible for the selection and discussion of the findings and recommendations that follow.

16. The relevant conventions are the Convention on the Protection of Rights of All Migrant Workers and Family Members (1990), the Protocol to Prevent, Suppress, and Punish Trafficking of Persons (2000) and the Protocol Against the Smuggling of Migrants (2000). Mika Mervö contributed to the discussion on Korean and other minorities in Japan.

17. The relevant international human rights conventions to which Japan is a party include the International Covenant on Economic, Social and Cultural Rights (Japan acced in 1979); the International Covenant on Civil and Political Rights (1979); the International Convention on the Elimination of All Forms of Racial Discrimination (1996); the Convention on the Elimination of All Forms of Discrimination against Women (1985); the Convention on the Rights of the Child (1994); the Convention Relating to the Status of Refugees (1981); and the Protocol relating to the Status of Refugees of 31 January 1967 (1982).

18. Wage gaps between migrant workers and native workers who perform the same task are not unique to Japan. This is a pattern observed throughout Asia, indeed throughout the world. See *International Labor Conference*, p. 44.

19. In 2001, there were 224,000 overstayers in Japan. Ibid., p. 12.

20. Gregory Clark, "Barbaric Immigration Policy", *Japan Times Online*, 22 August 2004, available at ⟨http://www.japantimes.com/cgi-bin/geted.pl5?eo20040822gc.htm⟩ (accessed 22 August 2004).

21. Yukio Takasu, "Statement", the Symposium on the International Movement of People and Immigration Policy towards the 21st Century, 29 November 2002, available at ⟨http://www.mofa.go.jp/policy/human_security/speech0011.html⟩ (retrieved 10 December 2002).

22. Daojiong Zha contributed to the discussion of Chinese migration to Japan.

23. Elizabeth Wishnick, Vilya Gelbras and Victor Larin contributed to the discussion of Chinese migration to the Russian Far East.

24. Tsedendamba Batbayar contributed to the discussion summarized in this paragraph.

25. We thank Jeanyoung Lee of Inha University, Korea, for contributing to the discussion summarized in this paragraph.

Index

Ageing
  population and labour force 17
Annan, Kofi
  migration, on 6

China
  Chinese migrants in Japan. *see* Japan
  cooperation with South Korea 245
  enforcement of emigration regulations
    242
  incorporation of legal standards 242
  labour migrants in Russian Far East. *see*
    Russian Far East
  migrant exports 237
  migration policy 84–86
  migration to Russian Far East. *see*
    Russian Far East
  North Koreans in 165–190
    accommodation 179–180
    assistance from other Koreans 185
    asylum seekers 173
    borders 167–168
    Chagang, from 176
    current assistance 182–185
    DPRK provincial boundaries, map
      168
    economic migrants 173
    employment 179
    estimating number of 169

  ethnic Koreans 167
  exploitation of women 180
  finding food 179
  geographic and social origins of
    177–178
  homeless children 180–181
  humanitarian organizations 185–186
  legal status of migrants 172–175
  migrants, meaning 166–167
  migrants' socio-economic background
    177
  most vulnerable 181
  North Hamgyong, from 175–176
  North Pyongan, from 176
  number of migrants 169–171
  papers 180
  pattern of migration 168–169
  plight of 179–182
  policy problems 174, 178
  policy recommendations 175, 178–179,
    181–182, 184–185
  political controversy about 165
  population of North Korea, table 175
  previous research 166
  reasons for migration from North
    Hamgyong 176–177
  refugees 173
  research on 173–174
  research problem 172

researching humanitarian organizations 186
Ryanggang, from 176
solutions to 178
terminology and politics 166–167
Yanbian, in 167
Yanji City 171
population trends 25–27
Chinese mafia 56
Chongryun 144–145
Corruption
Chinese labour migration to Russian Far East, and 78–79
Crime
Chinese in Russian Far East, and 56
committed by foreigners 238

Diversity
Northeast Asia, in 20
DPRK. see North Korea

Economic security
China–Russia regional relations, and 86–87
Epidemiology
Northeast Asia, in 17
Ethnic characterization
Chinese, of 57

Fertility rates 14–15
Foreign nationals
rights of 34–35

Globalization
cross-border human flows, and 240

Hong Kong SAR
population trends 27
Host-community members
rights of affected 35
Huaqiao 58–59
distinction from huaren 80
Huaren 80
Human trafficking
Mongolia, in 224–226

International Labour Organization
foreign workers in Korea, and 208
International migrants
statistics 2

Japan
application of international conventions 240–241
Chinese migrants in 120–140
1945 Japanese invasion 121
aims of foreign trainee system 131
"China boom" 121–122
Chinese consulate in Niigata 138
Chinese presence 123–125
Chinese–Japanese marriages 124
City official's views of Niigata–China ties 134–137
crime, and 127–128
economic ties 122
favourable views of 127
impact on local communities 128
impacts on local area 132
improving mutual understanding 130
internationalization strategy 122
Japanese contacts with 127
Japanese views on 126–133
means of improving Japan–China relations 130
Niigata and China 121–123
participation in exchange programmes 127
passenger airline service 122
recruitment of Chinese "trainees" 122–123
reflections on presence of foreign workers 136–137
reform of foreign trainee policy 132–133
registered Chinese in Niigata, table 123
"Revitalize the Northeast" campaign 139
short-term exchanges 125
sponsored students 124
statistics 120
students 124
survey 120–121
views on Japan–China relations 129–131
views on presence of foreign workers 131–133
worsening of employment situation 132
demographic changes 95
immigration debate 95–96
Koreans in 141–162
1930s and 40s migration 141
1991 memorandum 150

Japan (cont.)
  assimilation 145–146
  Chongryun 144–145
  citizenship 147
  colonial collaborators 144
  community divisions 143–145
  cultural backgrounds 142
  demography 142–143
  education 155–156
  educational background of Koreans in
    Shimane, table 155
  experiences of discrimination 159
  future of 159–160
  granting of permanent residence 150
  hate crimes 144
  heterogeneous nature of 143
  Japanese friends 158–159
  "Japanese names" 147
  Japan's image in South Korea 150
  Korean community among Japanese
    ethnic minorities 141–142
  Korean customs at home 157
  Korean residents in Shimane, table
    152
  Korean schools 144
  language 156
  largest concentrations of Koreans in
    Shimane, table 152
  Marital status of Koreans in Shimane,
    table 154
  marriage 146–148, 154–155
  migration 154
  mixed marriages 146–147
  nationality 149–151
  naturalization 151
  new migration 148–149
  relations with Japanese 157–158
  respondents' facility in Korean
    language, table 156
  security risks 149
  Shimane Koreans' use of Japanese
    aliases, table 158
  Shimane Prefecture, in, case study
    151–160
  social life 146–148
  statistics 142–143
  voting rights 151
migration statistics 96
population trends 28–29
reform of immigration policy 241
Russian presence in 95–119

  developing business opportunities 104
  dispute over sovereignty of Northern
    Territories 114
  economic benefits 102–103
  entry at small northern ports 102
  factors behind growth in 103–105
  Hokkaido and Niigata, in 98–103
  immigration statistics 97–98
  importance of studying 96
  improving public perceptions 115
  internationalization movement 105
  Japanese antipathy to 96–97
  Japanese views of 105–111
  Kushiro, view of Russians in 108–110
  local-level contacts 115
  Nemuro, view of Russians in 108–110
  Niigata, view of Russians in 110–111
  "no-visa visits" 104–105
  number of new Russian visitors by
    purpose of entry, table 100
  number of new temporary Russian
    visitors, table 100
  number of registered Russians by
    prefecture, table 101
  number of Russian nationals entering
    Japan, table 99
  number of Russians registered in
    Hokkaido, table 102
  number of Russians registered in
    Niigata, table 103
  reasons for 98
  registered with local administration 100
  Russian community 103
  Sapporo, view of Russians in 106–107
  tourism 98
  transportation infrastructure 104
  views of Russian residents about local
    Japanese 111–114
  Wakkanai, view of Russians in 107–108
support for UN 241–242
technological revolutions, and 95
temporary worker programmes 236–237

Labour export
  Chinese labour migration to Russian Far
    East, and 74–76

Macao SAR
  population trends 27
Migrants
  meaning 5–6

Migration
  channels of
    China to Russian Far East 50–53
  meaning 5
  Northeast Asia, in 20
  policies 24–25
  trends 21–24
Migration patterns
  Northeast Asia, in. *see* Population
    trends
Mongolia
  criminal activity 226
  foreign migration issues in 215–235
    anti-Chinese laws 216
    China, and 215
    Chinese firms, number of 217
    Chinese trade 216–217
    current status of foreign presence
      218–219
    free elections 218
    historical perspective 216–218
    human security agenda 232–233
    legislation 219
    obtaining passports 218–219
    People's Revolution 217
    population density 216
    recommendations 233–234
    Russian commerce 217
    Russian presence 215
    settling Chinese nationals 216
  foreigners in 219–221
    cashmere industry 223
    ceiling on 219–220
    dual citizenship 221
    foreign workers 223
    government service 220
    increase in visitors 221–222
    legal status of 220
    "local Russians", problems of 221
    number of arrivals and departures in
      Mongolia, table 222
    number of 220
    number of permanent residents
      220–221
    overstaying visas 222
    Russian's employment 223–224
    trade 223
  human trafficking in 224–226
    North Korean defectors 225
    studies of 224–225
  population trends 31

survey of public attitudes towards
  foreigners 228–232
  attitudes towards Japanese and
    Koreans, table 229
  attitudes towards Russians and
    Chinese, table 229
  desirability of partnerships with
    countries and international
    organizations, table 231
  perceived changes in number of
    foreigners, table 230
  preferences in dealing with foreigners,
    table 231
  respondents 228
  travel of citizens 226–228
    "army of migrants" in Russia 226–227
    Chinese border 227
    democratic reform, and 226
    outbound Mongolian passengers, table
      228
    Russian border 227
    South Korea 227
Mortality rates 14–15
Multilateral migration policies 33–34

Nation-states
  role in regulating migration 69
North Korea
  Koreans in Japan. *see* Japan
  North Koreans in China. *see* China
  population trends 29–30
  refugees in South Korea. *see* South
    Korea
Northeast Asia
  crossing borders in 237–238
  development of regional identity 239
  growing migration in 3
    international research project 4
    opportunities and challenges for
      individual citizens 3
  international relations in 1
    cross-border migration, and 2
    new analytical paradigm 1–2
  population data, table 12–13
  population trends in. *see* Population
    trends
  signs of changes in 2

Origin countries
  impacts on relations with destination
    countries 35

Population trends 11–44
    affected host-community members, rights
        of 35
    migration patterns in Northeast Asia, and
        11–44
    affects 11
    disparity in population size of states 14
    failures of social contracts 11
    fertility and mortality rates 14–15
    global consequences of population
        dynamics 14
    population size estimates and
        projections, table 15
    migration policies 24–25
    migration trends 21–24
        human welfare issues 24
        migration indicators, table 22–23
        state security 24
        tiers relevant to Northeast Asia 21
    multilateral migration policies 33–34
    national cases 25–33
        China 25–27
        DPRK 29–30
        Hong Kong SAR 27
        Japan 28–29
        Macao SAR 27
        Mongolia 31
        ROK 30
        Russian Federation 31–33
        Taiwan (ROC) 28
    overcoming obstacles 37
    policies in place 36
    population change in Northeast Asia
        15–20
        ageing population and labour force
            17
        diversity 20
        epidemiology 17
        migration 20
        past conflicts 15–16
        population pyramids, table 19
        recent population transitions 16–17
        right of return 16
        urbanization 20
        vital rates 17
    possible policies 36
    regional security environment 35–36
    relations between origin and destination
        countries 35
    rights of foreign nationals 34–35
    source of problem 36

ROK. see South Korea
Russian Far East (RFE)
    channels of migration from China 50–53
        Chinese tourism, table 52
        commercial trips 52–53
        contract work 51–52
        illegal border crossings 51
        number of tourists 51
        overstaying commercial visas 53
        "temporary work" agreement 52
        three official 50
        visa-free group tourism 51
    China and Russia's migration policy
        84–86
    China's approach to 48–50
        contract workers 49
        expanding relations 49
        political tradition 48–49
        provincial authorities 49–50
    Chinese communities in 54–59
        border territories, in 55
        Chinese perceptions of region 58
        "Criminal Chinese" 56
        criminal offences against Chinese 56–
            57
        emergence of 54
        environmental damage 57
        ethnic characterization 57
        illegal presence in labour market 54–55
        number of Chinese in Russia 54
        official statistics 54
        police statistics 56
        scale and consequences 55–56
        survey results 58
        Union of Chinese and Huaqiao 58–59
    Chinese in 47–67
        demography and economics 48
        disintegration of Russia, and 47
        "Heavenly Kingdom" 47
        unique nature of migration 48
    Chinese labour migrants in 68–92
        categorization 69
        corruption 78–79
        economic security 69
        economic security dilemma 86–87
        employment in north-eastern China,
            table 73
        family members 80–81
        government contacts with 81
        history of 70–71
        huaqiao distinction from huaren 80

inadequate regulation 78–79
issue on bilateral agenda 79
labour cooperation 81–82
labour export 74–76
mid-nineteenth century, in 70
monthly salary of Chinese workers,
    table 75
needs of local economies 68
occupation of Chinese workers, table
    75
opportunity 74
overall purpose of 79–80
overseas workers, as 80
population of Chinese Northeast, table
    72
push and pull factors 72–79
reasons for, table 73
role of nation-states 69
tourism 76–78
trade 76–78
trade and shipping networks 70
Treaty of Aigun (1858) 71
Treaty of Beijing (1860) 71
underdevelopment 72–74
underemployment 72–74
xin yimin 80
perception of China in 59–62
    "Chinese threat", existence of 60
    fear of Chinese expansion 59–60
    interest in friendly relations 61
    local media, and 59
    real and perceived threats 60–61
    reasons for fears 60
    "yellow peril" 61
Russian perceptions of Chinese migrants
    82–84
    border relations 83–84
    complementary economies 82–83
    regional balance of power 83–84
    regional economic cooperation 82–83
Russian Federation
    absorbing Chinese labour 236
    migration policy 84–86
    population trends 31–33
    Russian presence in Japan. see Japan

Security
    impact of international migration on
        239–240
South Korea
    administrative reforms 245

asylum seekers 209–210
    acceptance of refugees, table 209
    amendment to immigration law 209
    process 209–210
cooperation with China 245
current trends in emigration 194–197
    countries with more than 2000
        Koreans, table 196
    globalization, and 195
    increase in overseas Koreans, table
        195
    Koreans "temporarily" going abroad,
        table 196
    overseas Koreans associations, table
        197
    overseas Koreans, table 194
    reasons for emigrating 195
foreign migrants in 204–208
    amnesty for undocumented foreign
        workers 207–208
    attempts to attract 205
    foreign residents in South Korea, table
        205
    government position on foreign labour
        208
    illegal workers 206
    increased number of illegal migrants   ·
        207
    industrial training system 206
    International Labour Organization, and
        208
    labour strife 207
    marriage 206–207
    policies towards foreign workers
        207–208
    policy discrimination 206
    social prejudice 206
    state of foreign workers 206–207
    three categories 205
history of overseas Koreans 192–193
    adoption of children 193
    Japan 193
    Manchuria 192–193
    United States 193
Koreans in Japan. see Japan
migration policies 191–214
    foreign immigration to 191–192
    Koreans living overseas 191
net migration loss 237
North Korean refugees 210–212
    China, and 210

South Korea (cont.)
 defectors 210
 direct defection 210
 "illegal aliens", as 211
 safety of 211
 "soft diplomacy" 211
 surge in recent years 210
 overseas Koreans
 better policies towards 203–204
 overseas Koreans policy 198–202
 definition of ethnic Koreans with
 foreign citizenship 200
 Department of Overseas Koreans,
 establishment of 199–200
 development of Korean emigrant policy
 198–199
 educational institutions abroad for
 overseas Koreans, table 201
 limitations of policies 199–202
 progress and tasks 198–202
 promotion of welfare 200
 population trends 30
 proposed revision of Overseas Koreans
 Law 202–203
 complexity of 202
 diplomatic tensions with China, and
 202–203
 reorganisation of legal framework 244
 status of overseas Koreans' associations
 197–198

 trafficking of women 212
State security 35–36

Taiwan (ROC)
 population trends 28
Tourism
 Chinese labour migration to Russian Far
 East 76–78
Trafficking
 human
 Mongolia, in 224–226
 women, of
 South Korea, in 212
Treaty of Aigun (1858) 71
Treaty of Beijing (1860) 71

Underdevelopment
 reasons for Chinese migration to Russian
 Far East 72–74
Urbanization
 Northeast Asia, in 20

Vital rates
 Northeast Asia, in 17

Waipai laowu (overseas workers) 80
Women
 trafficking of
 South Korea, in 212

Xin yimin (new migrants) 80